SUCCESS
BY DESIGN

The Essential Business Reference for Designers

DAVID SHERWIN

For more excellent books and resources for designers, visit www.howdesign.com.

16 15 14 13 12   5 4 3 2 1

ISBN-13: 978-1-4403-1022-5

Distributed in Canada by Fraser Direct
100 Armstrong Avenue
Georgetown, Ontario, Canada L7G 5S4
Tel: (905) 877-4411

Distributed in the U.K. and Europe by F&W Media International, LTD
Brunel House, Forde Close, Newton Abbot, TQ12 4PU, UK
Tel: (+44) 1626 323200, Fax: (+44) 1626 323319
Email: enquiries@fwmedia.com

Distributed in Australia by Capricorn Link
P.O. Box 704, Windsor, NSW 2756 Australia
Tel: (02) 4577-3555

Material from this book has previously appeared in a different form on changeorderblog.com, imprint.printmag.com, and designmind.frogdesign.com.

Designed by David Sherwin
Unless otherwise credited, images and illustrations copyright David Sherwin.

Edited by Amy Schell Owen, Lauren Mosko Bailey, and Scott Francis
Art directed by Ronson Slagle
Production coordinated by Greg Nock

also by the author:

*Creative Workshop: 80 Challenges
to Sharpen Your Design Skills*

This book is also for Mary.

Acknowledgements

I have to thank the following three contributors, who helped me in generating the majority of the material for this book:

David Conrad is a founding partner at Design Commission. Armed with over fifteen years experience in designing websites and user experiences, David currently teaches web design at the School of Visual Concepts and actively promotes the Seattle technology scene. *www.designcommission.com*

Erica Goldsmith is a seasoned strategist and client relationship manager with over twelve years experience in design, branding and advertising. She has a passion for doing the impossible on time, on strategy and under budget. *www.linked.in/EricaGoldsmith*

Fiona Robertson Remley is a strategic program and client relationship manager. Her business philosophy is simple: Outside the box thinking requires a box. *www.linkedin.com/in/fionar*

In addition to the above, I interviewed the following designers, businesspeople and consultants on everything from accounting to estimating to strategy to project management: Derin Basden, Steve Baty, Abby Godee, Jenny Lam, Ted Leonhardt, Justin Maguire, Matthew May, Nancy McClelland, Stefan Mumaw, Luke Mysee, Gabriel Post, Mary Paynter Sherwin and Wendy Quesinberry. And I must thank the following people for their formative perspectives, enriching discussions and willingness to provide feedback on the book in draft form: Christopher Butler, Matt Conway, Teaque Lenahan, Tom Manning, Timothy Morey, Andrew Otwell, Nathan Peretic, Andy Rutledge, Matt Schoenholz, Lauren Serota, and Sebastian Scholz. Plus, this project wouldn't have happened without the support of the HOW Books team: Megan Patrick, Amy Owen, Grace Ring, Lauren Mosko, Scott Francis, and Ronson Slagle.

Contents by Topic

DOING THE WORK **AFTER THE WORK**

Introduction

Warning: This book will not solve all of your design business needs

This book is not meant to be the last word about running a design business. That would require thousands of pages!

Instead, I hope this book will serve as an entry point to the essential tools and attitudes you'll need to work at a design business—or own one yourself. It may serve as a useful refresher on familiar topics or as a primer that will aid you in bootstrapping a new business venture. Depending on what you need help with, you can read it from cover to cover or jump from one topic to another.

This book is a peek under the design business "cone of silence"

In your design career, you may have been like me: Digging through blogs. Trying to keep my projects on the rails and my clients happy. Learning to translate bits of information into useful knowledge for running a design business.

But I always found that the best advice came from group therapy.

When I lived in Seattle, every Wednesday night was dubbed "Burger-Drama": An assortment of friends and refugees from various design studios, agencies and in-house design departments around the Puget Sound region blowing off steam in the middle of their work week at a local bar and grill. Every time we'd meet, there would be a point in the conversation where the "cone of silence" would lower over the table. While munching on onion rings and guzzling IPAs, we would share the successes, failures, trials and tribulations of running design businesses. No client secrets. No unverified gossip. Just lessons from the school of hard knocks and the occasional story of a crazy co-worker.

Over the first few months of conversation, it became apparent that the majority of our problems had nothing to do with the design work itself. They had to do with being a good businessperson.

Cue rant from the guy with chunky black glasses

I bet when you first began working as a designer you thought you would have uninterrupted time—full days, if not weeks—to lounge at your desk, leisurely scratching away at your next breakthrough design idea.

Perhaps you work in a magical place, where the halls are filled with game-changing conversations spawning reams of genius, and it all floats effortlessly into layout and graces your perfectly calibrated monitors with award-winning unicorns. Or, if you work in-house at a corporation, you're always in client service mode, ready at a moment's notice to turn any flaming arrow that *thunks* beside your head into creative fire.

But even for designers who fly solo, with the requisite dreamy dreams about "me time," no one can deny that both our increased connectivity and our heightened need for interaction with clients are rapidly changing how we construct "billable time" as part of our paid workday.

If we want to preserve the integrity and quality of great design work, we need to understand how to run our businesses like, well, a business. We need to know how to manage ourselves from the high-level work flow to the nitty-gritty negotiations that sneak their way into seemingly simple client conversations. We need to restrain our hand from reaching back to the mouse for the fifteenth comp that really isn't necessary to prove (to the client, to yourself) that you've explored every microscopic detail.

We can eat, sleep and occasionally dream in measurements other than pixels and picas. We can learn to speak in estimates and business strategies. We can open Excel to update a spreadsheet without bursting into tears or feeling like we've sold out. Not only that, but we can also put aside our chunky black glasses and speak frankly with our clients about our measured, expert opinions informed by our previous project work, innate emotional intelligence and our understanding of how to wield the design process effectively.

When we've brought structure and thoroughness to the business process that supports our ongoing creative work, there is a much cleaner balance between what we imagine we do (design!) and what it really takes to succeed as a designer (business!).

"Design is the human capacity to plan and produce desired outcomes," says Bruce Mau. The producing part? That's definitely design. And the planning part? Still a good bit of design, but the rest is business.

We can plan and produce better outcomes for ourselves when we act as design businesspeople. On the other hand, when we don't have effective conversations with our business partners or our clients, because we choose to hide behind our own designerspeak ... and when the way we present our concepts doesn't really describe how we've helped our clients with their needs ... and when we get sidetracked by the internet, and end up pushing our creative work into the wee hours to distract (or inspire) ourselves out of a rut ... when we do such things, we're actually struggling to reconcile what we feel doesn't fit the designer persona. Designers are supposed to be "on top of it all," but the truth is that we're usually just trying to avoid being crushed by the eight ball. We just want to get paid to make cool things. All this business stuff is ruining everything!

Well, I'm all for putting aside anything that might get in the way of great design. Risk yields reward, when managed with a light touch. Some processes can be put on the shelf.

But the *business* process—that's what keeps us up and running. For the sanity of both co-workers and clients, it can never be sacrificed. Never. Firms that are unwilling to box their creative inclinations into a stable business process blow through clients, staff and potential profit like Kleenex.

So, where are the resources to aid us in becoming better design businesspeople?

It's my hope that this book becomes one of them.

———

Over the course of this book, I will use the term "design business" to describe any business that includes design as one of its core competencies. The term "design studio" or "design firm" will describe a design business that bills for time. They are not always one and the same.

———

WORKING WITH CUSTOMERS

THROW BELL
FOR SERVICE

Client Service

You know good client service when you experience it. Think about Four Seasons Hotels and Resorts, Southwest Airlines, Virgin America, Starbucks Coffee—even low-cost restaurants like Waffle House. What all of these brands have in common is that they've deliberately *choreographed* the services they provide, satisfying their customers' needs and desires beyond any specific product they sell. They provide more than a plane flying you from Atlanta to San Francisco, a fresh cup of coffee or a night in an elegant room with a pillow-top bed. They've considered how their employees interact with you before, during and after you've experienced their products and services.

But if we're so good at helping companies strengthen their products, services and brands, then why are we so poor at applying the same deliberate choreography to our own business operations?

Many designers focus on the quality of deliverables they provide to their clients, thinking that this will fully satisfy their clients. However, client service professionals also consider the quality of the story taking shape *around* their deliverables. Properly managing this story, in concert with understanding the people who are your day-to-day clients, can improve the bottom line for your design practice. You begin telling this story and building this long-term relationship when you meet the client for the first time. It does *not* start with the paid work.

A studio employee with client service responsibilities can facilitate ongoing communications with a client over the life of a project, monitoring and encouraging the highest quality design work and growing the overall income from that client over time. This employee can be a studio principal, a designer, a project manager or client partner.

Strong client service is not an option. It should come standard with every client interaction.

———

Note that I'm avoiding the use of the term "account management." To quote Fiona Robertson Remley: "We don't handle accounts; we handle people. We are not looking for one-project stands; we are looking for long-term relationships."

———

Should I try to cultivate long-term clients?

It can be exhilarating to work with a new client. But major benefits come with sustaining long-term client relationships, as opposed to always pursuing new opportunities. For instance:

- **Repeat clients create a possibility of reliable profit.** Pursuing new clients and opportunities reduces the amount of time that you can bill for paid work.
- **Familiarity can breed ease of business.** When you've learned to speak a client's language, you can collaborate more efficiently and become a true strategic partner. And when your client has a new project, your team is already well aware of their client's overall business landscape and the key attributes of their brand. You may have even helped establish those attributes.
- **Your staff can be free to conduct other business development activities.** Instead of grasping at any old opportunity to fill an empty pipeline for your business, having a strong base of established clients can free you to pursue new clients in a targeted manner.

And even if your clients aren't *new*, it shouldn't mean that the resulting work is *old*. Every project is an opportunity for greatness.

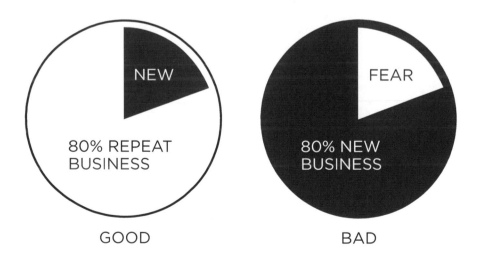

The 80/20 Rule of New Client Generation. It can cost your business more money to acquire a new client than to nurture and grow an existing one.

How do I provide effective client service?

While images of Pete Campbell from *Mad Men* may flash through your head, complete with boozy late-night negotiations over Scotch and cigars to land that big client deal, none of those activities are fundamental to creating great client service. These relationships are built on trust, which emerges from the following components:

QUALITY OF DESIGN WORK
Error-free, on brief and artfully executed design work is important in any client relationship. But delivering great design work may not matter if you treat your client poorly in other areas. (Did they tell you that in design school?)

FREQUENCY OF CONTACT
The speed and channel by which you respond to client communications can influence your client's satisfaction level, whether it's an in-person meeting or video chat or a text message. If they have an urgent question, you might need to send them a quick response to let them know when you can fully respond to their request (and not dilute your focus on your work).

QUALITY OF CONTACT
Quality of contact can be measured by how you utilize your client's time. When you have meetings with your client, do you use an agenda to structure the conversation? Are you aware of small project details you can share with your client on the spot, rather than filling them in through future meetings or conversations? A good rule of thumb: If the client begins to micromanage your time, there is a problem with your quality of contact.

MAINTAINING A PERSONAL CONNECTION
Learn which parts of your personality create winning situations for your clients. Clients hire people, not design robots—so be yourself and know what to share at the appropriate moment. That said, it's important to understand your clients as human beings, not just human doings. Leave space for them to be themselves too.

PROPER HANDLING OF OPEN ISSUES
When a client gives you feedback, how do you handle it? If an error crops up, how do you manage its impact before the client expresses a concern? Handling the situation poorly can lower the quality of your design work, your quality of contact and the perceived value of your services.

ESTABLISHING A MUTUAL WORKING STYLE

Is your client casual or formal, friendly or business only, buttoned-up or free-form? Don't impose your personal working style onto an organization that behaves in a different manner, or you may create tension. Follow their lead in the nature of the relationship.

PERSONALIZING YOUR DAILY INTERACTIONS

Personalize your client/account manager relationship after it is established, and find moments where you can add creativity and delight. Don't let your client feel like your interactions are scripted or cookie-cutter—even if you are working from a template that has functioned well for other clients.

PERCEIVED VALUE FOR THE MONEY THEY SPEND

How you price your services, and what is provided for that price, can influence how clients may value your services and what they expect from you. If you're the cheapest option for a project, does that mean your services are really worth less? If you're a high-cost bidder, are you always on call for any client question or concern?

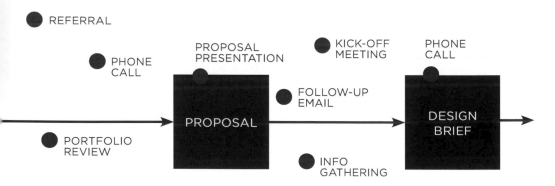

Define Your Touch Points. List all the potential ways you may interact with a customer throughout a project or product lifecycle. Then design each of those interactions with your customer so both of you have clear expectations regarding the quality of product and service you're seeking to deliver.

What should clients expect from me?

No matter what kind of client relationship you're trying to build, there are certain things every client will expect from a designer. Read what follows in the voice of the client who appreciates you most.

THE DESIGN CLIENT'S BILL OF RIGHTS

1. Timeliness

As your client, I should always know when I'm receiving deliverables, how long I have to review them and when I need to pay you for them. This must be clear from the start of our engagement.

In addition, my colleagues and I will keep to meeting times you have scheduled for me. You will not be late without warning. However, I am exempt from rebuke for slight delays, as I am working to ensure your work is approved and understood. If my tardiness is costing me money, please let me know.

Once a schedule is set, your work will never be late, unless an unforeseen circumstance arises. If this happens, contact me well in advance of the deadline. Otherwise, your delay might be considered unprofessional.

If we change the scope of our project, I expect you to negotiate a new schedule with me. This will allow the work to proceed to the best of your ability without compromising its integrity.

2. Transparency

I may need to know our project status at any time, as I may not be able to track the particulars on a daily basis.

I am your advocate in my corporation/organization and need to be able to understand and relate your perspective when I speak to my boss, my CEO, my peers and the general public. Do not assume that you will be able to participate in every meeting within my company to present your work. Even when I'd prefer that you do so, it may prove logistically impossible. For this reason, I need to know the thinking behind the work that you show me, the work that I choose to approve, and when necessary, the work that I decline to approve for appropriate reasons.

I want to know the impact my project will have on my customers, my company and the world at large, not to mention sustainability issues and ethical concerns that may transcend the work and damage our reputations.

And while I don't need to know exactly how the sausage is made, you may share details with me that help me understand why there may have been slight hiccups in the process.

3. Value

I seek fairness in agency/designer fees. I will be fair regarding minor fee changes if I have been responsible for changing the project's scope.

My organization will usually require me to request estimates from multiple agencies, so the cost of your work will always be factored into the overall value of our potential relationship. I will not always choose the lowest bidder. I will choose the best fit for the project.

Don't hide costs or penalize me for lack of forethought in your bidding, or lack of understanding of our communicated strategic approach. Work with me as a partner to help me understand where we need to meet, both fiscally and professionally, so that both of us can profit.

Be responsible if you find that you can't fulfill the contracted work for the estimate you provided. In such a situation, free me to engage with another designer before my boss fires me, or bring me options that both of us can live with.

4. Respect

We aren't friends. We are colleagues. I expect you to consistently convey that you care and respect for our shared partnership. We have a relationship that is predicated on our focus on creating meaningful impact on my organization through design. This can influence every aspect of our day-to-day interactions: How you dress, how you talk, how you describe your work to my boss, how we catch a beer after work and how you respect the client/designer boundary.

If I smell an oversize ego, or you tell me I just don't understand the ramifications of a recommendation you've put forth, then it is unlikely our mutual partnership will be sustained. I'm responsible for my business and have to live with the consequences of implementing your ideas.

Mutual expectations of our conduct should be established when we begin working together on a project. If you aren't going to be able to return an email from me within two hours, tell me. If you need flexibility on your project milestones because you're overloaded in your studio, tell me. Please don't surprise me along the way. Unspoken, unfulfilled or ignored expectations will diminish our trust in each other and our chances for success.

––––

Providing great client service is something you can be paid for, so be sure to include it in your project estimates and studio overhead costs.

––––

What expectations should I have for my client?

"The Design Client's Bill of Rights" provides a good understanding of what clients should expect from designers. But when you start work, your client conversations should also be about what you expect from them. If you don't tell your client up front about your expectations for their behavior, you may be scolding them for things they never knew they needed to do.

The best way to do this is to define rules of engagement for your clients. This should be provided in one written page, which includes the following:

- The type of feedback they need to provide for each deliverable, and when it will be due
- The key decision makers within their organization, and when their input will be required from deliverable to deliverable
- Who is assigned to collate their feedback (that isn't your job)
- The frequency and consistency of client contact: Who will respond, when and how
- What will happen if errors should occur

This document should function as a conversation starter and also guide you through any potential issues over the life of the project.

What kind of clients should I seek out?

Here's my personal take. The clients who I respect, admire and keep in touch with strike a perfect balance between personal respect and professional courtesy. When I show them creative work, they know that even if the work isn't perfect, I'm on my way to realizing a great idea. Either that, or they were once designers, and they see the process through my eyes.

These clients don't hire me because I have a pet giraffe or work at a factory that spits out lollipops along with design awesomeness. While I may have executed a gazillion logos and my working process is pretty sharp, my favorite clients are savvy enough to understand that I never step in the same river twice. They respect the journey that I take each day through the design process. They want to go on that journey with me.

These clients demand a level of attention and respect not because they continue to pay me and laugh at my jokes, but because I really do want them to succeed beyond their wildest dreams.

At a marketing event a few years back, I heard someone say: "Clients end up with the designers they deserve."

It's our job to prove them right.

Business Development

I remember working as a designer in a small studio and being stunned by their new business process. It was something like this:

1. Do great work.
2. Post your great work to studio website.
3. Hope your clients refer new business to you.
4. Wait for prospective future clients to see your website and call you.
5. Repeat 1 through 4.

While sitting around and waiting for the phone to ring may sound ideal, especially if it gives you more time to read design blogs, it isn't a dependable way of sustaining a business. You need to develop a more sophisticated process for how you secure new client relationships.

For most studios, finding new projects can be one of the most time-consuming, frustrating and rewarding parts of running a design business. Without nurturing a steady stream of new prospects and active leads, you risk having your studio staff sit idle for weeks or months of billable time. This can impact the stability of your business, or worse, lead to its demise.

My general rule of thumb is as follows: If you don't have a strong process in place for securing new business, it can take one hundred prospects to solicit ten new business conversations to mature into one new client. You heard me right: Sometimes it can take one hundred points of contact and conversation to land a single project!

What do I mean by prospects and leads?

A **prospect** is someone you've talked with who could become a client. They may not immediately send you work, but at some point in the future, things might turn in your favor. You may have had coffee with them or maybe a colleague gave you their name. Prospects are people you

———

You may be wondering: Can I just hire someone to find clients and projects for me? Well, if your name is on the door, you should be prepared to pound the pavement alongside any new business pros you've hired to support you. To quote Ted Leonhardt: "The one area of expertise you can never give up is sales."

———

can occasionally reach out to remind them that your services are available. They may be part of your personal or work networks, or someone you've met for the first time.

A **lead** is a potential client who has voiced that they have an opportunity for you. Leads can have a temperature. A hot lead wants to immediately enter into a conversation about a project, and ideally solicit a proposal from you. A cold lead might be someone who said they wanted to work with you but ceased returning phone calls or emails. These leads can be warmed up again by talking with them over a long sales cycle. To stay top of mind with a cold lead doesn't mean that you should pester them. Respect their boundaries. They'll let you know when to contact them.

Leads can also be repeat business from your existing client base. Ideally 80 percent of the ongoing work at any design business comes from returning clients. Working with your best clients can bring you peace of mind, especially if you don't have to bid against other designers to get the work.

Beware, however, that too much repeat business from too few clients can lead to account vulnerability. (See the sidebar to the right.)

How do I find new business prospects and leads?

There are many ways to initiate conversations with potential new clients. Direct methods allow you to initiate face-to-face or direct interpersonal contact, while indirect methods foster ways for clients to reach out to you.

DIRECT METHODS: YOU IDENTIFY AND CONTACT PROSPECTS

- Direct referral through your existing client base and friends in the community
- Pass-through referral, which means you ask clients and colleagues to introduce you to people they know, then you continue the conversation
- Networking through small business groups, where you can share perspectives with people from a range of unrelated industries
- Membership in nonprofit associations related to the types of clients you are targeting
- Meeting people at public events, such as conferences and trade shows
- Cold-calling, sending letters or emailing people at companies you would like to have as clients

WHAT IS ACCOUNT VULNERABILITY?

No single client should account for more than 25 percent of a studio's business. When it happens—and it will—immediately draw up a list of potential clients to call. This is known as diversifying your client base, and it's something that will help you reduce your level of vulnerability as a business owner.

Diversification allows you to sustain the loss of a client while protecting your studio overhead. If you hire more than one or two staffers to service a client that provides a high percentage of your revenue, and if that client leaves your studio, the one or two staffers you hired no longer have jobs. This is a risky business model for a small firm. Depending on the size of the client, it may result in the collapse of the entire business.

Diversification can reduce cash flow fluctuations that occur due to late payment from your clients. Any delay in client payment can potentially harm your cash flow. The fewer clients your business services, the more risk you bear if those clients are late in payment by even a few weeks. If you are offering credit rather than asking for payment up front, you invite this risk upon yourself.

Diversification can protect you from fee renegotiation. Agencies with lopsided client portfolios can suffer the following fate: The client discovers they provide the lion's share of your business revenue, and they ask to negotiate discounted fees in return for continuing or increasing their volume of business. The design business suffers, as there is little leverage in the negotiation with the client.

Diversification can lead to a more compelling portfolio. Design businesses whose portfolios contain work samples from only one kind of business or category of industry can struggle to attract new clients. A diverse portfolio demonstrates your curiosity, your range of skills in various domains of design and the desirability of your services.

Even if you become overwhelmed by project work, continue to call prospective clients and new business leads. If you focus all of your attention on making your sole client happy, in the short term you may profit, but the likelihood of harming your business in the long term will only increase.

INDIRECT METHODS: LEADS AND PROSPECTS CONTACT YOU

- Soliciting press in local and national media regarding projects you've worked on
- Blogging and placing articles on subjects in which you have expertise
- Podcasting or recording videos regarding subjects of interest to prospective clients
- Presenting at local or national events and/or online conferences to demonstrate thought leadership
- Online and print-based advertising where you know prospective clients may be looking
- Online, targeted search advertising

Many design businesses keep an internal database for tracking potential prospects and leads. Some use third-party tools such as Salesforce.com to manage this information.

What should I do when I talk with a lead?

Okay, you've got a lead, and you've scheduled a conversation with them to talk about a new business opportunity. What should you do to prepare for that conversation? How should you conduct it?

BE SENSITIVE TO THE TONE OF YOUR FIRST CONTACT
Gauge the difference between these conversation starters from two potential clients:

Call #1: "Hello, I'd like to see if your firm would be interested in taking part in a request for proposal (RFP) for Big Fancy Technology Company's new website redesign."

Call #2: "Hello, I was passed along your name by our mutual friend, Lorrie. She said that you create amazing websites, and since we're looking to overhaul ours, I thought I'd give you a call."

It's possible that the budget and time frame could be exactly the same for these two projects. However, from the tone of the first call, it seems you might be part of a shortlist of vendors that a client wants to bid on a potential project. The second call began with a mention of a personal connection before the business was presented. These cues can help you use the appropriate tone and approach when gathering information about a possible project.

TRY TO MEET IN PERSON

If possible, try to have at least one face-to-face meeting before submitting a final project estimate or initiating a project. Geography often doesn't permit this, but meeting face-to-face with a prospective client—or setting up a quick video chat—will speak volumes.

CONNECT AS A HUMAN BEING BEFORE YOU GET TO BUSINESS

If you're looking to develop a strong working relationship with any new client, you need to relate with them on a human level as well as on a professional level. Before you dive into business, you need to make sure their basic needs are cared for—coffee or tea, parking validation—and some brief small talk.

UNDERSTAND HOW THEY HEARD ABOUT YOU

I like to do this either at the very beginning or at the end of the conversation, to gauge the strength of the referral. This also helps me to remember to send an appropriate thank-you to the referee.

DISCOVER WHY THEY'RE CALLING OR MEETING WITH YOU

Create a space for the client to immediately start sharing. You don't need to describe your professional experience or talk about yourself until you've fully heard why they're interested in your help.

"SO, MR. CEO, TELL ME ABOUT YOUR VALUE PROPOSITION..."

Active listening is one of the most important skills you'll use when seeking out new clients. Don't assume that you completely understand your customer's needs after your first conversation, even if everything sounds familiar. Try to get at the root cause of any underlying issues or pain points. In the process, you'll likely uncover useful information for formulating an approach to satisfy their needs.

BE AWARE OF WHAT YOU WEAR

If you're a designer, you should dress in a manner that complements the impression you want your work to make.

PROVIDE AN AGENDA FOR THE MEETING

If you've initiated the meeting, confirm how much time your client has to talk. Casually relate to them a brief agenda of what you'd like to explore during the meeting. Even if you're working with a client who is savvy about design, shape the conversational focus. You're responsible for the work.

ACTIVELY LISTEN AND REFLECT

Be prepared to redirect the conversation as appropriate: "Before we talk about our relevant work experience, I'd like to explore some of the details around why you're embarking on this website redesign." Then you can share with the client appropriate case studies or examples.

ASK ABOUT POSSIBLE COMPETITION

"So, are you talking to any other designers/agencies for this project?" Don't be afraid to take it further. "May I ask which ones? I'm just looking for a clear understanding of the different options you're considering." These details help you understand whom you may be bidding against for a project and whether you may be favored for the project.

DISCUSS BUDGET RANGES

Never let a client escape an in-depth meeting without a budgetary range for your estimate. Be firm about garnering that information. If the client says they don't have an idea of how much money they have to play with—which happens often—you should still strive to pin them down to a general range. One of my former colleagues, Kara Costa, used to say something like this in client meetings: "Do you have $5 for this project or $1,000,000?" When provided with such a wide variance in cost, some clients will say, "No, it's more like $12,000." Other clients may become uncomfortable, so don't push them too far.

―――

Bill your new business activities as an overhead expense. If you don't account for your time in this manner, the time and cost you expend in acquiring new clients will go right out the window or be applied against the client project budget.

―――

ESTABLISH A POTENTIAL TIME FRAME FOR DELIVERY

You aren't asking for a firm deadline for delivery. You only need a point of clarity regarding project scope (how much needs to be done) and project time frame (how much time you have to complete the work). In future conversations, you'll connect the two and establish an appropriate time frame for the client's budget and scope.

GAUGE THE INITIAL LEVEL OF TRUST

Every successful client relationship is built on mutual respect and trust. If you don't hear a glimmer of client honesty in your first contact—an honest description of a business challenge they're trying to solve—it may be difficult for you to serve their business effectively over time.

BE UP-FRONT ABOUT QUALITY OF FIT

If the client is concerned that you're the right fit, they may be guarded in conversation. If they are rooting for you to get the gig, they may be truthful about where you stand in the running. You can often solicit their direct opinions by being honest about whether the services you offer are truly appropriate. If the client is considering you alongside a range of multiple studios and/or individuals, you don't need to sell yourself immediately as the right person for the job. If you rush in, you might miss critical inputs or subtext in the conversations that, in hindsight, were the first warning bells of a bad fit.

DON'T OVERSELL YOUR CAPABILITIES

Of course your client wants to hear you say, "Sure, we're great at creating websites and applications that are responsive for mobile devices and tablets using HTML5, and your budgetary range sounds perfect for the scope." But don't get caught saying, "Sure, we can do all of that! I'll get back to you with a timeline," if it's not actually true. You'll hang up the phone and begin to sweat over how you can acquire years of expertise in a matter of weeks. If you're still learning *how* to produce the work, then you're wasting time that should be spent on *doing* the work.

DON'T BE AFRAID TO MENTION YOUR PARTNERS

As your business grows, you may build an external team of collaborators you can tap as you generate a proposal. If you use outside help for your work—even if it's just the occasional photographer—let your client know that outside partners might be involved.

DON'T LET THE CLIENT DICTATE YOUR VALUE

Your first negotiation can often point the way that the client relationship is going to evolve, regarding the value of your services. The same applies for schedule. So, if the client says: "My website should cost $15,000 and take three weeks to design and build." You say: "I can't guarantee that, Joe. Let me work up an estimate and a timeline, and I'll send it to you by the 11th. Will that work for you?"

REFLECT ON HOW THE MEETING WENT FOR YOU

After your first meeting, it helps to ask *yourself* some very tough questions to calibrate where the relationship may go from here. What areas will you need to explore to formulate a strong proposal and start your project? *(See the questions in "Proposals.")* You should reflect on the first fifteen minutes of conversation you had with your new business prospect. That conversation can tell the story of your future business relationship.

If you're ready to move to a proposal, you'll need to estimate time and costs. *(See "Estimating.")*

Should I respond to requests for proposals or turn them away?

When a client is looking for a design professional to hire, they may be required to send out a request for proposal (RFP) or request for information (RFI) that is intended to help them select the best partner to fulfill that project. These documents will specify a set of needs that the client requires from any interested design partner. These partners will respond to the RFP or RFI with their own appropriate document.

If you run your own design studio or firm, you should have a blanket policy for how you respond to RFPs and RFIs.

Many design businesses choose to decline RFPs, because the amount of money offered may not offset the time and money spent creating a response in order to win the project. There is a risk that six to twelve other businesses may be in competition with you for the project, which may put the odds against you. There is also a risk that in order to participate, a design business will be asked to provide design services for free (i.e., spec work), which is considered unprofessional. *(See "Spec Work.")*

Other design businesses respond only to RFPs that require a limited amount of effort (in time and materials), as long as there is a strong possibility that they may win. If you don't have a bid/win rate of at least

50 percent—whether you're responding to RFPs or not—you should take a hard look at your proposal process and the kinds of work you are pursuing.

How do I decline client work and still generate future business opportunities?

The failure we most frequently face in the business of design is not recognizing a client project we should decline.

Declining a project is a subtle art, especially in the midst of any critical negotiation. "The trick is to turn down work but to have the client remember you as a positive person that they want to work with in the future," says strategic program and client relationship manager Fiona Robertson Remley.

"It can be advantageous to offer a conditional 'no' rather than a direct refusal," says Nathan Peretic, co-founder of Full Stop Interactive. "It's easy to see a project as a poor fit because one or more variables aren't right. The temptation in that case is to decline the project outright. However it can be worthwhile to offer a different solution that is more favorable to you: more money, smaller scope, phased work, etc."

If you need to decline a project, go about it carefully.

NOT ALL NEW BUSINESS COMES FROM NEW PEOPLE YOU MEET
Set up recurring times that you reach out to former clients and colleagues. Stay aware of and acknowledge the niceties, such as birthdays, big business wins, holidays and notices about events of interest. Even sending a thank you note for a small favor can contribute to staying top of mind for work down the line.

Happy Holidays

(Just don't use Zapfino.)

SHOW HUMILITY WHEN YOU SAY NO

Declining work is showing that you have power over the client/designer relationship. Never let the client feel like you are declining the work because of ego.

LEAVE THE DOOR OPEN FOR THE POSSIBILITY OF NO

You should make it clear in your early discussions that a project may not be a good fit for you. Leaving the door open for saying no to a project can lessen the chance of more-for-your-money negotiations.

SAY NO EARLY IN THE NEW BUSINESS PROCESS

Once you've moved too far into the sales cycle—for instance, to the point where you've already generated a proposal—it is unprofessional to say no.

ENCOURAGE FUTURE OPPORTUNITIES—DON'T JUST WALK AWAY

"No" should never be the last thing a client remembers about their interaction with you.

Declining an opportunity is not a sign of weakness. Use your refusal as a chance to describe what kind of work is a better fit. Be willing to refer the client to someone in your network who can fulfill their needs and return the referral in the future. Such a dialogue would sound something like this, delivered via a phone call or face-to-face meeting:

> I'm sorry, but it looks like the project we've been discussing isn't a good fit for us at this time. Let me refer you to another designer (or two) who would be able to help you with it. And we should put something on the calendar for coffee in a month, because it was really great talking with you about our love of web analytics.

"HAVE YOU THOUGHT ABOUT ADS ON SEARCH ENGINES? IT MIGHT HELP."

"NO, I HADN'T. I'LL GO THINK ABOUT THAT. THANKS!"

Be strategic in how you provide favors. Don't give your new business prospects and leads free design work. Instead, give them guidance in moderation.

How do I recognize opportunities I should decline?

In the process of sifting one hundred prospects to land one solid project, you may end up in one of the following situations:

THE CLIENT THINKS YOU WANT THE WORK THEY'RE OFFERING, NO MATTER WHAT

This is the beauty of establishing strong client relationships from your first meeting. If you and the client connect during those initial dialogues, there will be a strong reservoir of trust to fuel your first projects. In this case, you have a client who likes talking with you and expects that working with you will feel the same way. She genuinely cares about your shared success. She just doesn't realize that what she's throwing your way is not the best fit. Right client, wrong project.

THE CLIENT KNOWS THERE AREN'T OTHER CLIENTS COMPETING FOR YOUR ATTENTION

Your client has become aware of your increased focus and attention on the possibility of working with him. You have been throwing in bells and whistles whenever possible. By lavishing too much attention on him, you're training him to expect more for his money. Savvy clients, whether con-sciously or unconsciously, know this is when they can negotiate hardest on their own behalf.

THE CLIENT DOESN'T KNOW YOU LACK COMPETENCY IN AN AREA

This client loved the work you did for their logo and business papers. Now they want you to design a database for their website. Designers don't like to admit weakness in a specific area, especially if they are hungry to keep work rolling in from a client. Sometimes you will have strategic partners to help you out with these projects. In other situations, however, the work might be too much for your skill set, and you have no capacity for a compli-cated partnership with multiple external teams. Respect your limits and be honest with your client about them.

THE CLIENT WANTS YOU TO DO WORK THAT'S PART OF THEIR JOB ROLE

Designers are often hired to do things that are outside their client's core of expertise. But sometimes jobs come along that are part of a client's every-day work responsibilities, and you don't recognize that you're doing their job until you start the project. As an example: Your client has been having trouble getting content approved due to internal politics and asks you to help, even though it's clearly outlined in your contract that it's their responsibility. You may be able to move more nimbly than your client, but you will still have to work through the same internal politics to have the content approved. These kinds of requests can quickly make a project unprofitable, and they can be avoided by saying no and enforcing the boundaries set in your contract.

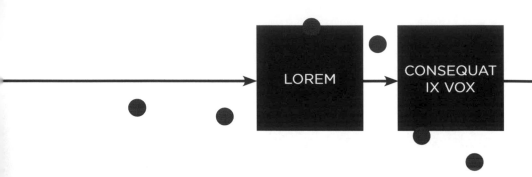

THE CLIENT FEELS ENTITLED TO YOUR HELP

Perhaps your client is thinking, "If you say no, there are plenty of other agencies yearning to get started on this project." Such a threat is half true. If a client threatens to take her work to another agency, she's taking this tack because she wants something from you: Your participation, your investment or just your attention. She knows you'll do it better than another agency. Being in this situation proves that you have more leverage than you think.

YOU REALLY DO NEED THE MONEY

Yes, you need to pay rent. No, this work is not beneath you. Yes, the work will hopefully lead to better things. You have staff you need to keep busy. It'll be over quickly, and you'll be on to better things. It's true that some projects that stroll through the studio are purely money makers. They'll never appear in your portfolio. No one needs to know.

Don't be a motion graphics specialist who finds herself pigeonholed as the PowerPoint designer. Don't take on search engine optimization projects if you just want to do logos. If word spreads that you're really good at the projects you don't want to specialize in, you'll risk landing those projects over and over again. Can you afford to promote yourself as an expert in one area and spend your time working in another?

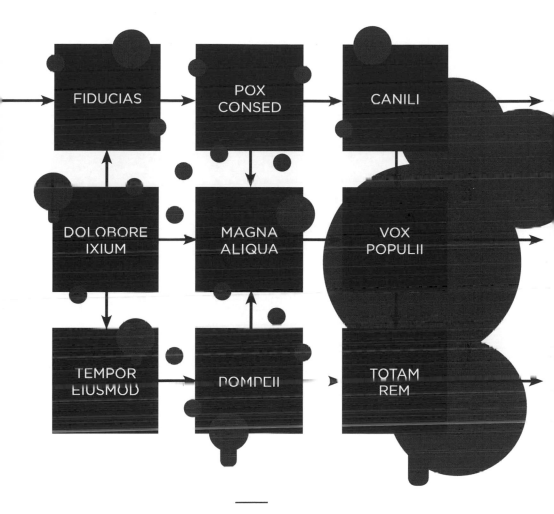

How do you turn a new business meeting into a bloodbath? Use specialized designer lingo. In your conversations, avoid this jargon. Speak your client's language: Everyday English. Otherwise, it'll sound like you're only fluent in Lorem Ipsum.

PROJECT AGREEMENT

With this ring, we are wedded to delivering your corporation a fully functional website (up to 10 pages) built in HTML5/CSS3 and cross-browser compliant, in return for $10,000 and a long-term retainer for upkeep ($500/month).

Witnessed this 3rd day of November by two parties who negotiated for weeks to bring this to fruition.

SIGN HERE QUICK:

X_____
CLIENT   DATE

X_____
DESIGNER   DATE

Proposals

Now that you've met with your next great client, bonded over your love of poodles or craft bourbon and identified a potential design project you can help with, what do you do? You write a great proposal.

Proposals are crafted documents that describe how you'll help a potential or current client fulfill her stated business needs. I enjoy writing proposals because they set your project up for success. They are often the first point in your client relationship where your client sees tangible evidence of how you're going to help them solve a problem.

Here's what you need to know about creating a proposal.

What are the contents of a great proposal?

Every proposal you generate should include the following content, whether it's a returning client or a new business lead:

- Your clear, articulate understanding of the client's business problems
- Your proposed activities in the form of a set of deliverables and technological/media considerations (aka the scope of work)
- Your professional experience and how it will help the client
- Your stable, successful business process for executing the proposed deliverables
- An agreed-upon timeline with a potential work-back schedule that describes high-level project milestones (subject to change)
- The cost estimate for the deliverables
- An outline of the overall budget required to fulfill the deliverables, based on the fee structure you've chosen and the payment terms both parties have agreed upon
- A list of shared working assumptions and contingencies that govern the project deliverables

If your proposal is missing any of the above components, your client is at risk of misinterpreting what you will provide. In addition, your proposal should include boilerplate considerations such as:

- Your client's name, address, information and main point of contact
- An area for both parties to sign and date
- Terms and conditions, process for overages and clarification regarding out-of-scope items such as licensing for stock photography

The conditions in the proposal are not legally binding until they are signed and dated by both parties. At that point, you are both contractually obligated to the terms of the proposal—unless you both agree to change the terms via a more in-depth contract or a change order, or you both agree to exercise a clause to end your relationship.

Some agencies use an extended version of the proposal as the contract. This format is used for larger projects or for establishing a retainer-based relationship. Like a proposal, it requires signatures from both the client and the agency. The extended proposal may also be accompanied by other legally binding documents, such as nondisclosure agreements and master services agreement documents.

A proposal should expire if not signed within a provided deadline. Mark your estimates and proposals valid for only thirty days. If an unsigned proposal has expired but the client is still interested in having the work done, you should revisit the terms of the document to make sure they are still applicable. An agency's business conditions can change quickly; an expiration date on your proposals can protect you.

How do I write a truly great proposal?

Here are some tips and tricks I've learned from working with great client service professionals and creative directors.

GREAT PROPOSALS PREDIGEST THE BUSINESS PROBLEM AND HINT AT AN OUTCOME

When you write a proposal for a new project, begin the document with a brief description of the client's business case and strategy. This shows the client that you understand her company's position. Your proposal should then explain what the client needs to solve their problem and how your firm will meet those needs. Always try to answer the questions: Who? What? When? Where? and Why?

It's not enough to restate what you heard in discussions with the client. Show your understanding of the competitive landscape by describing how the client is perceived. You can demonstrate your competence by doing some simple research and then providing a bit of analysis.

As you craft this paragraph or two, be aware of your potential audience. Make it as easy to understand as possible, without being overly simplistic. I like to imagine what would happen if the CEO of the company read my proposal. Would what I've written make sense to her?

GREAT PROPOSALS DO NOT INCLUDE SPECULATIVE WORK
You don't need to give the client speculative work to show that you understand his business and have a solid project plan in place. There are other ways to show your creativity and expertise. *(See "Spec Work.")*

GREAT PROPOSALS DESCRIBE THE CLIENT EXPERIENCE OVER THE LIFE OF THE PROJECT
When you write about schedules and deliverables in a proposal, consider crafting a narrative that explains in plain English what would happen from week to week over the life of your project. The narrative approach can work especially well when you're entering into a long-term client relationship or if you need to corral multiple stakeholders with differing perspectives. You can keep your "story" abstract enough so that it can't be easily negotiated until the proposal is signed. You shouldn't have to speak to day-by-day activities on a calendar.

GREAT PROPOSALS SHOULD REFLECT THE CLIENT/DESIGNER CONVERSATION THAT LED TO IT
A strong proposal reflects the give and take of the discussions you had with your client during the new business conversation. Stating your shared assumptions in a proposal not only demonstrates an understanding of your client's needs, but it also paves the way for the creation of a strong creative brief.

GREAT PROPOSALS SAY JUST ENOUGH TO MAKE THE SALE
Overwrite the overall document first, then edit it mercilessly. Don't repeat or reiterate elements. Show your progression of thought whenever possible, but remember that you aren't getting paid by the word.

GREAT PROPOSALS ARE LASER-SPECIFIC REGARDING WHAT IS IN AND OUT OF SCOPE
There should be no wiggle room in how you describe deliverables and rounds of review. Be clear regarding the following:

How many design concepts, templates or other deliverables you will generate
Ten (10) page HTML-based website. The website design will be derived from a home page and secondary page template.

How many rounds of review are allowed throughout the process
We will provide one set of wireframes for primary and secondary page templates. There will be two rounds of review to reach approval. After approval

of the wireframes, we will generate two concepts for the home page visual design direction, single direction will be chosen. There will be two rounds of review to reach approval.

What technology platforms are prescribed for implementation
All page templates will be built on a WordPress blog platform. A JavaScript slideshow will be included on the home page.

What the client must provide in order for the proposed deliverables to be fully delivered
Client will supply content for all pages. If full content is not provided before home and secondary page templates are approved for development, then development work may be halted, and restarting work will result in a $1,000 start work fee.

GREAT PROPOSALS DON'T GIVE AWAY YOUR DETAILED ESTIMATES, ONLY COST ESTIMATES
Be mindful of what the client needs to see in order to perceive the value of your services. If you're fully transparent about how you estimate your projects, you're asking for prospective clients to start chipping away at the total bill. *(See "Estimating.")*

GREAT PROPOSALS CLEARLY DESCRIBE WHAT ISN'T INCLUDED
Clients never enjoy finding out that certain critical items are absent from the bill, especially if that information comes late in the game. If you are taking a phased approach, describe in detail what is included in each phase.

GREAT PROPOSALS NEED TO BE JUST GOOD ENOUGH
Don't be a perfectionist about every proposal. Your next proposal isn't going on the side of a soda can or being displayed in a museum. Writing it shouldn't take more than 1 to 2 percent of a project budget you've proposed. David Conrad from Design Commission advises three to five hours on a proposal once a project has been qualified.

———

Sometimes you can't clearly limit project scope until you've been through the discovery phase of your project. You can include a clause in your proposal that makes deliverables contingent on what you learn or sets a ceiling for the number of elements you will provide. Additional work or deliverables would then require a change order.

———

GREAT PROPOSALS MOTIVATE YOUR CLIENTS

When they finish reading your proposal, a client should be emotionally moved. They'll know you're prepared, and they'll be excited about your journey together.

What should you ask your client before completing your proposal?

Before you can write a proposal, you have to know what to propose. You need to ask the right questions to estimate and fulfill a project profitably, while also satisfy your client's desired project outcomes. With this in mind, here are some of the topics you'll need to explore in your discovery process, organized by how they usually come up in conversation. *(For more on how to approach new business conversations, see "Business Development.")*

BUDGET AND TIMELINE

If you don't ask about the budget during your first conversations, you are making a big mistake. You are not required to automatically fit within that budget. A good relationship starts when you can negotiate a fair set of deliverables for a fair budget. "Fair" equals an appropriate level of profit for the designer within a manageable time frame. You can't negotiate this unless you know where to start.

You should never deliver an estimate without a clear idea of the money available and the time required for project fulfillment. Clients like to dictate what a project costs. They usually have an approved budget before they contact you. They won't tell you up front how much money they have until you ask them.

REQUIREMENTS

Requirements are the large and small details, fully implemented, that your client will want to see in what you create for them. A project requirement may look like the following:

- Expected features: "We want a blog on the website. And an email newsletter sign-up form."
- Technology constraints: "We have to use SharePoint for our intranet redesign."
- Budgetary concerns: "We'd prefer to have only two colors on the business cards if it saves us money."

Stated requirements will become a laundry list that you end up itemizing in your estimate—and where the most haggling occurs around setting a project's scope. When discussing requirements, know how to sift the sacred cows from the details that may be sacrificed to preserve a delivery window or keep within a budget.

COMPANY GUIDELINES

Clients often have guidelines—both formal and informal—regarding how their business should be represented in the wild, woolly world. You will probably have to ask them about:

- Legal review: "There's no way legal will let you launch an alternative reality game. We should have discussed that with legal from the very beginning."
- Brand and design style guides: They are floating around the organization somewhere.
- Design samples and examples: These can illuminate how a client brand is evolving—or how it's contradicting their stated style.
- Informal best practices and a list of concurrent projects: Will any of these impact the work flow?

Brand and design guidelines can often be on the lowest rung of importance for your client, especially when she's trying to launch a new project. For this reason, ask her as early as possible for things like this—even before the proposal has been signed.

VENDORS AND COMPETITOR INFLUENCE

Besides working with your direct client, it's likely that your project will be influenced by a host of third parties: Other design businesses, production resources, printers and hosting services, to name a few.

Some questions you should consider asking your client include:

- Do you have vendors that you partner with that I'm expected to work with?
- What is the relationship you currently have with those vendors (e.g., multiple bids required, no overage on estimates, 10 percent "friend" discount)?
- How am I expected to interact with these vendors?
- What influence do these vendors hold over your final work product?

Discovering such constraints late in the process can have undue impacts on project scope, schedule and cost—and make you look like you haven't done your job by asking the right questions.

ASSUMPTIONS

All clients make assumptions about what you can and will deliver—even if they don't realize that they do. You might hear clients say the following:

- Expectations regarding performance: "This is going to go viral, right?"
- Poor communication of requirements: "I thought that was included in the estimate. It should have been."
- Relinquishing responsibility to the designer: "I assumed you were the experts on [insert technology type or marketing need here]."

Assumptions need to be actively managed. Be clear with your clients as to what you can and can't deliver, what is or isn't in your estimate and what results may be realistic from your endeavor. Otherwise, unspoken expectations may wreak havoc on project fulfillment.

PROMISES

In your initial dialogue with clients, you will uncover promises that your client may have made to other important stakeholders, his boss and other vendors or partners. It will be your task to determine if these are unofficial, informal expectations or deal breakers that can (and will) affect your project. Clients may say the following:

- Schedule is dictated to the designer: "You can get this done in four weeks, right? I told my boss you could, because we've got a trade show coming up where we need to show this."
- Possible results for your project are predefined: "Our CEO thinks this will increase our sales by 2 percent in six weeks, guaranteed."
- Client is blinded by shiny trophies: "We want to win the Big Fancy Marketing Award with this project. That's why we hired you."

You don't have to agree to any of these promises. Schedules are always negotiable. Metrics for success should be carefully considered. And winning awards should never be the primary goal for your design work.

BUSINESS GOALS

Your clients may set the overall strategy for their business, which your proposed design project should support (or evolve). When talking with your client, ask them to speak about their goals. These are just as valid as their desire for a great website:

- Increased brand impact or value: "We're going to overtake our two main competitors for mindshare with this new website."

- Improved market position: "We want to increase sales for our primary product line by 3 percent by 2014."
- Mergers and acquisitions: "We're seeking to have our company acquired in the next six months to one year."

Before you sign off on a proposal, you need to be aware of these goals. Your project should align with them or help define them more rigorously. The following questions can help designers clarify these goals:

- Are you seeking to augment a currently existing product/service solution?
- Are you seeking to displace a competing product/service with a new product?
- Are you seeking to be acquired?
- Are you seeking to create a completely new product/service?

What you might recommend for a company hoping to be acquired is quite different from what would help them establish an ownable, defenseable and marketable product or service offering. Choosing the appropriate strategy will help you to focus on what problems you can solve by design. The answers will also provide you with a requisite list of skills and tools you will need to bring to bear on the project.

Occasionally the client answers, "We just want to create awareness," or "All of the above and chocolate for everyone!" Promoting a new brand position or launching a broad range of products and services may touch upon a wide variety of strategies. However, a designer's first task is to help clients focus on which options make the most sense and to generate actionable goals for the immediate project. Otherwise any solution that you suggest may be ungrounded, regardless of the popularity of the chocolate idea.

CUSTOMER NEEDS

Your client's business goals don't always align with their customers' stated or unmet needs. You'll want to explore these goals as part of your paid

———

Based on the complexity of the project you're being asked to tackle, you may need your client to pay you for discovery and project definition. What you learn from discovery can then be used to craft a clearly defined scope of work tailored to your client's needs.

———

project discovery process—but sometimes you'll have to form a working hypothesis as part of your proposal in order to secure the work.

When talking to your client, uncover whether they have research that will contribute to your project's point of view. If they don't, you may need to include this research as part of your project scope. If you are conducting research, know that you can insert a contingency in your project plan so that your project scope can change based on your research findings.

PROJECT PERCEPTIONS

Projects can be budgeted and approved, but sometimes your direct client or their business unit isn't really invested. This can create challenges for you, as your client's perceptions of the project and its potential impact on their business—or the world at large—will color how they engage with your work.

You can ask your client some questions to gauge their level of input and investment in the project. These questions include:

- How is the project perceived internally?
- Is the project essential to the well-being of the company?
- Is the project integral to the success of the company?
- Is this project urgent to fulfill or something they are finally getting around to?

CLIENT AND CORPORATE POLITICS

Wouldn't it be nice if you could just ask your clients what may go wrong over the life of a project? With the right questions, you may be able to sniff out the information necessary to understand what political hurdles may stand in the project's way. You can group the questions like this:

Understanding your direct client contacts (and their bosses)
- How do your clients see themselves, personally and within their team and organization?
- How is your direct client contact perceived by his bosses?
- Is "boss input" considered integral to project success, compared to market acceptance?
- Are the people you are working with at a level within their organization to affect the nature of change they seek?
- Does your client possess the skills to solve the problem at hand?
- Is your client savvy about design?
- Are you straddling a gap in the company's organizational skill set?
- Who's really in charge? (It may not be the boss.)

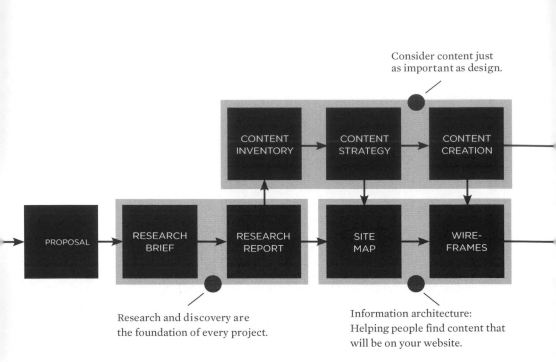

Consider content just as important as design.

Research and discovery are the foundation of every project.

Information architecture: Helping people find content that will be on your website.

Exploring what your clients think about their company
- What does your client's company believe they are great at?
- Is there a difference between what they say and what they do? At the office? In the eyes of their customers?
- What are people within the organization and team saying about each other?
- What do they believe their competitors can't steal away from them?
- What do they believe they know versus what they believe they don't know? Is their view shared across the company?

Shared understanding of the problem you've been asked to solve
You need to agree on the right problem to solve before you can fulfill the desired design work. Some questions include:

- Does everyone involved understand the root cause of the problem they are trying to solve?
- Is the problem a static or moving target? Just how complex is it?

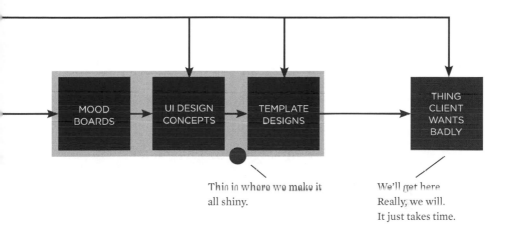

MOOD BOARDS → UI DESIGN CONCEPTS → TEMPLATE DESIGNS → THING CLIENT WANTS BADLY

Thin in whoro wo make it all shiny.

We'll get here
Really, we will.
It just takes time.

- Is the organization ready to deal with the impact of the solution you will provide to their problems?
- What hurdles might stand in your way? Are they avoidable?
- Most important, is the client looking to solve the right problem?

WOW, THAT'S A LOT OF QUESTIONS TO ASK ...

Imagine what would happen if you didn't ask any questions during the proposal process! When you create an estimate, allow time for information gathering as well as a buffer in your studio overhead to accommodate for the times that you don't land the work.

———

Don't mystify the process. Explain where things may get messy in helping your client achieve their goals.

———

Contracts

A contract is a legally binding version of the proposal that you provide for your client, and it includes the complete terms and conditions of your client relationship. A contract outlines a detailed cost estimate, a complete scope of work describing all the deliverables you'll put forth over the life of the project, a simplified schedule and other elements that clarify the terms of engagement between designer and client.

You should never start work on a client project until you have a signed contract. If you design with a handshake instead of a contract, you have no recourse should anything go wrong along the way.

How does a contract protect a designer?

When I think about how a contract protects a designer, I think about rock climbing. A rock climber will insert protection (metal hexes and cams) into cracks in the rock face. These points of protection serve as anchors that he clips his rope into as he works his way up the rock face.

Now replace each piece of protection with each design deliverable that you've included in your contract. Replace the climber with yourself (a designer). The rope that's protecting you from hitting the ground is the contract you've agreed upon with your client. And the belay partner is someone who's working with you, such as another studio principal, a project manager, a client services professional, a lawyer—someone who can help you should anything go wrong.

If you skip steps in your process for convenience or comfort, you increase your risk. If placed properly, the protection will catch you if you slip. The closest piece of protection will serve as a top anchor, and you'll dangle in space while your partner below supports your body weight. But if the protection is poorly placed or untested, it will fail if you slip and you'll continue falling until your weight hits the next piece of protection. You'll drop another 8 to 10 feet to the next deliverable, but you'll gain extra momentum. The next piece of protection will then take on a much greater load, and with that additional stress, you can just imagine. In the worst-case scenario, your rope will snap and you'll go into free fall, taking out everything on the way down and squashing your partner once you land.

If your client pulled out some or all of the protection along the way by not formally approving earlier rounds of deliverables, you're only going to speed faster toward an overall collapse of the client engagement. You risk something worse than scope creep. Let's call it "scope repeat," which is when you find yourself redoing a sizable chunk of work because of unaddressed feedback or new input that completely changed the outline of the project. Each time you deal with scope repeat, you risk going over budget or losing the project completely. Some falls you can't recover from.

A CONTRACT SERVES AS PROTECTION, NOT INSURANCE FOR INATTENTION

Your contract is only as strong as your work over the life of the project, and the quality of your relationship with your client. Your contract must ensure that you will get paid for time spent on the work—provided you fulfill the terms of the agreement in a professional manner, of course.

Be sure to specify approval of your work in writing through each round, and capture and respond to all client feedback. A contract can't always protect you when it comes to measures of client satisfaction, but if you have documented proof of approval, then your protection will hold firm in a negotiation.

What kinds of contract terms will protect me?

You need to work with a lawyer to establish contract terms that will protect you. And the terms may differ by city or state, even by specific market. Lawyers are experts at helping laypeople wrangle with the nitty-gritty details of contract law. They will help you understand what points in your contract should be verboten, no matter what a prospective client may say.

Now, that said, after living through a good number of stumbles, I've started to mandate a few critical contract terms in my client agreements. If you're looking to be professional and also clear about intellectual property (IP) ownership in the midst of a medium- to long-term design engagement, you should check to make sure you include these kinds of terms in your standard design contract.

––––

Disclaimer: I am not a lawyer and these clauses are written in plain language. I can't guarantee how they will hold up for you in a court of law or arbitration. Go over them with your attorney to ensure that they will support your business needs before using them in a contract. Did I mention that you should be working with a lawyer? Good.

––––

CLAUSE #1: YOU DON'T HAVE RIGHTS TO IT UNTIL I'VE BEEN PAID

"After receipt of final payment for [deliverables in contract], [client name] will retain [level of rights granted] for [intellectual property and/or materials] created under this contract."

In plain language: Retain all rights to your work until you are paid in full for all work outlined in your contract.

Why would you use this clause? It protects you from a client balking on payment for services rendered at any time during the life of the contract and attempting to use deliverables that you have provided without due compensation. This is especially important in cases in which you are generating intellectual property, such as naming, brand positioning, identity and brand systems, websites and so on.

CLAUSE #2: IF YOU CANCEL THE CONTRACT PAY ME FOR ALL THE HOURS I'VE WORKED

"Upon cancellation of services after having engaged [my design services], the client will be billed for all hours worked at [my hourly rate]."

In plain language: If the client halts or cancels a project midstream, all hours worked to date will be billed to the client.

Why would you use this clause? To help your client understand that there are repercussions for engaging a designer's professional services, then freezing or canceling a project. The designer should not be held responsible for the costs incurred due to the client's request.

CLAUSE #3: I WON'T EXTEND YOU CREDIT, SO PAY ME BEFORE I START THE WORK

"Designer will be paid for [services rendered] with the following schedule. First payment is due before work will begin on [name of first deliverable]..."

In plain language: Don't offer credit to any new client, no matter what. Provide a payment schedule that mandates a payment in advance of each phase.

Why would you use this clause? You should never start work for a client without a deposit. If they can't pay you up front to start your project, then warning bells are ringing. Run a credit check on your client to be sure they can pay the rest of that $200,000 fee. This is not outside the realm of possibility for any designer to request, especially when you are seeking to secure large-scale projects. This may be less of an issue for clients who have established a firm payment history with your firm.

CLAUSE #4: WE SHOULD GO TO MEDIATION IF THERE IS A DISPUTE
"Any unresolvable dispute between designer and client will be settled by mediation in [your place of jurisdiction]."

In plain language: If a conflict becomes insoluble, protect yourself by entering into mediation instead of the court system, which will cost both parties a large amount of money in lawyers and fees.

Why would you use this clause? Taking this route can save smaller design businesses from the major legal fees contract disputes can incur. However, if a client still fails to pay after coming to an agreement in mediation—and this does happen—you might end up in court anyway.

SOME CONTRACT BATTLES JUST AREN'T WORTH FIGHTING
Nathan Peretic, cofounder of Full Stop Interactive, has this partially tongue-in-cheek list that he uses to remind himself of the value of building a healthy relationship with a client alongside having a strong contract:

1. Anything can be litigated.
2. Anything that can be litigated will be litigated.
3. Being right doesn't guarantee a ruling in your favor.
4. Everyone believes he (or she) is right.
5. If a dispute goes to court, everyone loses.

The last item on the list is definitely true. "It may be worth taking a hit by surrendering to an angry client, rather than stubbornly losing money fighting for a point of honor," says Nathan.

Spec Work

You should not do free design work to win projects. If you're providing free design work, or "spec creative," you're making it harder for yourself and everyone else in our profession to run profitable design businesses. It's possible to communicate the value of your design without actually designing client-facing deliverables.

Why should I avoid doing spec work?

Jeffrey Zeldman of Happy Cog wrote a powerful blog post about speculative creative many years ago that has held true. (Read it here: www.zeldman.com/daily/0104h.shtml.) In it, he notes three things you should keep in mind:

FIRST, IT'S A LOT OF UNPAID WORK

That's right: You're doing the work that you would be paid for during a real project—except you are gambling that the client will like your work and pay you for it after you've already done it. To paraphrase the designer Gunnar Swanson: It is a sucker bet. You're paying for the privilege of playing at a casino table whose odds are stacked against you. This is time that you could be spending looking for paid work, fulfilling paid work or creating your own products or services that you could be compensated for. Where would you rather invest your time?

SECOND, DESIGN IS ONLY PARTLY DECORATION

For many design disciplines, the visual design is the last element you'd show in a well-measured design process. Showing design work to your client before you have started the paid project implies, whether you like it or not, that your process is a sham. Your client could think that you skip over

———

A recent trend that gets around this issue involves giving agencies under consideration token payments for spec assignments or dressing up the same activities as "design competitions." In these situations, the amount paid to the agencies is usually far lower than the cost of the billable time necessary to complete the speculative work.

———

measured research and forethought to solve problems that you only half understand at the outset.

THIRD, IT'S UNSAFE FOR AGENCY AND POTENTIAL CLIENT ALIKE
Until you've been paid or foolishly signed away your rights, you hold copyright for everything you create in a pitch situation. Your potential clients, however, may not understand this. In my former agency life, I presented speculative design work to clients who had not hired me, and in a matter of months, watched our agency's concepts hit the market. This is bad business for all parties involved.

Why do so many designers still do spec work?

Professional organizations such as the AIGA and the Graphic Artists Guild consistently lobby against the perils of speculative creative, as well as crowdsourced design work. But plenty of people are willing to generate spec creative, to deliver game-changing strategy in the pitch and to take part in any number of other questionable activities necessary to land new business. Just who are you, spec-friendly designer?

YOU HAVE FOCUSED YOUR EFFORTS WITHIN A SPECIFIC NICHE OF DESIGN THAT DEMANDS SPEC WORK
Many agencies specialize in niche mediums, such as motion graphics for film and video. It is common in some of these industries to pitch ideas up front to obtain client work—and agencies that handle these mediums are fairly open about it. Some clients consider it the way design studios "pay for the privilege" to receive plum projects, and studios factor this pitch work into their project costs. Even the most respected practitioners in the field are not exempt. During a talk I saw Kyle Cooper give, he described how when he exited Imaginary Forces to found Prologue, he was still regularly pitching spec work in order to be considered.

YOU WORK AT A BIG ADVERTISING OR MARKETING AGENCY AND WANT AN ACCOUNT THAT JUST WENT INTO REVIEW
Pitch and bitch, as the saying goes. If you want to be a Mad Wo/Man, you may be required to roll up your sleeves and give up big-money thinking for the privilege of being considered by Fortune 500 accounts. The use of search consultants, who are paid to facilitate these agency reviews, adds another set of flaming hoops to the process.

YOU MAKE MONEY FROM MARKING UP MATERIALS, NOT TIME
I have worked at more than one agency where profit was made from the markup on printing. Our pitches followed a rigorous formula, contingent on showing big idea concepts with reams of completely designed executions, often in the hope that the client would pick one direction wholesale so we could move immediately into production.

YOUR CLIENT HAS A POLICY THAT REQUIRES SPECULATIVE CREATIVE FOR PROJECTS OF A CERTAIN SIZE
Most design studios trip over this issue when they lust after big projects with marquee clients. A large client's procurement-focused mentality can turn agency discussions into cattle calls.

YOU WANT TO TRY TO GENERATE ENOUGH REVENUE QUICKLY TO FORESTALL LAYOFFS
I have freelanced at agencies where they have been in the throes of massive pitches that included spec work for the simple reason that if they didn't secure the revenue, they'd have to lay off everyone on the floor. Desperate times called for desperate measures.

ANOTHER DESIGN BUSINESS PROVIDES SPEC WORK IN THEIR PROPOSAL FOR THE SAME PROJECT
If one of your competitors happens to show spec work, you might be offered the "opportunity" to match their contribution before the client makes a decision. Use your best judgment in these situations—though you already know what my advice is.

COMPANY OWNER / CEO

Raise My Baby   Make More Money

MIDDLE MANAGEMENT

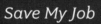

Save My Job   Get Me Promoted

LOW-LEVEL STAFF

Fear for Future   Ready for Change

Politics

What you create as a designer will advance the interests and needs of your client's organization, but it will also influence the status and advancement of your direct day-to-day clients. As a result, no matter how large or how small your client organization, you're always going to have to consider situational politics when you propose and fulfill design projects.

Here's how to consider the role of politics in your new business process, your client service efforts, your project management approach and your stance as a strategic partner to your client.

How do I identify politics when pursuing new business opportunities?

In your meetings with a client, politics emerge when addressing the following questions:

WHAT ARE THE CONDITIONS FOR PROJECT SUCCESS?
Consider the metrics you'll be measured by, both in terms of hard numbers and softer, more qualitative improvements. Desiring an increase in the annual revenue per user (ARPU) of a company's customer base can require different tactics than having a nicer-looking mobile application than their direct competitor. These metrics are directly tied to how you frame and fulfill your projects.

HOW IS THE CLIENT REALLY BEING MEASURED FOR SUCCESS?
The CEO may want you to "save their ugly baby," while their staff might want to throw it out with the bathwater. Or your client may be desperate to show progress on a long-running project in order to receive a promotion. Tease out these contradictions before starting a client project, though some may only emerge in the flow of the work.

WHOSE ASS IS ON THE LINE IF THINGS GO WRONG?
If a problem crops up during your project, who will deal with it? Is there a risk of that problem being exploited? Not all clients will openly support your efforts to mitigate an error. Not everyone in your client organization may trust you. There may be external partners or vendors waiting in line to take your place.

DOES THE CLIENT FORESEE ANY HURDLES OR OBSTACLES?
Your client knows what internal storms are brewing in her organization. Discuss ways to help steer you clear of them, or address them, if appropriate.

HOW DOES THIS UPCOMING PROJECT FIT INTO THE CLIENT'S BRAND AND/OR MARKETING STORY?
Politics often emerge from the friction between the client's brand story, as perceived by its customers, and the stories that clients tell themselves to preserve their company culture or ways of working. Be aware of how to help align your clients with customer need.

DO YOU KNOW WHO NEEDS TO BE IN THE ROOM?
Be aware of the emotional and logical drivers of your clients, and what is at stake for each of them. Different sizes and shapes of client organization dictate the kind of politics you'll need to negotiate over the course of any project. One way to mitigate political influence is to build a RACI Matrix with your client. *(You can find this matrix in the "Stakeholders" section.)*

How can I protect my project in progress from political impacts?

The business strategy shifts during a project midstream, forcing a change in your direction—and potentially a change order. A surprise decision maker is revealed too late in the process. You are blindsided by a manager with a bone to pick.

These situations should be the exception, not the rule. You can't always control politics, but you can control the following:

CONTROL PROJECT DEADLINES AND AGREED-UPON SCOPE
When politics force changes to your overall project work flow, do not try to fit the necessary changes into the scope of your current contract. Instead assert a new schedule that takes the changes into account, and consider the additional scope or cost that may be required to accommodate those changes. It is not appropriate for you to adjust how you deliver your work in order to accommodate unforeseen factors.

Have a backup plan for projects that go over schedule and may require pulling your team away to address other paid projects. It's better to have a contingency plan well in advance of the close date of the project than to leave a client high and dry or to bring in freelancers to finish out the work at a loss.

CONTROL THE IMPACT OF FEEDBACK

When client feedback comes in, you need to sniff out where specific requests originate, and how they relate to the project brief. If they don't speak to the brief, they may be subjective or motivated by politics. Client requests are not marching orders. There is often room to discuss alternatives.

At the end of your project, your goal is for the client to "own" the work as if they created it themselves, as a personally invested client is often the best kind of client to have. Good client feedback should state the goals that you need to attain without telling you in mathematical detail how to reach them. *(See "Feedback.")*

Consider leaving space in key deliverables for a client to "add value." It can help to think through how your stakeholders make decisions. Does everyone look to one person in the room for the final say? In these situations, it isn't always the boss or CEO who weighs in. The key decision maker can be a middle manager or project contributor that has been given a chance to lead, the organizer of a task force or even an outside consultant. It may not become apparent until you've had your first client presentation, even with a RACI matrix in place.

With some clients, however, the opposite may be true: You won't get an approval without everyone weighing in. All seventy-two of them. Organizations that depend on a collaborative decision making process, or "design by committee," will hinder your efforts at creating a cohesive design. Make sure there is one client representative who coordinates that feedback. They should manage differing perspectives and focus the rest of the group on defining specific action items. Otherwise you may risk receiving a chorus of competing opinions and demands, which will only dilute the quality of your work.

When sitting with clients through my first and second face-to-face meetings, I watch how people discuss key action items. Based on what I've observed, I confirm an appropriate presentation strategy with my primary client before presenting future rounds of work.

HELP VARIOUS STAKEHOLDERS CARE ABOUT YOUR WORK

Clients don't always recognize great design work. You should strive to wrap a compelling story around your deliverables. Some of the reasons we do what we do as designers aren't immediately clear to those outside of our profession. Without a strong storytelling component, your project will continually struggle to gain acceptance.

Deliverables should be shaped for your audience
You may need to adapt or shorten your story, depending on your core audience. An executive presentation for the CEO will be a dramatically different beast than what you send to your regular client contact.

Always point back to the strategy
Your story should define and clarify the connections between the deliverable and the insights from the design brief.

Deliverables should speak for themselves
Ask yourself, "Will my client understand this work without me there to provide a voice-over? Is everything (objectives, outcomes and next steps) communicated clearly in the deliverable?" Consider showing your deliverable to someone who has no knowledge of your project. Can they repeat the story back to you without too much effort?

ACTIVELY COMMUNICATE WITH YOUR CLIENT
Actively listen and overcommunicate when it comes to understanding client fears. This is not about encouraging high-frequency or neurotic contact with your client. Instead, encourage active dialogue so you can understand any worries your client may have regarding the project. Your client doesn't need to tiptoe around the realities of what makes their day job difficult, and you can make these conversations productive by documenting and revisiting client worries as the project progresses.

BE A RESPONSIBLE CONSULTANT
If a client asks you to make changes to your work for political gain, rather than for the purpose of improving the quality of the end product, he is not being a responsible client. If you are dealing with this kind of situation, you must remain a responsible consultant at all costs.

What does being a responsible consultant mean?

1. We never confuse our point of view with our client's task.

2. We seek to align the client's view with our own, if our view is properly informed.

3. We practice integrity, which means that we respect the needs of the client's customer throughout a project.

Be cautious not to overstep your bounds. If you've been asked to define the company's strategy, then do so. If you've been asked to follow it instead, then only challenge it if you feel things are going down the wrong path. It's possible that the work you provide may create opportunities for organizational change within a client's company, but you can't expect that it will always be the outcome or that you know better than your clients.

In most cases, you will know less than your clients about the business strategies they are executing out in the market. And if you do have more knowledge, then you don't want to be the therapist who on the first appointment with their new client says, "You don't have to tell me any more. Quit your job, go back to school. By the way, your boyfriend is cheating on you, so move out now."

Competing political priorities can cover up the most innovative design solution in the same way that dust dulls a diamond. If you help your client sweep away the political debris throughout the design process, your work will sparkle just as it should.

Negotiation

When first striking out on their own as businesspeople, many designers don't know how to bargain or strike a deal. Consider this story from creative consultant Ted Leonhardt, cofounder of The Leonhardt Group and a consultant for design businesses. What would you do in this situation?

My associate, Tim, had the opportunity to redesign one of the great American brands. It hadn't been updated for years, and the company needed to present a revitalized brand at an upcoming event.

Tim was chosen because of his packaging expertise. While not known as a brand design house, his firm had significant experience with packaging that overlapped nicely into branding. He was desperate for this job, because brand design has more status than packaging design. This assignment would launch his firm into that heady, highly profitable world.

So, Tim's leverage was spectacular. His firm was the only one being considered. His skill set was a perfect match. He was the perceived expert, and, even better, the client had only three months until the unveiling of the new brand. There was no time to source a new design firm.

Tim presented his fee proposal. His direct client approved it and they began work. At the next meeting, while discussing the results of the discovery phase, his client mentioned that Purchasing had questions and would be calling in to the meeting to talk.

Enter Mr. Procurement. He called from his car, apologizing for not being there and mentioning that he has been extremely important to the company's turnaround by streamlining divisions and vendors globally. (A classic power play.)

"We can't wait to see your solutions. We are thrilled to have you on our team. Hitting a home run on this will launch your firm into big-time branding. But there are a couple of things we must address before I sign your purchase order...." (Another textbook power play.)

You can guess what happened next. The client's purchasing policy required a 20 percent discount on fees over $300k, and payment 180 days after completion. Before he really knew what was happening, Tim had agreed to the terms.

What went wrong? Tim was vulnerable. He needed the job and had his team going full speed. He was confused by the new conditions and afraid of losing the work. However, he forgot that he had the leverage of expertise. Time was on his side. The company could not meet their deadline without him. Instead of negotiating from this position of strength, Tim let his client take advantage of him.

When working with any new or existing client, you need to be prepared to address situations like these. Whether you're negotiating the payment terms for an upcoming project or amending changes to a design based on client feedback, negotiation skills are required in the conversations you'll carry out with a client.

The following tips will help you next time you enter into a negotiation with a client. Similarly, they can apply to internal negotiations within your company.

How do I best negotiate with a client?

HAVE A POSITION BEFORE YOU ENTER THE ROOM

Good negotiation starts with knowing what you want and putting it forth in conversation. This requires a substantial amount of preparation and asking the right questions through the discovery process, rather than improvising responses in calls and emails. When you negotiate from a position of strong preparation, the other party will be more comfortable meeting you on your terms, based on your expertise.

UNDERSTAND WHAT KIND OF LEVERAGE YOU HAVE

Design firms bring a range of skills and hard-fought experience to bear on client problems. This is expertise that our clients rarely have within their own organization. "The most important leverage any design firm has is expertise," says Ted Leonhardt. "Each of us has our own mix of history, skills and experience. A client can only get the unique skills you provide from you."

Beyond expertise, you also have leverage with regard to schedule, scope and other variables that are necessary for client success.

MAKE SURE YOUR POSITION IS REALISTIC

If you wanted two million dollars and a platinum-plated Rolls Royce, negotiations would be difficult. However, if you're presenting an estimate for a design project and have some strong logic behind your pricing, or some ground as to why your audience will prefer green instead of blue for their new logo, you shouldn't change your position.

COMMON SELF-DEFEATING NEGOTIATION BEHAVIORS

Charles Wiggins—a lawyer and expert in negotiation—and Ted Leonhardt, recommended in an article in *Graphic Design USA* that designers watch out for the following "tells" designers often exhibit when negotiating with clients:

Intimidation: A representative of a powerful company brings her positional power to bear on you—the beautiful office, the 20-foot conference table, executive assistants, the works. But, remember, if you are sitting at that conference table, you are there for a reason. You have something they need. Something that is not widely available. Use that knowledge to your advantage.

Talking Too Much: Nervousness can lead to talking too much, a sign of discomfort and neediness that a trained negotiator can exploit. Talking too much at the bargaining table can get you into trouble. Be honest, but don't give away all of your secrets.

Insecurity: Our "product" is personal, and we need praise and affirmation for who we are and what we do. But in competitive situations, many talented people concentrate on their weaknesses, not their strengths. They discount their own accomplishments and fear that their credentials are lacking.

Rolling Over: Designers can be so eager to get past the uncomfortable bargaining stage to where they feel in control—doing the work— that they just throw in the towel.

Cutting Deliverables: The creative firm puts together the perfect team, approach and deliverables to precisely meet the client's needs. Then they freak out at their own price, and cut out steps before the presentation. Why would we not want to present our best, most thoughtful approach, and explain the benefits when challenged?

COMPROMISES SHOULD BE AROUND SHARED INTERESTS

Don't give up in your negotiations until you've exhausted possibilities that meet your shared interests and help your firm create a quality product. Push for your best-case scenario, preserving your project's schedule, budget, creative direction and so forth. Know what other cards you can place on the table or return to your hand before considering a compromise.

ALWAYS KEEP THE BIG PICTURE IN MIND

Know which decisions require formal negotiation and which are just potholes in the road. Changing a headline or swapping out a photo shouldn't be a drama. Spiking a killer concept to play it safe? That's another story. If you have a strong creative brief and a strong contract, these points shouldn't become issues. Don't treat every single discussion and point of feedback with the client as a potential conflict.

DON'T AGREE TO A DEAL UNTIL YOUR TEAM AGREES

When discussing action steps, withhold agreement when necessary. Avoid saying yes on anything related to schedule, scope management and other contractually-required action steps until you can review the discussion with your internal team. Make sure that your team's goals and your client needs are aligned. To quote Robert Solomon in his excellent book *The Art of Client Service*: "Make no commitment without consultation."

BE AWARE OF CULTURAL NUANCES

I once worked with a foreign client whose method of negotiation was to state in every deliverable review that there were always things that could be improved. We found ourselves increasing the project scope and number of deliverables in order to compensate for the perceived lack in quality. Their negotiating position wasn't unusual in their country, but it was for our team. After a few nerve-racking weeks, we realized that the client's escalations were an opportunity to set up clear approval criteria to demonstrate how our design work had merit and was on brief. In our final presentation, the success of our project was clearly evident to everyone within their organization.

DON'T RUSH TO AGREE WITH A CLIENT NEED

If the stakes are high, take your time and hash out the finer points in detail. The longer and more drawn out the negotiation, the more important it is to never show your "settling point." Get some time and space to think it over. Don't jump on the phone and immediately try to iron it out. Otherwise, whomever you're negotiating with may think that they can push their position even further. These situations are very hard for designers; we love to solve problems as quickly as possible!

KEEP YOUR DIALOGUE HUMANE, RESPECTFUL AND HONEST

When negotiating with clients or your boss, make sure you don't turn your negotiations into an "us vs. them" scenario. Our clients and co-workers have the same set of human needs that we do, and relating with them on a human level will strengthen your continued working relationship. It will also cement the expectation that no matter what happens in your work, you'll always be on equal footing as people.

BE PREPARED TO LEAVE THE TABLE AT ANY POINT

Be willing to walk away from a negotiation if you think the options available are going to hurt you in the long term. Being willing to say no is important in contract negotiations, and the natural human desire to avoid conflict is a something that potential clients may exploit. It's okay to say no.

IF THE NEGOTIATION FAILS, DON'T TAKE IT PERSONALLY

Hindsight is 20/20. If you don't land a project because it wasn't the right fit, or the client overrules your beautiful color scheme because they dislike purple, learn from what happened and move forward. Don't let your conscience eat a hole in your gut. Analyzing these failures can have a big impact on improving future negotiations.

FAILURE TO LAND A PROJECT CAN LEAD TO A FUTURE WIN

Relationships between your co-workers and your clients continue, even if you fail in your first negotiations. If you've been cordial and truthful about your position and the experience that you bring throughout the entire negotiation process, you'll gain respect. Mutual respect comes from establishing clear boundaries and reinforcing them throughout the life of a relationship. This is the currency that will yield future work and support you when you get down to business.

FURTHER READING ABOUT THE ART OF NEGOTIATION

Getting to Yes: Negotiating Agreement Without Giving In, by Roger Fisher, William Ury and Bruce Patton
Influence: The Psychology of Persuasion, by Robert B. Cialdini
How to Win Friends and Influence People, by Dale Carnegie

Discounts

The word *discount*, the last refuge of the desperate marketer, should never enter the designer's lexicon except at great peril.

I can't recall the last time I phoned a lawyer and asked to engage his services for a deep discount on his amicus curiae brief so I could make budget. If a designer is providing strategic insight and business value, then clients should treat them with the same respect they would afford a consultant. As the saying goes: You pay a consultant to tell you about the problems you already knew you had. Swap consultant for designer, and you get the added value of professionals who work in tandem with the client to solve those problems.

However, let's get real. Inevitably one of your clients will ask you for a discount. These requests will come in several forms:

- **I only have so much money:** "I can't afford $2,000. I can pay $1,500."
- **I know you, so please give me a deal:** "What about a 'friends and family' discount?"
- **I'm not sure how valuable your services are:** "You are far too expensive. Can you do me a favor and reduce the cost?"
- **I think I can get more for the money:** "Can you throw in a brochure for free?"

Don't let these requests offend you, being the fine consultant that you are. Having little understanding of how designers make money—except in billable hours and flat-rate costs in an estimate—some clients may try to squeeze the most "efficiency" out of their contracts.

But efficiency is an illusion. When you snip hours out of your contract, you end up working them anyway, just to fulfill the ideal process you'd articulated in the initial contract's time estimate.

So you might be able to provide your client with a discount, but only in the following circumstances:

- You want to win a new client
- You want to win a client's trust to gain bigger/better projects
- You want to win back a client's trust, which was lost through a poor prior performance

Here's the rub: If you are absolutely certain that you can deliver a strong product that will be successful, on time, on budget and at a profit, then a discount is probably possible. But if you can't maintain your profit margin or ensure success, you can provide a discount only by changing the deliverables associated with the project:

- **Reduced deliverables:** "We can deliver the website but not the collateral template."
- **Reduced scope inside a deliverable:** "We can do two design concepts instead of three" or "The website will be built on a blog platform instead of a custom content management system."
- **Use direct-to-bill vendors:** "We can use your vendors, and you can pay for them directly."
- **Spread out deliverables:** "We can create the brand direction and the website now, and if you decide to do the print campaign later, we'll see if we can honor the estimate you approved for those specific deliverables."

Clients most frequently ask you for a discount after you've provided them with a proposal. There is nothing wrong with revisiting the cost estimate in your proposal, i.e., providing a discount retroactively. Design businesses do it all the time. However, if you reduce the cost of a project without reducing the deliverables, the project will still cost what you estimated originally. It's just a matter of how much of that cost your client is still paying and how much you're absorbing into your own budget.

It's always better to negotiate on the amount of hours you will provide or on the scope of the deliverable you're being asked to deliver. Your hourly rate should not be negotiable, unless you are asking for substantially more than the market value for your services, or your client is asking to retain you for a long period of time. But even then, there's a risk that for future projects, they would try to hold you to the lower rate.

Be aware, though, that reduced-rate projects rarely benefit any design business. Here are reasons why:

- Cutting corners on a project undermines its overall value for everyone
- By giving a discount, you will have established a rate with the client that can be hard to change in the future
- You will still need to pay contract resources their rates, or work hard to get them to reduce rates
- Resentment can creep in very easily, and you might find yourself saying things like, "That client is cheap!"

DESIGNER EFFORT

CLIENT SATISFACTION

Expectations

Projects can be terrifyingly complex for designers. But projects can become a horror show when clients don't know what to expect as they progress through them.

What follows are some ways you can help clients understand what to expect when working with a designer.

How do I set expectations with a new client?

A few years back, I received a call from a potential client who expected that within two days of kicking off an identity redesign project, he would be seeing fully executed comps—in full color, no less—from which he and his co-workers would provide critical input and choose a direction.

These conversations are known, in client service parlance, as opportunities to "reset expectations" or "fully outline our process," meaning it's time to spend a good fifteen minutes with the client meticulously, but not condescendingly, describing a set of activities that can seem nebulous if he's never worked with a designer. Usually a client has no idea what to expect from a designer until he is reacting to project deliverables.

So, if you want to save yourself time and set client expectations in a matter of seconds, start projects off with your own variant of this chart:

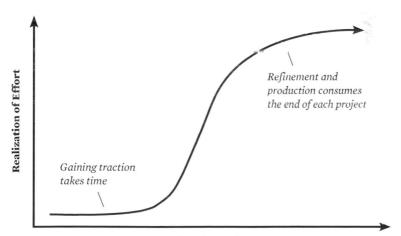

Refinement and production consumes the end of each project

Gaining traction takes time

Realization of Effort

Time for Project

The Design Investment Curve

As you move from discovery (on the left), to concepts (the middle), to the final executed design work (the right), you can point out to the client how the deliverables that you're sharing in that review fit into the overall process of realizing the design work.

If you don't set expectations in this manner at the start of the project, it's likely that no matter what you say or do, your client's expectations are going to look more like the following:

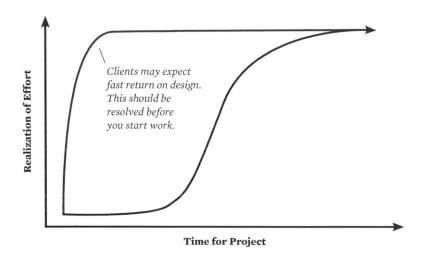

Clients may expect fast return on design. This should be resolved before you start work.

Realization of Effort

Time for Project

The Design Investment Curve Versus Client Expectations

How do I educate a client during a project?

Weave your methodology and process through the work, preparing your client for key moments they may not understand and defining those elements in plain English. They should understand key phases they'll be moving through over the life cycle of a project, as well as how specific activities fit into those phases. This can begin as early as your first proposal, especially if you see or sense that your clients don't understand why you are fulfilling a particular activity.

For example, I conduct design research for many of my clients. Some of the methods that I use seem complex to clients from outside the world of product and service design and development. My clients might not understand what happens when I conduct a contextual inquiry or facilitate a card sort. As a result, I have a cheat sheet of plain-English descriptions for research activities. The descriptions are provided at the appropriate point in a project life cycle to explain an activity's context, value and how it informs ongoing design efforts. The following is the entry for "Paper Prototyping."

PAPER PROTOTYPING

What it is in plain English:
Simple versions of your website pages printed on paper. Customers can use them to give feedback on your proposed designs.

Real-world example:
Bank of America's site visitors aren't signing up for the new AmEx card as the bank had expected. After reviewing site metrics, it becomes clear that visitors give up when they get to the sign-up form. So you draw up sketches that represent different form design options. You put the sketches in front of users and ask them how they would prefer to sign up for a credit card, moving papers around as necessary to "load" new screens. Based on this user input, you make a more informed recommendation on the AmEx card sign-up form design.

Business value:
Witnessing customer reactions to simple paper prototypes will validate critical interaction points and help you protect your web site investment without having to write a single line of code. This is especially important when you want to create seamless transactions for your customers.

Provides input into the following deliverables:
Navigation schema, wireframes, user flows, interaction storyboards, the UI design, the content map, the content strategy and the site map.

This level of detail isn't always required, so don't always feel like you have to overdescribe your work or your process. Some clients don't want to know. In some cases, however, you may be hired to demonstrate best practices and working processes for your clients. If this happens, make sure the time required to provide proper documentation is part of the estimate.

How do I prepare a client for challenging work?

The account director Erica Goldsmith taught me some important lessons about managing client expectations on large-scale projects, especially when taking on work that impacts a company's business strategy.

Clients are used to seeing their business function in certain ways. They have established patterns to assess and manage their customers' expectations—familiar product lines and consistent marketing are only the beginning. Assumptions about customer relationships with a client's product or service can run deep into the heart of a business.

This is partly why your clients may be surprised (or downright shocked) when you present major deliverables such as a new branding strategy, information architecture for an enterprise-level website or a provocative advertising campaign. Your deliverables might generate new insights or opportunities that your client hadn't considered before. They might also bring new data into the client's worldview or reframe aspects of the client's brand or product experience that the client had taken for granted.

If you think this will be the case, inform your client in advance of the meeting what type of approach they can expect from you. You need to let them know that the content is going to provoke dialogue, not that you're going to give them the opportunity to pre-vet or critique the material.

This also gives you a chance to further probe what people (and politics) may emerge from a robust, challenging discussion. You can also establish, as part of your agenda for the meeting, the key points you'd like to drive toward in gathering constructive feedback.

How do I meet client expectations for quality?

The quality of execution on a design deliverable can be subjective to clients if you have not established expectations for what makes a deliverable acceptable. The criteria can be established through simple discussion with your client and through the structuring of your project process so your clients understand the evolution of the solution, from idea to execution.

However, situations will emerge where shared criteria somehow fails. For example, your client approves every deliverable over the life span of a design project. You think everything is fine, but when you provide the client their final deliverable, they say they are not satisfied with your work.

Either of the following two options in this situation can hurt your business. Choosing Option 2 may cost you time and money, but choosing Option 1 may cost you your reputation.

OPTION 1: YOU CAN APOLOGIZE FOR THEIR DISSATISFACTION AND EXPLAIN WHY YOU CANNOT BUDGE ON YOUR FEES

If you take this approach, you are entering into a negotiation over whether the client will pay you for your work to date or agree to a change order to pay for additional revisions to the work. While your contract may fully protect you, there is a risk that the client will want to take you to mediation or court rather than fulfill the terms of the contract or pay you to rectify the situation. This situation is more likely to happen if your immediate client contact did a poor job of socializing your work throughout the project.

OPTION 2: YOU CAN APOLOGIZE FOR THEIR DISSATISFACTION AND ASK THEM TO DESCRIBE HOW THE PROBLEM MAY BE FIXED

If you choose this path, you will negotiate with your client regarding the criteria required for them to accept the balance of the work to date. You will then need to determine the overall cost to you, from a time and materials standpoint, to satisfy the changes they are requesting. You may require the client to pay a portion of that cost.

HOW DO YOU ASSURE PROJECT QUALITY?

If you're sometimes surprised by major errors in your projects—such as websites that don't work or typos slipping into deliverables—you should establish a quality assurance process for your studio. A quality assurance process includes explicit instructions on how you can test your deliverables against specific functional requirements and benchmarks.

Quality assurance should happen before you take any interactive deliverable live. Give yourself enough time to fix any errors and retest. You don't want to cause new errors in the process.

For example: You've created a mobile application for your client that lets people send audio files to each other via SMS. As part of your delivery process, you would carry out rigorous testing to ensure each feature of the application worked across a broad set of use cases and usage scenarios, such as having no signal on your phone, dropping out of the application midtask and so forth.

STEP ONE

STEP TWO

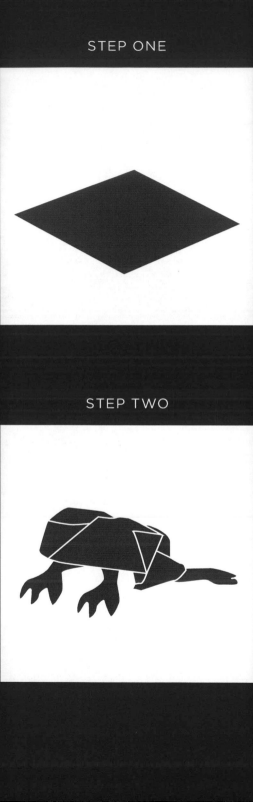

Design Briefs

The essential foundation for every design project is the design brief, *not* the creative work. A design brief is a tool used to clarify and focus what should be created for clients over the course of a design project. You'll know you have a great brief if you start imagining design ideas as you read it. The same goes for when your client reads it.

Crafting a compelling, accurate brief can take substantial effort. Don't expect to cough one up in a few hours—it will take days. However, a well-written and properly informed brief will save your design team countless hours by aligning their efforts with the client's expectations.

If your client has not approved your brief in writing, you should not be designing. A signed brief should be an ironclad must in your practice. Otherwise you run the risk that each round of deliverables is merely an aid to iterate your client's business thinking rather than the quality of your creative work. If you have a well-crafted brief with a very specific key insight, there's no way to change the strategy without incurring costs to the client, both in terms of money and time.

You should refer to the brief in every presentation. The litmus test of a compelling brief is when you polish up your designs, stick them on boards, meet your clients in the conference room and introduce your work by sharing one to two succinct sentences that summarize the entire strategic direction of the project. At this point, their heads should be nodding expectantly, as they wait for you to reveal how you've clothed their business needs in compelling artistry.

The characteristics of strong briefs

While there is no one template that all designers use for design briefs, there are certain characteristics that exemplary briefs share.

COMPELLING BRIEFS ARE BRIEF

A brief is digested, in all senses of the word: It is a condensation of thought indicating a succinct strategic direction and the main reason you're going to expend so much energy over the course of a project generating great design work. This can be conveyed in one or two pages. Support material, such as foundational research, should not be distilled from some twenty-five page PowerPoint deck into pages three through six of the design brief.

The best design briefs are narrow. Scarily so. They make clients sweat a bit under their collars, because they pin clients to one extraordinarily specific business strategy and key insight. There's no wiggle room! Killer creative thinking comes from focus. You need a bull's-eye to aim at, not a wall.

An inverse correlation exists between the length of a design brief and the quality of thought that goes into it. I have haunting memories of being handed design briefs, then realizing that the author was requesting work that communicated three or four different ideas within one piece. The creative process can be easily co-opted for the purpose of focusing the client's marketing or branding strategy in the work itself. This is a waste of time and money for the client and the designer, and no way to run a profitable business. A design brief is a place for clarity, not contradiction.

If a client isn't willing to pin herself to a key understanding (which has been supported by research) about her business needs, then how can you judge the efficacy of your work in the first place?

THEY STATE THE BUSINESS CONDITIONS THAT REQUIRE DESIGN
Have you ever had to sit in a client meeting where the first thing a client says about the brief is: "Do you understand what we're trying to accomplish here? From the brief, it doesn't seem like it. Let's go over the business problem again." You must succinctly and accurately describe the client's business problem in the brief. This should be a distillation of how you stated the same information in the proposal, informed by what you've learned since you started work. Keep it simple, so everyone knows why the project is necessary. Otherwise they may wander off and solve a problem you didn't need them to solve.

THEY CONTAIN ONE WELL-ARTICULATED KEY INSIGHT
The dictionary defines insight as "an accurate and deep intuitive understanding of a person or thing." In the world of design, insight is the bridge from a business challenge to a stated design opportunity. Without an insight, there is little investment in a shared outcome for any large-scale

——

Here are some key insights I've seen in sample creative briefs about the internet: "Big events in London are closer than you think with British Airways." "Pot of Noodle: Your dirty secret." "Mattel: Endless expression."

——

project, especially when working with a diverse set of stakeholders who have their own stated (or unstated) political goals.

An insight, however, is not a summary of a singular research source. An insight emerges from the synthesis of information gathered from a multiplicity of research sources.

And a well-articulated insight is artfully concise.

If it takes you forever to explain the key insight in your brief, you're not doing it right. A good insight should be communicated in two to five seconds flat. "Our product is the best because of x, y, z and x features ..." Nope. Not an insight. If there's a lot of commas, em-dashes, colons or other punctuation in your key benefit statements, you're cramming too much into what should be a simple imperative sentence.

Say one thing. Own it. Keep it simple.

THEY SUPPORT THE KEY INSIGHT WITH REASONS TO BELIEVE

Reasons to believe can be both emotional and rational in nature, and they should be extracted from your research findings. This is usually the area in the brief where thickets of details emerge, oft requiring a machete or a blowtorch. However, these details are secondary to the goals of the project and will further complicate why your target audience will believe your key insight. Plus, if you spend all your time talking about your competition, you're not doing it right.

THEY STATE WHAT EMOTIONS SHOULD BE INSPIRED BY DESIGN

Understanding what your target audience should feel when they encounter one of your studio's designs is a valuable way to calibrate your design team's efforts and create a shared understanding in design critique regarding what makes a specific concept or execution "on brief." Key emotions should not be ambiguous, such as "engaged" or "happy." Dig into your heart's thesaurus and uncover emotions that can inspire your team.

Consider this key insight for Pot of Noodle: "Your dirty secret." Some of the (conflicting) emotions the audience might feel are ashamed, fulfilled and lustful. These emotional drivers may sound absurd for the marketing of an instant soup, but they were rooted in understanding their audience.

THEY DEFINE AND DESCRIBE YOUR AUDIENCE

Yes, it is a good idea to know that your audience is made up of fifty-five to seventy-year-old retiring baby boomers that love to fly home to see their folks and who earn $75,000 a year on their pensions.

But it's even better to know Polly.

She lives in Boca Raton, Florida, in a retirement community, plays tennis twice a week at the club, has a weak spot for QVC, spends time on Facebook with her sorority sisters from college and regularly looks for travel bargains for impromptu trips to see her new grandkids. She is also a technology maven, having started and sold fourteen companies before her early retirement at the age of fifty-nine.

Is she your target audience, or an outlier? The latter often deliver the most valuable insight, especially if you are seeking to disrupt by design. Moving beyond the "mass audience" your client wants to reach and exploring select customer segments can be liberating for your designers. It can also help focus your client conversations regarding just who the audience is for whatever you create. "Everyone who lives in Canada" is not a valid audience segment. Neither is: "Everyone who wants to buy a great can opener." If that were the case, then Smart Design would never have met with arthritis patients and young children while researching potential designs for OXO Good Grips—and created a breakthrough product line.

How you describe your audience should be just as narrow as how you define your single takeaway, and it should show up either in the brief or in supporting documentation that the client approves. You need to know the behavior of your audience and how it may differ from other people out there in the world. (We'll get to research briefs in a minute.)

If you're sharing thoughts about your audience at the same time that you're showing concepts, it's too late. You're giving your client another thing to critique besides the creative work. Have the client agree to your audience within a research summary, and reference the research summary in the brief.

THEY OUTLINE HOW AUDIENCE BEHAVIOR CAN CHANGE

Communicating an idea is nice, but unless people act upon the new information that you've provided them with, nothing is going to change for your client's business.

THEY CONVEY A CLIENT'S BRAND VOICE AND EXPRESSION

Whether or not your client has established brand guidelines, you should call out exactly what constraints will be placed on your designers regarding brand voice and personality, and bring up any unique graphic elements that may be required in the final visual expression. This doesn't mean you should include a laundry list of every element. Point the designer, even if the designer is you, to other documents or information, as appropriate.

THEY PROVIDE HIGH-LEVEL SPECIFICATIONS FOR WHAT TO MAKE

Are you looking to create an online advertising campaign, a new identity system or the interior design of a bus? This should be noted in the brief, as it will let the team know what kind of output they should generate. If you need to run the team through twenty-seven different deliverables associated with the design brief, you should prepare a separate deliverables brief. (See the next section.)

THEY READ AS PLAIN ENGLISH, NOT MARKETING JARGON

Cleansing your briefs of marketing and researchspeak can clarify some key points for your creative team. If you have to leave jargon in the brief to demonstrate understanding or market expertise to a client, then have a glossary attached that defines the lingo you've used. Even long-term clients who have evolved a common language with your account management and creative teams should be patrolled. What happens if your designer is out sick for a week and you need to bring someone in to help? You'll be playing "decode the brief" for hours.

———

An amazing design brief won't save a bad product or business strategy. Sorry. Just had to say it.

———

Different briefs for different moments in a project

A design brief is most frequently used as a focusing tool for designers who need to understand what they should be designing. However, there are other types of briefs that may be employed at different points in the design process. You probably won't need all of these briefs on a smaller-scale effort, but a massive design project may require each of the following.

RESEARCH BRIEF

With an approved research brief and/or plan, a designer can forge ahead, conducting research activities to inform and guide the design work. Outputs that may be expected from agreed-upon research activities may include audience segmentation, personas or archetypes and a project's creative brief. A research brief should:

- State the client's business problem as it is currently understood
- Identify the gaps in knowledge that you're seeking to fill

- List the specific research activities that will serve as inputs into future design work
- Qualify the audience that you're seeking to reach

EXPERIENCE BRIEF

An experience brief is the foundation deliverable designers can use when crafting large-scale interactive experiences. Gaining approval on an experience brief before diving into site maps and wireframes helps support key decisions around a website's information architecture—well before a design brief and visual design direction are established. An experience brief should:

- Reframe the client's business problem with new data and insight derived from research
- Establish a "parti," which is a central idea or metaphor that serves as a foundation for the structure of an interactive system—the same way that a key insight serves as the core of a design brief
- Describe the story arc your team is seeking to create for a person who visits the website or uses the application
- Convey story concepts and themes that will weave into the visual execution
- Describe the activities that site visitors will take part in and the emotions that those activities should evoke

DELIVERABLES BRIEF

Deliverables briefs are most useful when a team that is familiar with an approved design brief and set of design directions is continuing onward to design additional, complementary elements. A deliverables brief should:

- State the agreed-upon strategy (from the design brief)
- Restate the key insight and reasons to believe (from the design brief)
- Describe the relationship between a previous project's output and new deliverables that must be created
- Provide in-depth specification for each deliverable, as well as any messaging that may be required for each deliverable

Deliverables

A design brief is only one of a range of deliverables you'll provide a client over the course of a well-formed design project. Strong deliverables are chapters in a story that you are telling over the life of a client project. If you do a good job of shaping deliverables for your audience, they will embrace your story and convey it to others.

You should collaborate with your client to understand their needs as you become fully immersed in a project, and tune your deliverables when appropriate to help communicate the quality and fit of your design work.

However, you should not allow the client to dictate your deliverables or change your necessary design process in a manner that jeopardizes your project output.

Project deliverables should have been clearly outlined in your proposal with your client, and they should have also been tied to a payment schedule that follows the course of the project. For example, a website design and development project may have some of the following deliverables, with payment triggered by delivery of visual design and the code at the end:

- **Design Brief (one to two pages):** Describes agreed-upon strategy for project. Two rounds of review, with edits.
- **Content Strategy Document (two to four pages):** Defines critical content for website to be generated by client before entering development. Two rounds of review, with edits.
- **Site Map and Low-Fidelity Wireframes (up to three page templates):** Shows information architecture across site and placement of key content. Includes light annotations. Two rounds of review, with edits.
- **Mood Boards (two):** Establishes foundation for visual design direction for website. One round of review, with edits.
- **Visual Design Templates for Website (two page comps):** Visual design for two website templates in Photoshop (PSD) format. Two rounds of review, with edits.
- **HTML and CSS Templates (up to five pages):** Coded page templates that may be repurposed for key content areas across website. Two rounds of review, with edits.

Meetings

In the name of providing great client service, it can be tempting to encourage face-to-face contact as often as possible. However, meetings cost money. Stuff the room with twenty-seven important people who want to weigh in on a pressing client problem and then count the billable hours you've consumed in order to have everyone be part of the process.

Next time you think about placing a meeting on anyone else's calendar—whether co-worker or potential client—consider the following. Everyone will thank you for it.

How do I plan for and manage a meeting?

DETERMINE IF IT NEEDS TO BE A MEETING
Make sure a formal meeting is necessary before you expend the energy required to plan it. The content of most meetings can be covered in a quick face-to-face conversation, a phone call or Skype conversation, or through a brief email or IM exchange.

DON'T DEFAULT TO THIRTY MINUTES
If it does need to be a meeting, how much could you accomplish in four minutes? Two minutes? Some issues can be addressed in microincrements.

CONTROL WHO NEEDS TO BE IN THE ROOM
Before blasting out an invite, determine critical attendees. No, you don't want to leave out anyone on the team. But be honest: Don't they have better things to do? Touch base with them and see if they want to be included in the meeting, and if doing so will cut into their workday productivity. If they are going to attend, assign them an agenda item.

ALWAYS PREPARE AN AGENDA AND GROUND RULES
Any meeting you have with a client or your team should be planned in advance. When you're creating the agenda, understand what kind of meeting you're seeking to create: Standup/status meeting (i.e., who's doing what today), start work/kickoff meeting or presentation of a deliverable. At the meeting, make sure the agenda is distributed to everyone involved. Enforce the agenda. It also helps to have clear ground rules for everyone to follow, independent of the topics you'll discuss. For example, information architect

Bram Wessel recommends the following guidelines he uses for meetings: "No devices. Time-boxed agendas. No decks. Call it a 'workshop,' not a meeting. Limit attendees and make them stand."

PROVIDE FOOD OR DRINK, AS APPROPRIATE
Providing coffee, tea, water and other small snacks can go a long way for any meeting, whether it's a client meeting or just an internal one. I like dropping a dark chocolate bar on the table after a tough meeting is half over. It always brightens conversation and helps people relax.

RUTHLESSLY CONTROL THE SCOPE OF THE CONVERSATION
Keep an eye on the clock to keep attendees honest regarding how much time each uses on a specific topic. If the meeting has more than a few people, one person can play the role of timekeeper. If a topic simply won't die, ask if you can "park" it in the parking lot, a space on the whiteboard for items that require further discussion after the meeting.

PLAN BREAKS IN YOUR MEETINGS AND HOLD PEOPLE TO THEM
Control any breaks that you factor into your agenda. A five-minute break can easily slide into fifteen minutes and derail planned activities or topics of discussion.

ASSIGN A SCRIBE TO DOCUMENT THE DISCUSSION
One attendee of the meeting should capture key points of feedback, clearly outline action items, and at the end of the meeting, read aloud a list of what must be clarified or followed up after the meeting. (See "Feedback.")

DON'T SPILL YOUR CONVERSATION INTO ANOTHER MEETING
If anyone in the room requests scheduling another meeting to continue the discussion, it probably won't be another meeting with the same people at the table. Step outside of the meeting to consult with the appropriate people and determine what next steps are required to keep moving.

START ON TIME AND END FIVE MINUTES EARLY
Acknowledge the commute that attendees have before and after meetings, whether from hours away or across the hall. Graciously accommodate their travel by leaving space at the end of your agenda for them to reach their next destination on time. No one likes to rush—especially if they're having to run to another meeting.

Presentations

Designers are afraid of many things: Poorly kerned type, color palettes that seem to have been constructed by an angry toddler and presenting design work to clients. But don't fret. Promoting your firm and presenting your deliverables are skills that can be learned the same way you can learn how to draw clipping paths in Adobe Illustrator.

How can I become a better presenter?

I happen to be married to a professional speaking coach, Mary Paynter Sherwin, so I asked her for her perspective on how to become a better presenter of design work. Here's what she said.

EVERYBODY ON YOUR TEAM NEEDS TO KNOW HOW TO PRESENT

Everybody needs to know how to hold a board properly, how to gesture at a PowerPoint without pointing with one finger and how not to rock back and forth like they're trapped in the basement in a horror movie. But the only way you're going to learn all of this is if you become familiar with how you talk.

ANYONE CAN LEARN TO BE AN EFFECTIVE PRESENTER

The first obstacle is getting over saying to yourself, 'I'm just not comfortable doing it.' Comfort has nothing to do with it. Were you 100 percent confident when you designed your first logo? Are you 100 percent confident now, even after all of your years of experience? Why should presenting work be any different? You can be a really good presenter and not be comfortable doing it. You can be confident and efficient and informative, and still not like doing it. It's a skill, just like making wireframes.

BEING A GREAT SPEAKER COMES FROM FINDING YOUR OWN AUTHENTIC STYLE

There are so many different speaking styles and techniques for giving presentations that most people don't even know exist. You can learn all the different styles and tricks, but what's important is to remember that speaking is a lot like designing. It takes time as a designer to develop a style, and to be able to recognize the tools you are most comfortable with and the individual way you use them. Like the dozens of keystrokes you learn for shortcuts in After Effects, there's a similar shorthand for how you can become a better presenter. But without authenticity, you aren't going to progress. Something will always be off and your audience will see it.

This isn't to say you can't design in a style you're not familiar with or use a tool you aren't an expert at. But you do have a preference and that preference or aesthetic says something about who you are as a person. You have to spend the time exploring ways of talking about the work until you find the way that works for you ... because it's just like your design work. It's your sweet spot. So if you have to sit down and read from notecards, that's your style. And that's totally okay.

PRESENTATION STYLE SHOULD BE INVISIBLE TO YOUR CLIENT
When you're presenting the work, your presentation of the work cannot become an additional component of the work. You don't want your clients saying, 'I would have liked that work if he hadn't used that laser pointer, or if he wasn't fidgeting all the time...' You want your presentation style to be invisible.

PRACTICE YOUR PRESENTATION UNTIL YOU CAN IMPROVISE
Even if you've practiced a hundred times, you will get nervous. Being nervous is perfectly fine. Something would be wrong if you weren't! Presenters get worried because there's no undo. You can't revert to a previous version. You have to be okay with that.

How should I prepare for a presentation?

Here are some additional tips and tricks I've personally gathered over the years that have helped me make better design presentations.

BRING A CHEAT SHEET FOR THE CONTENT YOU'LL BE PRESENTING
Just formulating what should go on your cheat sheet will help you remember what key points you want to hit in your presentation. And if you've practiced your speech as well, then you won't need it. (Though cheat sheets will come in handy if you get laryngitis and another team member has to present your concepts.)

PARE AWAY ANYTHING EXTRANEOUS TO YOUR ARGUMENT
You don't need to tell your client about the process by which you reached the comps, unless it supports your strategy from the brief or helps build trust in a process your client hasn't been through before. In either case, consider how concisely you can provide this information without burning up forty minutes of an hour-long presentation.

RECORD YOURSELF PRACTICING THE SPEECH, THEN WATCH IT

The only way to catch some of your nervous tics and unintended vocabulary—uhm, ah, like—is to record your presentation, and then watch it. Once you've done this a few times, deliver your speech to one of your co-workers or a disinterested party. Listen to their feedback. You may be surprised to discover that when watching your video, you only caught a fraction of your problem presentation habits.

CONTROL WHO IS GOING TO BE IN THE ROOM

Part of a great presentation comes from having the right audience to receive what you've prepared. Everyone in the room should have a good reason to be at the meeting and should participate in the presentation. If they don't, they shouldn't attend.

IN THE PRESENTATION, PROPERLY FRAME THE THINKING BEHIND YOUR DESIGN

Describe each idea before you show any visual executions. Don't over-describe the details after the reveal; two to three points per comp is enough. Emote a little, but don't overload the room with your excitement. Feel free to clarify when clients ask questions (after the presentation), but don't go down the rabbit hole on extraneous details.

DON'T WAIT UNTIL THE LAST MINUTE TO PRACTICE

If you're driving to the client meeting and haven't practiced what you're going to say, it's too late.

DON'T TELL YOUR CLIENT WHICH IDEA YOU LOVE MOST

Don't push a specific direction when presenting a range to your client. Says project manager Fiona Robertson Remley: "When the client asks you which idea you like best, smile and avoid answering. Use language such as: 'This concept echoes the focus on health and the outdoors described in the brief.' Or: 'This logo maps to your request for a strong, vibrant identity.' Try to avoid picking the design for the client. It is ultimately their project, not yours, so they need to take ownership of the design."

REQUEST #2:

MAKE THE LOGO BLUE

REQUEST #3:

STOP SEEING RED

Feedback

Clients deliver feedback on everything we create for them: proposals, deliverables, project schedules, email communication styles, what we've worn to a meeting with their CEO and so forth. Soliciting and receiving feedback from clients is a crucial part of any ongoing collaboration between a client and a designer. To quote Robert Allen, "There is no failure. Only feedback."

The inability to manage client feedback causes your design work to suffer. Here are some ways to work with feedback that will help keep your design projects running smoothly, while reducing the tension that poorly considered feedback can cause in a client relationship.

How should I manage client feedback?

1. PUT THE FEEDBACK IN WRITING FOR ALL PARTIES TO APPROVE

For every project, you should schedule a date by which clients are responsible for providing you feedback. Often clients will want to deliver this feedback face-to-face or over the phone. Document everything discussed during those meetings, then send it to the client as a record of your conversation. Otherwise you're going to forget details and nuances.

2. CLARIFY AMBIGUOUS FEEDBACK BEFORE MAKING CHANGES

When receiving written feedback from a client or discussing the nuances of their perspective, strive to turn ambiguous comments into directions instead of opinions. Don't say in your email, "Client dislikes green color, wants us to explore other options." Tack on the end of that sentence a way to focus and narrow the comment's implications. Instead, try "Client notes that green background in sidebars might be too similar to green in competitor's site." Ask them to agree to your interpretation before starting on the changes.

3. DESCRIBE WHAT FEEDBACK MAY IMPACT PROJECT SCOPE

The client may not be aware that requested changes will influence the scope of the project. Describe potential impacts to schedule and scope with every major round of feedback and approval. Be clear about how her input is contributing to the final goal or possibly changing that goal. This will help everyone involved stay on the same page. No surprises!

What are common issues with client feedback?

Here are a few examples of issues that can come up when receiving client feedback, even if you follow the process outlined above.

YOU'RE CONFRONTED WITH FEEDBACK THAT IS ACTIONABLE BUT HAS A NEGATIVE TONE

> "I hate the color scheme. You should have used yellow instead of purple. And the stock photo is all wrong. Find someone who looks older and richer. What the hell were you thinking?"

Put the client's tone aside for the moment. Don't let it cloud your judgment.

Take the client email and strip it down to what really needs to be addressed: "Explore new options for the color scheme, especially surrounding the purple in the tertiary color palette. Assess photo on page 2 and see if you can find someone in their forties wearing fashionable clothes."

Then write back to your client with this clarification of your original intent, what action items have arisen from her feedback and a query as to why she questioned your intent with such language. Finish up with the type of feedback you would appreciate in the future based on your rules of engagement.

If you manage a team, this is your job. Be cautious that you don't make your team expend emotional energy to resolve these types of ambiguities around what a client wants from them. They may be distracted from better uses of their time and talent.

THE CLIENT ASKS YOU TO MAKE CHANGES COUNTER TO THE CREATIVE BRIEF, BRAND STYLE GUIDE AND SO FORTH

> "I think for this one, we can ignore the style guide and bring in some new visual elements that contrast what our competitors are doing. I'm really excited about this, so I don't think you need to worry about a brand review."

These situations can happen when clients become busy and pass along what seems like actionable feedback from other stakeholders. However, once you really start thinking about the feedback, red flags begin to wave frantically in your mind.

You should initiate a direct conversation with the client regarding why he is contradicting agreed-upon standards, and capture that rationale in writing. If you feel the feedback will adversely impact their brand or quality of project execution, you should propose alternate actions that preserve the integrity of the project strategy and the client's brand.

YOUR CLIENT TELLS YOU SHE DISLIKES EVERYTHING YOU HAVE CREATED SO FAR

"I think you've missed the mark. Maybe you need to start over."

This kind of feedback isn't immediately actionable. Take a deep breath before crafting a response.

Ask the client for discrete reasons the design you provided was not appropriate. Make sure these reasons point to specific places in the agreed-upon brief, brand guidance, functional specifications and so forth. Her feedback needs to be tangible and quantifiable, not just emotional. You will need to establish clear constraints and boundaries in order to target what needs to be rethought or revised. Otherwise you may burn additional hours toward an uncertain goal.

OVER TIME, RECEIVING FEEDBACK BECOMES EASIER

Through repeated practice, you can gain greater tolerance for receiving and reshaping client feedback.

Whenever I receive client feedback, I think of stress tests for rock-climbing ropes. In a stress test, you tie a weight to the end of a rope, secure the other end of the rope and drop the weight off a tall building. You observe how far the weight can drop and how much force the rope can withstand.

Note that a rock-climbing rope doesn't reach an instant breaking point. These ropes are designed to stretch, then bounce back. The amount of flexion, or give, that the rope demonstrates is a measure of its resilience. No one wants a rope that snaps under pressure.

A seasoned designer has a deep reservoir of resilience. This leads to a higher tolerance for change and ambiguity, as well as a certain level of professionalism around negotiating client feedback. This is a learned skill, and it will be critical for improving client service and project management for your business.

Networking

Build time into your busy schedule to find the people and companies that will help you fulfill your projects. Your network should always reflect your own skill level or higher.

Some ways to build your network of collaborators include:

- Staying in touch with people you worked with at a previous company or design studio
- Meeting with people at local and national industry events
- Working on-site in a freelance capacity
- Being willing to help a colleague find a resource, with no profit to yourself—they will return the favor
- Reaching out to people through well-crafted email
- Starting conversations and keeping tabs via social networks such as Twitter, Facebook or LinkedIn
- Looking outside your discipline of design for inspiration and potential partners in crime
- Fostering dialogue through instant messenger and video chat

Networking should be part of your studio overhead, as it contributes to new business development, hiring, culture and your thought leadership.

Competition

You and your competitors drive each other to do great work. You should celebrate when your competitors are successful in landing a project that you bid on.

Poor sportsmanship occurs when your eight-year-old child won't shake hands with the competing soccer team because they scored fourteen goals in the first quarter. You are better than that. If you can't recognize that what your competitor did was better, and learn from your failure, then you aren't a good competitor. There may even come a time when you end up collaborating with your competition on a future project.

To quote Nathan Peretic, cofounder of Full Stop Interactive: "Your competition may well be 'bad design' and not the other guy in town who happens to make good websites. When you don't sell a physical product, the goal shouldn't be to capture a percentage of the market; it should be to find enough good clients to support the business you enjoy."

So don't spend too much of your time worrying about your competition. If you change what's unique about yourself to emulate a more successful studio, then you're not being true to yourself or your studio's current strengths. It's those unique qualities that can help you win the kind of business you want in the future.

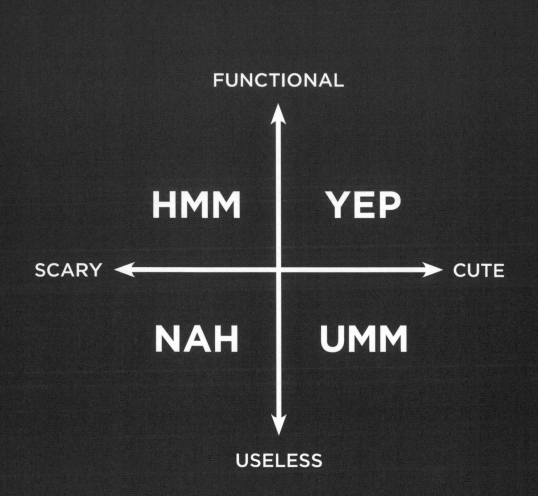

SEGMENTATION STRATEGY

Strategy

So far, we've spent most of our time uncovering the secrets of how designers can provide strong service to their clients. But in the process of doing so, we increase the likelihood of becoming a strategic partner to our clients. We finally have a seat at the table when the client is talking strategy—and we can offer a range of strategic services that verge outside what may be considered a designer's core area of expertise.

This is a good thing. With the ongoing expansion of design's role in business, today's designers are helping to solve problems that transcend mere decoration and instead impact the core functions of a client's business. But in our haste to be strategic partners, we've added a host of new services to our capabilities that we may not fully understand: Design strategy. Brand strategy. Content strategy. Interactive strategy. Media strategy. Business strategy. We may have overstepped our reach.

If you're going to run a design-led business, it's inevitable that you will need to talk strategy with your clients. So let's take a brief interlude and explore the types of strategies you might create as a design businessperson, as well as how they may support the efforts of your clients. It's my hope that this information will come in handy as your business grows.

What exactly is strategy?

The dictionary says: a strategy is a "plan of action or policy designed to achieve a major or overall aim." Intention leads to action, which hopefully yields a desired result.

But don't get too excited about the word design appearing in this definition of strategy. Even though plans or policies may have been designed, that doesn't mean strategies are about designing or are created by designers.

Instead design businesspeople who want to create strategies must be able to both intend and realize strategy, says Henry Mintzberg, Joseph Lampel and Bruce Ahlstrand in their book *Strategy Safari: A Guided Tour through the Wilds of Strategic Management*. The realization piece can be hard for some designers, as our clients are often responsible for the deployment and upkeep of what we create. To quote Timothy Morey, an associate vice president of strategy at frog, a global innovation firm: "Business strategists can't agree on how exactly firms make their strategy. The emergent schools of strategy favored by Mintzberg (and backed by my experience!)

suggest that there is a lot of room for clever designers to surreptitiously impact their client's strategy through design and design research."

Unintended consequences also influence how designers create strategies. "Strategies... have to form as well as be formulated," says Mintzberg, in reference to the ways companies react to continual fluctuations in the behavior of their competitors, customers and culture as a whole. For example, a soft drink manufacturer plans to release a new pink-colored soda that tastes like watermelon, but it will take at least a year for its product to reach the market. An article in *The Wall Street Journal* says that their competitor is rolling out a line of fruit-flavored sodas, starting with a watermelon flavor in just one month. Both companies may have similar strategies for how they will roll out their products, but the late entrant to the market will have to reformulate its strategy in order to establish a successful position. A strategy has no value if it can't be acted upon.

In your work as a designer, you will be asked to take many positions with regard to what strategy means to your clients. You may perceive new patterns through your research and recommendations. For another client, you can suggest a specific position or change their perspective. You may also find yourself recommending particular tactics for your clients to assume a better position in the market.

Just by fulfilling design activities you are often realizing strategies, whether you intend to or not. But this does not mean that you are practicing strategy. Compare the above definition of "strategy as a plan" with how Charles Eames defines design: "Design is a plan for arranging elements in such a way as best to accomplish a particular purpose." If a designer's actions are aligned with a particular purpose, then they may be strategic. This does not mean, however, that they are intending that strategy or able to fully describe the course to get there. This is the domain of a design strategist.

How does a designer practice strategy?

I asked Abby Godee, an executive director of strategy at frog, for her definition of design strategy. This is what she said:

> Design strategists will help any design team create the why and the how that will lead to a more meaningful what.

> Design firms are generally good at addressing what should be made, but their abilities may vary based on the how and the why.

Many designers, in their design training, are not initially prepared to address what a client needs to understand around the why, and design firms can often leave a client hanging regarding the how.

What does Abby mean by the what, the why, and the how?

WHY?

We need to understand our client business problems and identify where they should explore solutions to those problems—which segments, which user needs, which markets and which opportunities?

A designer practicing strategy must be able to explore and describe why certain conditions have led to the need to create new things in the world, or to change or remove existing things from the world. These conditions could be related to customer behavior, market competition, cultural trends or other factors. The design strategist must be able to discern patterns and identify competitive positions in order to establish a more holistic perspective for their clients.

WHAT?

We have identified opportunities regarding what to design, supported by insight. These opportunities clearly indicate possible design solutions that will influence a client's business for the better.

As Abby noted, most design businesses spend the majority of their time intuiting what should be made, but they may not always know why what they are making will have a meaningful business impact. A strategist should be able to work with a design team to plan a future state for a business's customers with the inclusion of new or improved products and services, as well as any new branding approaches, marketing or advertising positions. These plans should help clients focus attention on a specific position in relation to their competition.

———

Gabriel Post, a design strategist, suggests that the strategist should understand "where the client is in their own development process—what decisions have been made and which can be influenced—so the energy going in is aligned with what is needed and challenges what can be overcome."

———

HOW?

Based on agreed solutions, we determine how possible design solutions will be designed, implemented and brought to market. A design strategist would also assess how prepared the client organization is to realize those solutions and the potential impacts of doing so.

A design strategist should help a company understand how to realize the solutions they've envisioned and designed at a high level. This could require anything from creating implementation road maps to designing, building and shipping products, services, new brand guidelines and advertising campaigns. The design strategist may not be an expert in all of these domains. Instead she may serve as a sort of general contractor to connect design teams with the appropriate partners throughout the implementation process. At this point, a design strategist's careful planning gives way to a deep understanding of what tactics will fulfill intended strategies.

How does design strategy align with your client's business aims?

Now that you have a sense of what design strategists provide for their clients, you can begin to explore the roles that designers can play in helping to formulate and realize strategies on behalf of their clients. Designers may influence strategies within the following areas of a client's business operations.

CORPORATE STRATEGY

Corporate strategy governs how a company intends to sustain its operations over time. Corporate strategy seeks to answer one question: What business are we in? The corporate strategy is manifested through the mission, values, goals and aspirations that a company has set for itself. You'll also find it in the client's plans for partnering with favorable firms, merging with competitive firms or acquiring companies or IP to support its interests.

"This area has traditionally been the domain of management consultants, but designers bring a clarity of thought and the power to reduce complicated strategies to digestible images, frameworks and stories, which makes them good candidates to play here," says Timothy Morey.

BUSINESS STRATEGY

Business strategy is a broad umbrella that encompasses the most important ongoing considerations for any corporation, from process optimization to product/service portfolio management to operations, finance and market-

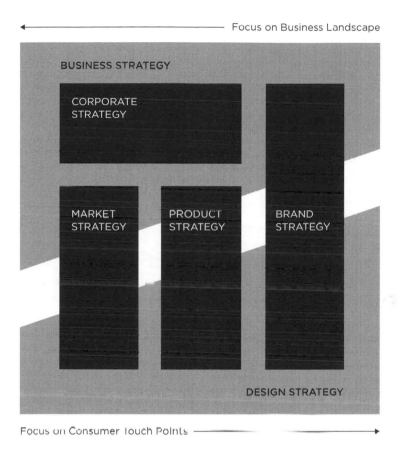

Focus on Business Landscape

BUSINESS STRATEGY

CORPORATE
STRATEGY

MARKET
STRATEGY

PRODUCT
STRATEGY

BRAND
STRATEGY

DESIGN STRATEGY

Focus on Consumer Touch Points

A framework by Gabriel Post. This illustrates the overlaps between the domain of design strategy and business strategy.

ing. However, it can almost always be summed up as an attempt to answer this question: How are we going to make money within our market?

Business strategies support corporate needs: Meeting revenue targets, achieving desired market positions, rewarding shareholders, fulfilling stated corporate strategies and more. Many services that design businesses provide, such as product/service strategy, brand strategy and marketing strategy are flavors of business strategy and may be generated by a design strategist who has the appropriate expertise.

BRAND STRATEGY
Brand strategy is the practice of formulating how a company's brand—the sum of how the company is perceived through all of its interactions with its

customers—is manifested through corporate marketing, communications, product and service design, interactive design and business operations. Designers who work on a company's brand translate corporate strategies and business strategies into a brand position, which may then touch a company's product/service strategy and marketing strategy.

PRODUCT/SERVICE STRATEGY

Product and service strategies help to define and shape the evolution of a company's portfolio of salable products and services. I use the word *portfolio* very deliberately, as a corporation's business strategies are realized through proper investment in their best-performing products and services. While product strategy is often depicted as an outcome of corporate and business strategy, in reality it is often the driver of those "higher order" strategies. A designer with a great product strategy can end up surreptitiously changing the business or corporate strategy of an organization. Think of Apple's initial foray into the music business with the iPod, or Amazon's impact on the publishing industry with their Kindle products.

MARKETING STRATEGY

Marketers explore a client's business strategy and product/service strategy, then determine what actions should be taken in the market to better sell a company's products and services to reach stated business goals. Designers who play in this space may influence product/service strategy and business strategy.

WHAT SKILLS DO STRATEGISTS EMPLOY THAT DESIGNERS MAY NOT HAVE OR MAY NOT BE ABLE TO ACQUIRE?

- Design strategists have an interpretive role: They must speak fluently about various disciplines such as business, marketing, technology, design and culture
- Design strategy works with design research: Good strategists understand how to translate the information gleaned from research into insight. Then they blend it with perspectives from the other disciplines
- Design strategists focus more on the framing than on the actual design making: You may not hire design strategists in order for them to execute designs, but they should be expected to collaborate with teams to generate design ideas

STRATEGY AS A SERVICE THAT DESIGNERS PROVIDE

A designer may provide even more flavors of strategy that impact a client's business: interactive strategy, content strategy or media strategy, just to name a few. Many of these strategies are closely tied to what should be realized, and how, but they may not be offered by a business strategist.

While it's tempting to elaborate these strategy types in depth, I think it's more important to note that these are services that support the delivery of design strategy. Design strategists must be able to string tactics together into a plan that every person at the table can agree upon and execute with confidence. Much of what we design can create new patterns in behavior and can cause business strategies to form in an emergent fashion. But we can't create a media strategy and claim to be a corporate strategist. Nor can we completely revise a company's business strategy when formulating a content strategy. What a design strategist can do is help clients visualize how they can reach a set of agreed-upon objectives, with the appropriate tools and resources at their disposal.

How do I help set strategic direction for a client project?

BFAs advising MBAs regarding their business strategy may seem a bit strange to both parties involved, but as you've read so far, designers can have great influence on how a company's business strategy is realized in the market. To act as a strategic partner for any organization means reaching a place where both of you agree on the problem you are trying to solve—while remaining flexible enough to accept that this agreement will likely change as the project progresses, due to market forces.

But the most critical part of solving business problems through design requires investing in learning about a client's business and its competitive space. We often forget to approach our client's problems with the same level of rigor that we would approach the formal design process. Over time, this is how a designer becomes a strategic partner for her client. This process often begins with asking the right questions during the proposal stage or while writing a brief.

The secret sauce in these long-term sustained conversations is to think about problems as a space that both people and companies maneuver through over time. Designers can help companies define where they stand within that space—as opposed to grasping at problems to solve—and help business stakeholders find a consistent language to describe the challenges they face and how they interrelate, from organizational units and market segments to long-term goals and brand style guides. Do not underestimate the power of design and storytelling to rally organizations behind a well-articulated strategy.

Designers are well equipped to work with strategists to achieve this aim. To quote Gabriel Post, a strategist I have worked closely with:

> Given that designers are typically highly visual people, or at least model makers, I highly encourage strategists to co-develop visual models... with the designers of the products that will live in it. Some common models used are ecosystem models, value-chain models and "marketecture" models ... each has a slightly different take on what is described in its "landscape."

> The better the understanding of the world which a product is being designed for, the more meaningful the resulting product. And since I'd argue the value of design is in the degree to which the result is meaningful for the end user, being part strategist is becoming an essential part of being a designer.

And lastly: As a strategist, it's not your job to just say yes. It is often said that strategy is as much about deciding what not to do, as it is about selecting what to do. Having a high-level, strategic impact on any company requires a deep level of commitment, trust and a sustained relationship over time. None of these emerge instantly on day one of your very first project. And none of them come from being a yes-man. You need to choose to ask the hard questions early on, in a way that can be heard and responded to, and every compromise you make should be clear-eyed and shared.

And if you don't? You may obtain a well-paid client engagement, but you won't be invited back to the table as a strategist.

STRATEGIC RELATIONSHIPS ARE BUILT ON TRUST

Trust is earned in a client relationship, not given. If you expect a strategic role in your client's business too early in a relationship, you can create situations where you overstep the bounds of that relationship. In such situations, we can say to our clients: "Trust me. Have faith that we'll succeed!" But faith and trust are not the same thing.

I asked Stefan Mumaw, creative director and author of *Chasing the Idea Monster*, for his point of view on this subject:

> Trust and faith are close concepts, but I believe they can be defined separately.
>
> In terms of design and clients, I think you can define trust as the ability for a client to experience our work in some way—whether that's by viewing the problems we've solved for others or by some form of known recommendation—and believe that we can solve similar problems or achieve similar results for them. It's a form of self-application, to experience that which we have created and apply it to their personal situation. Faith, on the other hand, is blind. It's a client's ability to have nothing in which to apply to themselves other than our word, and to believe we can serve them wholly.
>
> It takes trust for a client to hire us to solve a problem we've solved for someone else. It takes faith for a client to hire us to solve something we've never solved previously.
>
> Which should we encourage from our clients? I believe it's entirely dependent on what they are hiring us to solve. Philosophically, it's rare for us to be hired to solve that which we haven't solved previously, but I believe it's an integral part of growing as a creative. Learning to sell process and philosophy rather than goods and services is a fundamental shift in how we've defined ourselves as designers. How we think, and how we insert the client and their goals into that, is our greatest asset and our greatest value.

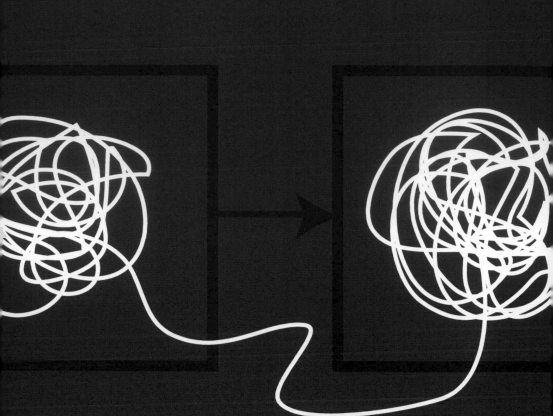

MANAGING YOUR
PROJECTS

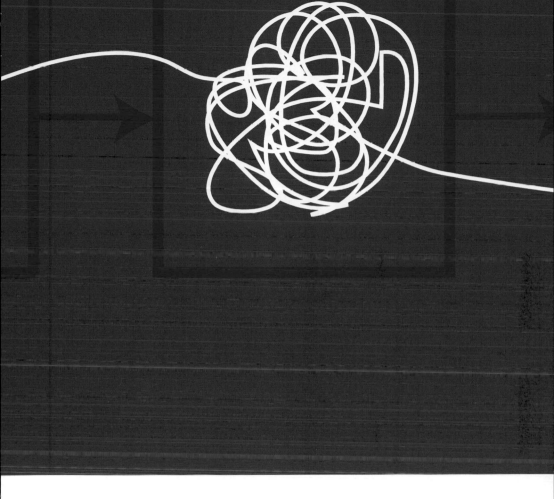

DOING THE WORK

AFTER THE WORK

FOOSBALL

FINANCES

MANAGING
PEOPLE

SCHEDULING
& PLANNING

CLIENT
SERVICE

ACTUAL
DESIGNING

HOURS PER WEEK ON STUDIO ACTIVITIES

Project Management

"If only I could spend more time designing and less time doing [insert name of mundane task that doesn't seem design related at all]" is a constant refrain for most designers. But it's those mundane tasks that allow your design business to stay in business. Most big projects today are complex enough that the percent of time spent actually designing them can be less than 30 percent of the total time the job requires. The rest falls under the domain of project management.

Project management is what keeps design businesses successful and profitable. For the sanity of both your co-workers and your clients, it can never be sacrificed. Your clients will expect this service from you. Your business will demand it. "Agencies and designers are usually hired for their design skills, but they are nearly always fired for lack of project management skills," says strategic project manager Fiona Robertson Remley.

What is project management?

I talked with Derin Basden, an associate director of program management at frog, a global innovation firm, to explore what project management is and what designers need to know about project management as a discipline for their business.

WHAT WOULD YOU EXPECT A PROJECT MANAGER TO DO?
First, it helps to define what we mean by a project.

I define a project as a defined series of steps intended to achieve an agreed-upon and stated outcome. These steps usually need to be performed in some kind of predefined order and meet certain defined specifications at particular milestones.

Every project has a few basic parts: defined scope, deliverables, timeline, budget (and payment terms, if via third party) and the list of assumptions/caveats. These, in fact, are the basic pieces that go into a contract or scope of work. It is not by accident that the Project Management Institute makes no distinction between a construction project manager and a software project manager. They study the same material and take the same test. The basic parts are the same, no matter the industry.

Project management is the careful guidance and execution of the project plan. It encompasses everything from initial planning to final delivery.

It is a project manager's job to ensure that the final deliverable meets the needs and expectations of the client, and fulfills the terms of the agreed-upon contract, inclusive of all of those other elements: Scope, deliverables, timeline, budget and assumptions.

A good project manager ensures that the plan is solid (or at least a solid start), the contracts are signed, the correct people are assigned to the project, the deliverables are being created per agreed-upon specifications and timeline, and the budget is in line. If any of these are not lining up, the project manager pulls various levers and switches to get things back on track, including changing the overall terms of the contract.

A great project manager has the pulse and confidence of his team, can motivate them to do better when they should, knows when to change course, knows how to keep the team focused on the end goal and prevent individuals from going down a rabbit hole. He can proactively challenge the client, set their expectations, and game the system to get the project done.

WHAT IS GREAT PROJECT MANAGEMENT? HOW IS IT DIFFERENT FROM OR SIMILAR TO GREAT CLIENT SERVICE?

A project manager's responsibility is to the project and to the project team first, then the client. There, I've said it.

In my experience, the client often doesn't know what they want, and can't see the forest for the trees. They can get bogged down in detail, or

———

If you don't budget time for project management into your eight-hour day, you'll end up working late nights and weekends to account for activities that support your formal design work.

———

8 AM   11 AM

they aren't paying attention at all. They come in with an idea and have no idea how to execute. Then, when you start executing, they can try to take the reins—often with disastrous results.

A great project manager gets the project done the right way, helping to foster collaboration and teamwork despite any self-destructive efforts on the part of the client. An old project management joke is: "If it weren't for clients, the job would be easy."

In the end, it's the final deliverable that matters to the project manager. His major focus should be on the project and the internal team, with minor focus on the client. Good project managers deliver as-scoped quality projects on time, on budget and with a happy team. That's the Holy Grail.

Client service is another beast altogether. At some companies, it is the job of a good client partner or account manager to continually set and manage the expectations of the client. Great account managers help keep clients happy by ensuring that the client is being heard by the project team, the team is being heard by the client and the projects meet the overall client goals. Ideally the client is never surprised by anything; they are continually pleased by your team's results. Client service professionals help build relationships and accounts, identify opportunities and consult with project managers on how to make decisions. Their focus should be on the client, with minor focus on the project.

Of course, project managers can provide good client service through honest communication, attentiveness, responsiveness, regular status reporting and solid logistics. Clients should never have to think or worry about any of these things. As far as the client is concerned, the project should just work.

At one of my previous jobs, the developers would often complain about feature requests from clients. At this company, clients would make silly

1 PM   3 PM

| Estimating new projects | Design | Phone calls | Design |

Thar be overtime ⟶

requests (as they often do), and the developers would either satisfy those requests grudgingly or push back and say they wouldn't do them, while the project managers crunched numbers in the background. A great project manager, however—often working with a client service professional—understands what the client really wants and proposes a solution that meets the needs of the client and the approval of the team doing the work.

Think of it this way: If a client walked into your restaurant and asked one of your staff to prepare a meal differently, how would you respond? There are many more options besides yes or no. Sometimes just saying yes is a disservice, sometimes saying no is good service, sometimes just listening to the client meets their needs. That is just good service: knowing what is going to work best for the client in the long run.

WHAT HAPPENS WHEN YOU DON'T HAVE A PROJECT MANAGER?
Many things can happen. Usually all bad.

The project spins and spins
There is no one to put a foot down, push back or help make a logical choice. Spinning could happen due to internal perfectionism, client shenanigans or general uncertainties.

Too many cooks on the team
If there's a power vacuum or a lot of uncertainty surrounding a project, a few people on the team may elect themselves as leaders. Conflicting

———

Know how to distribute project management responsibilities appropriately across your staff, so you aren't carrying the full burden of both creative and project management duties.

———

ALWAYS BILL FOR PROJECT MANAGEMENT

No one loves a project manager, especially when he starts questioning why the project is $5,000 over budget and the developer is freaking out over the back-end services that don't exist yet and a strident voice interrupts: Wait a minute! Did you forget to make the logo green because the client requested it in the feedback document, didn't you read it, go back to page 3, down there at the bottom, how did you miss it, can you get it done in seven minutes, cause the deliverable is already late and then we'll figure out how things ended up wrong and I'm sure we'll all learn something from your epic fail—

This fear of project management is a ruse. This imaginary combat between the left-brain, rational number-crunching beast that screams at us because we're going over budget, and the right-brain, crafty part of our mind is engaged in some heavy-duty creative flow, busy affixing gold stars to layout comps with star stickers matching PMS 123, is an albatross that we gingerly hand from designer to designer.

This is not a strategy that I advocate, for you or anyone else.

Instead, consider what roles and responsibilities you hold through your workday. What do you do that keeps your projects humming along? How many hours a week are consumed while doing those tasks?

Add up those hours by project—be sure to include project management, client service and other nonoverhead roles that you provide as part of your workday—and add those responsibilities into your billable hourly fees. Carve them out of your design time, and tack those hours onto the end of the project.

This is how much you should be estimating and billing, at your top-line rate.

It's also how hard you should actually be working, amortized across each forty-hour week.

Of course, you have an alternative. You could just spend sixty hours per week cursing at the clock and preparing your baggage for a fast trip to Burnoutland.

direction and confused deliverables ensue. Frustration, marred by the lack of a cohesive voice to the client, leads to misaligned expectations with the client and client unhappiness with the product—even if the product is good.

No one watching the store
No one's paying attention and timeline, budget, deliverables and resourcing all go by the wayside. Project managers help make sure that contractual obligations are met.

Lopsided deliverables
There's no mediator to help different leaders and doers get along. The loudest voice wins and subtle points are missed. The end deliverable is lopsided—development wins over design, design wins over usability, etc.

No one listens to the client or ensures their expectations are met
The team is proud of end product. The client is furious. Clients, for all of their silliness during the process, are pretty good judges of the quality and effectiveness of the final deliverable.

All of these problems result in cost overruns, unmet deliverables and unhappy clients.

———

Hire someone to provide the necessary project management responsibilities if you're struggling to keep up or if you have a lot of new projects coming into your studio.

———

1 AM   3 AM

Design, peering at monitor
in weary haze

HOW CAN I LEARN HOW TO BE A GREAT PROJECT MANAGER?

A new project manager is going to make mistakes. A lot of them. What counts is how you react to making those mistakes. Ask questions. Watch others and how they work. Learn, adjust and take mistakes in stride. Next time you see a similar problem, you can be more proactive. If it only takes one mistake for you to learn, you're doing well.

What people typically associate with project management—number crunching—is just one piece of the puzzle. Project management is a strange combination of number crunching, organization, people skills and content comprehension. Listen to your clients, your team and your instincts. If you don't understand why you are doing the project, what the client wants, what a great deliverable feels like or how to help your team get there, you are missing the point entirely. Great project managers are always playing what-if scenarios, logging risks and playing out mitigation strategies, like some elaborate simulation or real-time strategy video game.

Communication is the single most important skill of a project manager. And good communication means you are able to speak, write, listen, perceive, read body language, present, wrangle, badger, charm, threaten, dismiss, greet, and more. You know your audience and pick the right medium, format and structure. You aren't afraid to pick up the phone or meet face-to-face, when warranted. Of course, you also need to know things like scoping and costing, scheduling (i.e., tasks over time by resource), resource management, quality control, contracts, financials and negotiation, which all involve communication as well.

Consider shadowing an amazing project manager in your downtime, and perhaps you'll add a few tricks to your bag.

5 AM   7 AM

Decide to hire   Sleep soundly
project manager   on desk

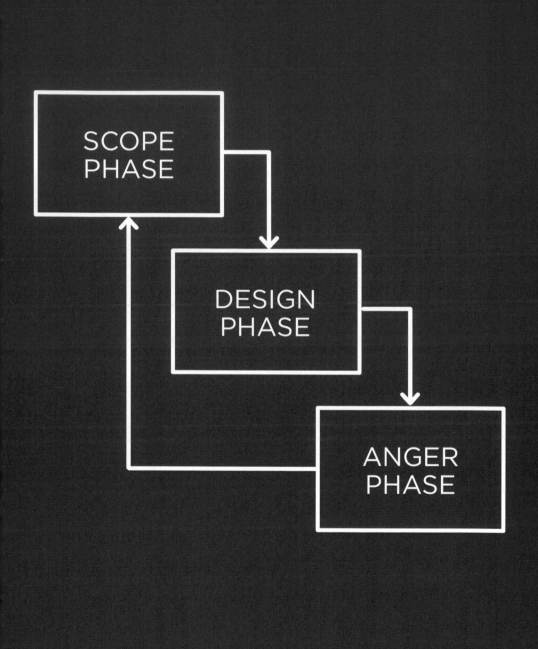

Process

The dictionary defines process as "a systematic series of actions directed to some end." Design businesses often have deliberate, branded processes that are splayed across their websites and marketing collateral. You see their FancyNames™ referenced above tidy charts on their websites that describe exactly how their design studio's product is manufactured.

This is the designers' attempt to fuse her creative process to some form of business process. Often discussions of process can be used as a way to comfort a client: "We've done this before. This is how we did it. In the end, we'll have your two perfect widgets and a microsite describing its awesomeness." But do studios actually follow these processes to the letter? Do they have an in-depth manual they use to guide their designers through Step 4A? Do clients swoon at the process diagrams when you're competing for a project? Or is this packaging of process solely a way to pitch and secure business?

Instead of establishing and following rote guidelines for how to design (and sell your firm), become a perpetual student of your process so you can design the design process. Each time I design a project, I learn something that I fold back into the process, changing how I may approach design in the future. Here I quote Hugh Dubberly, whose design studio compiled a free e-book that captures over one hundred of these process model diagrams from around the world:

> Our processes determine the quality of our products. If we wish to improve our products, we must improve our processes; we must continually redesign not just our products but also the way we design. That's why we study the design process. To know what we do and how we do it. To understand it and improve it. To become better designers.
> *www.dubberly.com/articles/how-do-you-design.html*

Clients, however, rarely take an interest in improving our skills. They want us to complete the project and provide them with what they need. I recommend that you share your work with your client through a clearly defined business process and shield them from the organic complexities of your creative process.

Before hiring you, your client needs to understand the following about your business process:

- Your studio has a record of delivering successful project work for your clients
- Your studio is happy to provide references, so clients can describe what it's like to work with you
- Your studio has an established business process, described in your project plan, that supports the creation of great work
- Your studio's business process is tailored for each client's specific needs, both in the work that needs to be generated and how your client's organization may consume and respond to work
- Your studio's business process contains the appropriate amount of time necessary for discovery, design, quality assurance and production (whether via development in Objective C for iOS or setting up and running a letterpress)

Everything on this list should be expressed in your proposal and schedule. You then realize each one of them as the project is fulfilled. If you skip anything from this list, you're in trouble. And if you give more information, you're probably overcomplicating things for your team and your client.

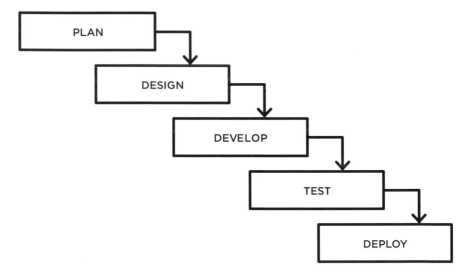

The Waterfall Methodology

What's the difference between design methodologies and design processes?

The waterfall and agile methodologies (and many others I haven't listed) may be appropriate for reaching an agreed-upon goal with your client. However, they shouldn't be words that you casually throw around in your proposals, as they have very specific meanings regarding how you may execute your work.

Read through the descriptions of the models below, and consider how you may adjust your business process based on the problems you're seeking to solve for your clients.

WATERFALL

Otherwise known as "Big Design Up Front," the waterfall methodology for a design project requires a team to comprehensively plan, design, produce or develop and then test everything in delineated phases. This process requires the client to approve the work for each phase before moving on to the next.

Most print design work is generated using the waterfall process: From the start, when the client approves concepts, to the final polished execution released to print. The waterfall methodology also makes sense for well-defined projects with a limited scope, such as websites with a handful of pages, a brochure or a logo.

One risk of the waterfall process is that, while it's intended to increase quality and control risk before moving too deep into a design project, a team can waste months on design ideas that fall apart in code. For this reason, it's becoming less common to see large-scale interactive or software projects created exclusively via the waterfall process. Exceptions might occur when very tight requirements are in place or in cases that have a high possibility of project failure without client approvals.

AGILE

The agile development methodology works by letting teams learn by making. Designers and developers create working code for software during short sprints that can last from one to four weeks. A sprint begins with the team agreeing to design and develop specific features for a software product, such as designing for user stories. A user story is a description of an experience that a person can have with the product being developed. During the sprint, the team translates the user stories into working, bug-

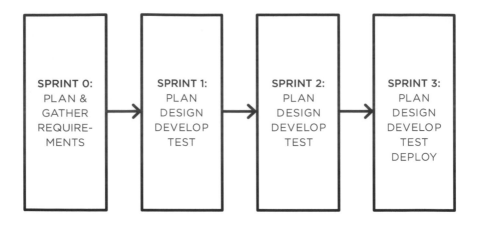

The Agile Methodology

free design and code. At the end of the sprint, the team and the client assess what has been generated and decide what the team will pursue in the next sprint, be it a new feature or the refinement of an existing one. At the end of each sprint, you can demonstrate what you've created, because the code already works.

You could use the agile methodology (or one of its flavors, such as scrum) if you have an established foundational design for software work. This design may already be in place, or your team could set it at the very beginning of the project. In agilespeak, this foundational design should get hammered out during Sprint 0.

Agile methodology can also be handy if you're creating software to fulfill an established long-term goal and your client is comfortable without any major up-front development targets except for what comes out of each sprint. A strong working team that's comfortable with ambiguity is essential. Whoever leads the team through sprints should have formal training in the methodology.

The most important thing to remember about the agile methodology is that there's a chance that any work you develop along the way will be thrown out. Sure, you'll better understand what needs to be made in future sprints, but the process can freak out both designers and clients if they aren't prepared. If you're not willing to take the risk of throwing away your hard work for the greater good, you aren't being agile! This methodology also requires working from a contract that allows for scope to fluctuate.

ITERATIVE VS. PLANNED

Many design businesses are seeing the value of converging planning, design and development into a single activity focused on creating prototypes of potential design solutions. This is a process that depends on fast iteration, like the agile process. But unlike the agile process, teams that work in an iterative process may not agree to having shippable product as an output. And unlike how things progress in the waterfall process, the information architecture or planning may not be fully established before the team begins to create potential solutions in code or visual design.

If your design team and your client are looking for novel design ideas, or seeking to leverage new technologies in ways that haven't been seen before, then a more iterative approach may be valuable. Generating a proof of concept prototype via an iterative approach can confirm for everyone involved that such ideas are feasible. These prototypes can prove through testing that they are functional and desirable before coding is complete. Some design studios will provide a single design solution up front, then iterate it substantially at increasing levels of fidelity. Contrast this to a traditional process of showing three to four concepts up front, where you have to spend extra time building a contingency plan for anything that becomes unworkable during implementation.

An iterative methodology may be a challenge if you need to move quickly from design ideas to shippable code, if your team is less experienced or if your client has little stomach for continuous learning and feedback.

YOUR METHODOLOGY INFLUENCES HOW YOU DEFINE SCOPE IN YOUR CONTRACTS

Most designers craft proposals that outline a set number of deliverables. You complete the deliverables, the client approves them, you get paid. "Deliverables can be easier to identify with a waterfall process and typically easier to sell," says Nathan Peretic, cofounder of Full Stop Interactive. For this reason, if you want a client to work with you in an agile or iterative fashion, you will need to include scope definition and management as part of your work process. This means, instead of defining deliverables, you will set stages in your work process where you'll evaluate and calibrate how much is feasible in the amount of time you have in your contract. Work from a variable cost estimate instead of from a flat fee.

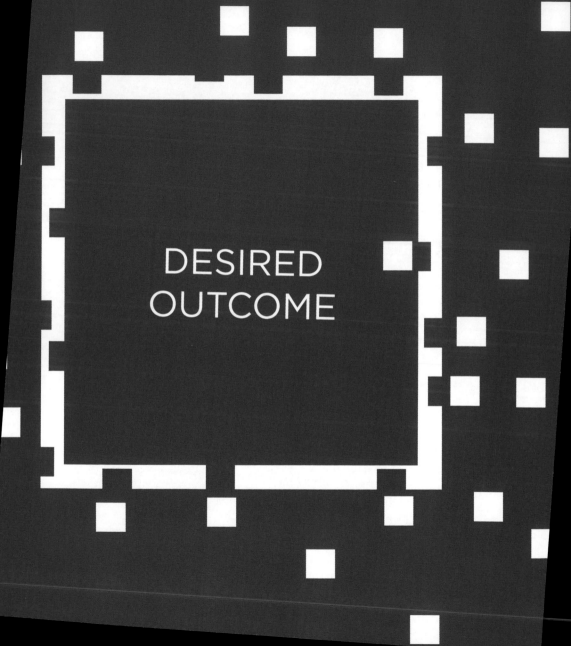

DESIRED
OUTCOME

Estimating

An estimate is a detailed list of deliverables with information as to how the studio will complete them. This information is then translated into hourly fees for each skill set required to complete the deliverables.

Estimates are not guesswork. I've heard countless designers say, "I haven't done this kind of work before. I don't know what to charge. So I just made a guesstimate, and if I go over budget, I'll just eat the difference."

Sadly, differences are not edible.

You can estimate how much a design project will cost by walking through the following five activities:

1. Project the number of hours the project will require
2. Set a schedule that accommodates those hours
3. Generate costs for resources, based on hourly rates
4. Select a pricing model to match your current business context
5. Translate your detailed estimate into a cost estimate for your client

Cost estimates are usually shown to the client in a summary form embedded in a project proposal. Detailed estimates are tools that are used within your design business and should not be shared with your client.

The more detail you use for an estimate, the better your chances of writing an accurate cost estimate and making a profit when the project is complete. This detail can be drawn from timesheets, estimates from past projects and other sources that help you determine how staff time has been utilized in the past.

Pull all of that information together, grab a cup of coffee, and close your office door. It's time to create a great estimate.

———

Before estimating, you should know your client's budget. "Even if the prospect tells us they don't have a budget—oh, they have one. If they're not willing to tell us what it is, we'll likely move on to the next opportunity," says Greg Hoy, president of Happy Cog Studios.

———

WHAT ACTIVITIES DOES YOUR DESIGN BUSINESS FULFILL?

Fiona Robertson Remley and I generated the following list of activities for a design business that specializes in interactive and video production. While it may seem that billing for all of these activities would require dozens of full-time staffers who have their own individual billing rates, this list could also apply to a design business with two staffers supported by third-party vendors and freelancers.

Running Your Business
Business Development
Account Management
Account Coordination
Project Management
Project Coordination
Administration
Logistics
Accounting

User Experience & Interface Design
User Research
Information Architecture
Interaction Design
Visual Design
Usability Testing

Content Creation & Management
Content Strategy
Content Writing
Copywriting
Copyediting
Proofreading
Social Media Management

Development
Technical Discovery
Technical Architecture
Back-End Development
Front-End Development
Bug Testing
Quality Assurance
Migration

Photo, Video, Film & Motion Graphics
Scripting
Storyboarding
Preproduction
Production
Styling
Videography
Video Editing
Sound Design
Motion Graphics
Computer Graphics & Animation
Mastering
Sweetening

Project Closure
Analytics
Archiving (Backup & Portfolio)
Follow-Up

1. Project the number of hours

As I am able to read the thoughts of design professionals worldwide, I can provide a transcript for what goes through your mind while you estimate a design project:

> "I think this project is going to take me twenty hours. Last time, it took about three days, and we only billed them for fifteen hours. If I make it twenty this time, that will work out perfectly!"

Time passes. One of your associates reviews the estimate and thinks it isn't cost-competitive. They want you to find places to cut your hours:

> "Hmm, maybe I can do the concepts in sixteen hours. I've designed a ton of web pages, so this one should be a little bit easier than the last time."

Sorry to break it to you, but you're probably going to spend at least twenty-four hours working on the project you thought you could squeeze into sixteen. On top of that, you're also going to lose money.

Why does this happen time and again? Because designers don't have good habits when it comes to how they project the number of hours an estimate may require. I see it as a point of maturity when a designer is pragmatic in constructing estimates. It's a skill that requires mindfulness. Here are a few things to consider.

KNOW THE ACTIVITIES REQUIRED TO FULFILL THE WORK

Designers bring a range of skills to bear on their work. Often we lump those skills under a single hourly rate, which we then use as the basis of a project estimate. But if you're trying to understand the relationship between fees, skills and hours, you should keep track of how these individual skills are utilized on a project-by-project basis.

Being aware of this level of detail will help you estimate how time will be utilized on future projects. It will also quickly tell you where you can hire support staff or bring in freelancers if your staff becomes over-whelmed. This contributes to more detailed estimates—which means they will be more accurate.

REFER TO ACTUAL HOURS FROM SIMILAR COMPLETED PROJECTS

Once you know the activities you're usually fulfilling for your clients, you can refer back to how you billed hours from previous projects. If you don't explore how your team has utilized their allocated hours, project by project, then you will make estimating mistakes.

Fiona Robertson Remley says, "Track your hours religiously. Keep data on what things cost, so each time you have to estimate, you have something to refer to." Ideally you should be able to review your final budget for similar projects, itemized by activities. There are software tools you can use to pull this information when necessary. *(See "Accounting.")*

CREATE A HIGH-LEVEL PLAN FOR YOUR DRAFT ESTIMATE

"You need to plan the steps and milestones of the job," Fiona says. "Lay out a map of how you are going to move through the project." For a solo designer or even a larger team, this can emerge from a quick whiteboard session that maps out the overall arc of the project. Be sure to include the core deliverables, a set number of client reviews and a list of the staffers necessary to complete those deliverables. At that point, you can start working on a list of assumptions, which you can include in the final proposal to protect your project from scope creep.

SHARE ROUGH NUMBERS WITH THE APPROPRIATE STAFFERS

The surest way to upset one of your staffers? Give them no control of the hours you provide for them in the design estimate. You should solicit their feedback on an estimate in its raw state. However, be aware that most creative people don't really know how to estimate their time. For this reason, you should take some precautions.

PROVIDE THE APPROPRIATE LEVEL OF CREATIVE "PADDING"

Designers, when self-estimating, can be off by as much as 50 to 100 percent on a new task or activity. With the pace that technology moves, and your client's ever-evolving business needs, you can never assume that everything will go your way on every single project. For this reason, add a creative pad of at least 20 percent for the hours you think are required, by activity, on every estimate you generate. Consider setting up a spreadsheet formula that adds this buffer automatically. You can estimate hours like you normally do, and the spreadsheet will give you some instant insurance without any extra effort on your part.

INCLUDE HOURS REQUIRED FOR MANAGING VENDORS

If clients want to use their own vendors, or they aren't willing to pay for markup on vendors that you're suggesting, you have to bill for the time necessary for managing their output. Otherwise you're just giving your time away, which equals more money out of your pocket.

BILL FOR THINKING TIME, NOT JUST COMPUTER TIME
"Make sure you allow a little time in your estimate for off-the-wall-thinking," Fiona says. Creating the time and space for dreaming in the midst of cranking out a big design deliverable can have a beneficial effect. And you should be paid for it!

DON'T BE AFRAID TO ASK COLLEAGUES FOR INSIGHT
"Talk to a project manager or someone who has done this frequently to get their perspective," Fiona says. That person may provide you with a crucial piece of information you wouldn't have obtained any other way.

ADJUST YOUR HOURS BASED ON PROJECT CONTEXT
Be realistic about how much effort it may take to work with a new client. Andy Rutledge, principal and chief design strategist at Unit Interactive, says the following:

> I expect that most design professionals tend to determine pricing and hours' calculations based largely on the relatively ideal project. And surely this is a benchmark that we need to be familiar with. However, this sort of hours' calculation should serve only as the basis of our determinations—to be modified based on the contextual issues specific to each individual project.

Keep your eyes peeled for levels of hierarchy and bureaucracy in your client organization, slavish devotion by your direct client to preexisting design ideas, poorly considered requirements and so forth. These should be factored into your estimate. For more on this subject, read Andy's article on calculating hours at www.andyrutledge.com/calculating-hours.php.

2. Set a schedule

After you've determined the number of hours required to fulfill a project, you will need to determine when and how those hours will be used. This requires the creation of a work-back schedule. *(For more information on generating detailed schedules, see "Schedules.")*

For the purposes of generating an estimate, you may not need a fully detailed work-back schedule until a project has been secured.

3. Generate costs for resources

Now that you've determined the amount of time a project will require for you and your team, and how those hours are translated into a work-back schedule, you're ready to establish how much to charge your client for that time.

The first and most important step is to multiply your time estimates by the cost per activity. In the illustration here, you can see how a studio can use a simple spreadsheet—or the appropriate software—to generate these costs on a week-by-week basis. Your hourly rates should be based on your studio overhead, desired profit margin and other considerations.

Once you've summed your hours multiplied by your hourly costs, you'll need to consider if the total cost you've calculated will be cost competitive in your market. Design businesses struggle at this point in the estimating process for a number of reasons.

Task	Win	Plan	Design	Build	Check
Creative Direction	8 hrs	4 hrs	4 hrs	4 hrs	4 hrs
Art Direction	2 hrs	2 hrs	8 hrs	8 hrs	8 hrs
UX Design	2 hrs	40 hrs	20 hrs	20 hrs	10 hrs
Visual Design	4 hrs	15 hrs	40 hrs	20 hrs	10 hrs
Content Strategy	2 hrs	20 hrs	20 hrs	10 hrs	20 hrs
Front-End Development	0 hrs	4 hrs	20 hrs	60 hrs	40 hrs
Back-End Development	0 hrs	8 hrs	40 hrs	40 hrs	40 hrs
Account Management	20 hrs	8 hrs	20 hrs	20 hrs	20 hrs
Project Management	12 hrs	10 hrs	20 hrs	40 hrs	40 hrs
Testing	0 hrs	0 hrs	0 hrs	20 hrs	40 hrs

Estimate Template. When estimating, it helps to estimate hours used by project phase, by task. Note: All rates and estimated hours are hypothetical and for purposes of presentation only; they do not reflect market rates. Download an Excel version here: www.SBDBook.com

THE VALUE OF YOUR SERVICES MAY BE RELATIVE

In most estimating situations, you are providing a competitive bid. And at times like this, the clients have the advantage. They gather their estimates, they know what each designer costs and they can adjust their negotiation tactics accordingly to get the best deal. However, clients only know your *relative* value. As a result, you may need to adjust your estimate to appropriately position yourself and your work.

You don't need to be the lowest bid. You need to be the bid that offers the client the most perceived value for her money. Here's how to determine what you should charge, comparative to your competition.

Ask what kind of competition you're up against

Ask the client what other types of companies are bidding—or, better yet, ask for names. Internet research and discussions with colleagues and associates in the community can also indicate the size and shape of those studios.

Deliver	Measure	Meetings	Hourly Rate	Total Hours	Total Costs
4 hrs	0 hrs	8 hrs	$170/hr	36 hrs	$6,120
8 hrs	0 hrs	8 hrs	$120/hr	44 hrs	$5,280
5 hrs	0 hrs	8 hrs	$120/hr	105 hrs	$12,600
5 hrs	0 hrs	8 hrs	$100/hr	102 hrs	$10,200
5 hrs	0 hrs	8 hrs	$120/hr	85 hrs	$10,200
40 hrs	0 hrs	8 hrs	$120/hr	172 hrs	$20,640
20 hrs	0 hrs	8 hrs	$150/hr	156 hrs	$23,400
10 hrs	4 hrs	8 hrs	$120/hr	110 hrs	$13,200
24 hrs	16 hrs	8 hrs	$120/hr	170 hrs	$20,400
20 hrs	0 hrs	8 hrs	$100/hr	88 hrs	$8,800
				Total	$130,840
				20% Pad	$26,168
				Grand Total	$157,008

Determine how your competition's size may impact their estimates
Distinct differences fall between pricing as a large agency or a small agency or bringing in freelance talent.

You should provide an estimate that is true to the scale of your business, supports the style of service that you hope to provide and is adjusted upwards or downwards based on the latitude for earning more profit.

Pick up the phone and gauge the market value of your services
How do you know if your estimate is on target or way off base? Ask people in the industry who aren't your direct competitors. It's fair to ask associates in your market to gauge whether your estimate is in the ballpark—but only if you know it's unlikely they are bidding on the same project.

Be aware of the location factor
Location can influence your studio's perceived value in the eyes of a client. "If you work in Pittsburgh and the client is in San Francisco, you may be bidding against San Francisco-based companies whose rates can be sometimes double your own," says Nathan Peretic, cofounder of Full Stop Interactive. "The supply and demand for your services will help determine your prices."

If you don't win the business, ask for feedback
If you don't win a project, ask the client for feedback regarding why he didn't select you as a design partner. Don't be too pushy in this conversation. What's most important is to learn the rough cost the client will be paying for the project and the size of the competitor. This information can help you reverse engineer the hours required by a competitor to fulfill the project, as well as determine who did the work when it hits the market.

YOU DIDN'T MARK UP PASS-THROUGH SERVICES
If you're billing to a client any service or tangible product from a vendor, you must mark it up. Otherwise you will not earn any interest on the credit you're extending.

However, there are situations where you will find it hard to mark up pass-through services. If you're a single-person agency, it's hard to pad an outsourced position's rate, as it can inflate your estimate beyond its market value. Large agencies get around this problem by billing hundreds of dollars an hour, and then hiring freelancers at $65 to $80 an hour. They can bill those rates at a double or even triple markup. But if you're a solo designer, this may not be possible. The appropriate thing for you to say to clients is: "We don't pad our outsourced talent. We pass on their rates

FOR COST ESTIMATES, SIZE DOES MATTER

Large agencies carry high overheads and require higher project fees, which are derived from a tiered pricing structure. When working with large agencies, clients receive big brains that contribute strategically, established working processes, a deep knowledge base, a consistent product and lower-level staff executing the balance of the work product. The junior staff will be billing lower rates than the senior staff or owners, but in general the blended rates for that studio will be higher than the market average.

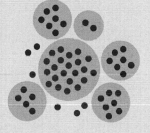

Small agencies often have studio principals doing the design work. This may reduce the bureaucracy and tiered pricing that is often found at large agencies. Clients of small agencies often want the studio principals to contribute in some part in every level of work. They also expect more nimble responses to their concerns and a focused skill set.

Freelance designers can choose to position themselves as a compelling alternative to working with an agency—though they can struggle to fulfill large projects comparative to other agency types. When working with a freelancer, clients receive undivided attention, specialization of skills, a dedicated resource and more intimacy in the business relationship.

In an estimate, a freelancer or smaller agency should highlight what about their services may be more intimate or appropriate. She should also potentially revise upwards her estimate, based on the competition. Revising estimates downwards to try and make a larger agency cost competitive with freelancers is not a good idea.

 Creative/Design Staff   ● Business/Studio Infrastructure

directly to you." (Note: If you start hiring staff and increasing your billing rates, this policy will have to change.)

Depending on the time you have to generate an estimate, you may not be able to include accurate hard costs for pass-through services such as printing, stock photography or photo shoots, color proofs, models and acting talent. Such services should be listed in your contract as outside the scope of the project and provided at an additional cost.

YOU DIDN'T COVER CONTINGENCIES WITH A PROJECT MARKUP

A contingency fee is between 10 and 20 percent of the total estimate you provide to a client. This markup is to cover possible increases in scope, shifts in schedule and negotiation over price. Project markups are shared with the client as a line item before the total estimated cost. They can be used as a "not to exceed" variance on the provided cost estimate.

YOU DIDN'T CONSIDER THE LONG-TERM VALUE OF YOUR WORK

Hourly estimates can be blind to the long-term value of what designers create for our clients. For example, Carolyn Davidson, a graphic design student, created the Nike swoosh in 1971 for $35. Carolyn couldn't have predicted the success of the Nike brand—but thankfully, her contribution was later recognized by the company with a significant award of company stock.

It's a designer's responsibility in the early proposal discussions with a client to gauge that client's business direction and estimate the long-term value of our efforts. We can then use that knowledge to adjust our estimate in the appropriate direction—usually upwards.

I spoke with Wendy Quesinberry, a principal at Quesinberry and Associates in Seattle, about her process for generating estimates to accommodate long-term asset value. This is what she said:

> There are a number of projects that fall into a predictable pattern and can only be determined by a history of careful tracking of hours. Each day, everyone in our office completes their timesheet. Because every project is different and seems to introduce a new

————

Remember: You aren't just selling design services to your clients. You're creating intellectual property that can have great value beyond the time it takes you to make it.

————

chaos factor, we are constantly refining the budget range for these types of projects. If it's a new client, we lean towards the high end to allow for bumps incurred building the new relationship. If it's a long-term client, we can determine patterns and whether most of their projects are quick and smooth, or not.

Some items, such as a logo, I can't estimate because I've done a logo in one hour, and then I've done some that take one hundred hours. I charge based on the value a logo is to their business—its long-term branding.

But, take something like a white paper. From concept design through delivery, a job like that will take us twenty-five to thirty-five hours. A large company won't blink an eye at a $5,000 budget, but smaller companies can't afford it. So if it's for a good client who sends a lot of business to us, I consider the value that white paper will be for their business and estimate accordingly. If it's a one-time client, or a client with perpetually small budgets, I refer them to a designer who can work within smaller budgets.

4. Select a pricing model

Once you understand how much time your studio requires for a project, how that time fits into a project schedule and the amount of money it will cost a client, you're ready to determine a pricing model for your estimate. The model you choose will dictate how your cost estimate will appear in the proposal you provide your client.

Some designers focus heavily on their pricing model as the differentiator in how they pitch and land new clients. But as you can see from this estimating process, the pricing model is the last thing you should determine when generating an estimate for a design project.

The most common pricing models include charging by the hour, asking for a fixed fee, establishing a retainer agreement or some hybrid of the three. On the following pages, I've outlined the pros and cons of the three most common pricing models.

$= \mathbf{\$15,000}$

[hours * rate + expenses] + markup

FIXED FEE

Fixed-fee pricing is an agreed-upon price for a set number of deliverables in a proposal. The price is determined by an hour-based estimate with expenses, plus any marked-up costs for pass-through services. With a fixed-fee estimate, the client will not see how many hours you will be spending on discrete activities in your proposal.

Fixed fee: Pros
- Allows value-based pricing and increased perceived value in the mind of your client
- Allows for an increase in budget from previously delivered projects of a similar type
- Allows overhead costs to be built into the budget, including time spent estimating and planning the proposal
- Potential for larger profit margin
- Allows greater flexibility in pricing
- Requires no budget reporting to client

Fixed fee: Cons
- Easy to lose money on a project if it spins out of control
- Requires rigorous adherence to deliverables—no room for "freebies"
- Invites lax internal reporting on the part of staff
- Requires deep estimating experience to "eyeball" a price accurately
- Client delays will force negotiating a change order

Fixed fee: When to use
- When competing with other agencies, as this is the standard model for larger projects
- When your project requires more than one skill set or resource: designer, writer, coder, etc.
- When you have more than one deliverable
- On any project that requires you paying for vendor-provided services or physical materials; it allows for agency markup on those hard costs
- To educate clients on the value of your agency and your services
- To help grow a client into a retainer-based relationship

=(hours * rate)

HOURLY CONTRACT

An hourly contract consists of a billable hourly rate multiplied by the amount of hours required to finish the project. The client is informed via the proposal of the hours allocated for you and your staff, as well as your billing rate.

Hourly contract: Pros
- Allows for accurate estimating, as you bill for the actual time worked
- Easy to formulate estimates
- Clients understand the model quickly
- Simpler to initiate change-order conversations when hours are exhausted
- Allows client to add hours to fulfill additional tasks
- Good for multiple projects on similar timeline
- Tracking and reporting stems directly from keeping accurate time sheets

Hourly contract: Cons
- Requires experience when estimating hours associated with new types of deliverables
- Can train clients to see you as a hired hand instead of as a long-term partner
- Invites bargaining over the number of hours required per project (and your hourly rate!)
- Can lock you into a poorly considered rate
- May require on-site work
- Can be cut off more easily midcontract

Hourly contract: When to use
- You are being invited to collaborate with multiple clients on multiple projects
- You are an extension of the agency's or client's in-house team
- Your client can't or won't define deliverables
- The project is open-ended with no deadline
- You're testing the water for a full-time position

= $15,000/mo.

$$\$\$\$/month - [hours * rate]$$

RETAINER AGREEMENT

A retainer agreement is an agreed-upon weekly or monthly bucket of billable hours associated with ongoing needs you fulfill for your client. You both agree to your hourly rates as part of a long-term contractual agreement.

Retainer agreement: Pros
- The retainer can be structured different ways depending on client need
- Guaranteed income: You're paid regardless of whether you complete the hours agreed
- Relationship based on trust
- Shows high value to client
- Can connote an agency-of-record status, meaning that you will be the only company helping your client with a specific set of tasks
- Encourages deep knowledge of client's industry and needs
- Can support hiring the appropriate talent required for the project
- Often associated with large dollar amounts

Retainer agreement: Cons
- Requires complex and mathematically accurate budget reporting
- The client "owns" your time—all that you agree to provide
- Can create boundary issues regarding when you work and how hard you work
- Can cause inflated expectations for work quality
- Often involves noncompete contracts, limiting you from other opportunities in the same field or market
- Requires expertise in negotiating retainer contracts and master service agreements (MSAs) to hold both parties accountable
- Can impact your company's health if it goes away; downsizing will likely be necessary if revenue is not replaced

Retainer agreement: When to use
- When you have established a position of trust with your client
- To become an effective extension of the company's business or marketing plan
- To act as a day-to-day consultant affecting company business
- To attain agency-of-record status
- For consistent, sizeable billings
- As a tool to build your agency
- When your client can guarantee long-term work for you but isn't sure of short-term deliverables (e.g., $500K of business over eighteen months, divided and paid monthly)

5. Translate your estimate for your client

After all of that, you can finally put an effective and accurate cost estimate into your proposal for your client. Congratulations! Step out of your office for a break and grab a refill on that coffee.

BONUS
ROUND

Budgets

A budget consists of the agreed-upon fees for each deliverable provided to your client over the life of a project. It is your financial bible for how time and materials will be consumed by your team, and it's derived from your project estimate. You'll want to start constructing your budget before kicking off any project—even internal ones!

Some designers feel that budgets are the bane of their existence— *the creative process takes as long as it takes, right?*—but without a well-constructed budget in place, it can be very hard to complete a project profitably. It's just like keeping a budget for your personal or household expenses: If you overdraft your bank account, you are going to have to bear the additional cost somehow. And if your checks keep bouncing, the bank is going to close your account.

How can I create a budget for my project?

Break down the allotted hours to certain milestones in the schedule, like this:

- First client presentation
- Second client presentation
- Client signs off on design
- Completed website build
- And so forth

It can help if you group these milestones into categories, such as discovery, design and development.

After you construct your budget, make sure each team member agrees to her allotted hours for each deliverable before, or at, your internal kick-off. Assign a percentage complete for the budget at the key points you've chosen to track. These percentages will differ per team member. If a team member feels there aren't enough hours allotted to accommodate a particular need, you can review the overall budget to see if hours can be shifted to accommodate her request.

Have team members fill out daily time sheets and track their progress against the budget. By monitoring how their hours are used on your project on a regular basis, you can forecast any risk of going over budget and adjust your efforts accordingly.

What if it looks like we're going to go over budget?

What's easy? Creating your budget, then tracking how project hours are used. What's hard? Keeping your staff to the budget and changing course if a project starts to get ugly. But don't fear: Here's what to do.

CALL THE TEAM TOGETHER AND DISCUSS OPTIONS

Can anyone shift some of her hours to another team member, without reducing the quality or quantity of work required?

CONSIDER WHAT CAN BE SUBSTITUTED IN THE FINAL DESIGN

You can't change the scope of the project just because you haven't run your budget effectively. But you may be able to reduce your efforts to meet that scope, especially if you're overdelivering on what you'd promised in the proposal.

LOOK AT THE REASONS FOR THE BUDGET SLIPPAGE

Based on what you've delivered to your client to date, is there justification for a change order? If so, begin to consider how to discuss this with your client. *(See "Change Orders.")*

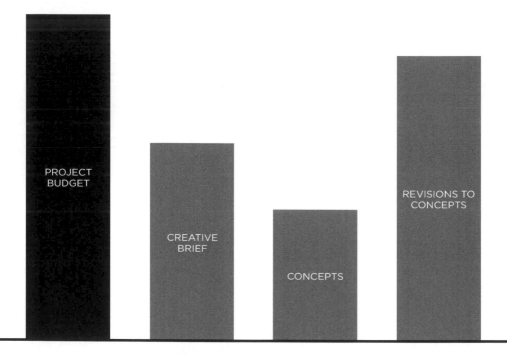

SEE IF LATER DELIVERABLES CAN BE FULFILLED WITH FEWER HOURS THAN YOU HAD ALLOCATED

Sometimes your designers will be working hardest on the first deliverables for a client project—i.e., establishing brand look and feel, initial concept development and information architecture—so fewer hours may be required later in the project. (Sadly, this only works on projects with multiple deliverables.)

My project went over budget. Now what?

Follow the simple three-step process below, and you'll be more likely to close out your project without completely risking your profit margin.

1. CREATE A SHADOW BUDGET

Write an estimate for the hours needed to complete the project. This is a new budget used solely for the time necessary to close out the rest of the deliverables under your current contract. Do this on your own, based on your knowledge of your team and their capabilities.

2. NEGOTIATE THE NEW HOURS WITH YOUR TEAM

"You had twenty hours to complete that web page template. You've used twenty-four. Can you hit thirty for the rest of this phase of the project, then stick to the rest of your estimated time?"

Other than poorly scoping a project, the main reasons that design studios remain unprofitable are improper budgeting and tracking of your team's time.

PRODUCTION

PRESS CHECK

LOSS

This isn't just about the time required to finish the work. This is about what's necessary to make sure your company doesn't lose money. The only exception is whether your original estimate was inaccurate. In that situation, try to negotiate a position where everyone wins a little—whether that means staying slightly profitable or breaking even and folding what you've learned from your estimating mistake into future project estimates.

3. RUN THE PROJECT TO THE SHADOW BUDGET

In managing the shadow budget and keeping your entire team aware of it, ensure that everyone is hitting their new hours. If they aren't staying on target, they should alert you immediately. Tensions are already high when you're losing money; don't let a team member's fear of reprisal make it worse. At times like this, honesty is the best policy, and people need to speak up if they're still overwhelmed.

A project that goes 10 percent over budget can still make a profit. The same does not apply for a project that has gone 50 percent over budget. So be aware of exactly how much give a project has when creating your shadow budget, and make sure you're not waiting until it's too late to react.

Remember: Shadow budgets can help you know when to ask for a change order. Be sure that all time is accurately captured via time sheet. Proper documentation is critical if you need to bill the client for work above and beyond what has been scoped. *(See "Change Orders.")*

How can I get better at estimating projects?

When your project is complete, generate a budget report and review it with a team leader. Summarize your conversation while the project is still fresh in your mind and post it with the budget. This information will be essential if the agency does a similar project or does more work for the same client. You also need this post-project budget report to prepare for a postmortem conversation. *(See "Postmortems.")*

———

Clear budget reporting is proper business. Without referring to actual financials on a weekly basis, your business is flying blind. Such practices can drive creative companies right into the ground.

———

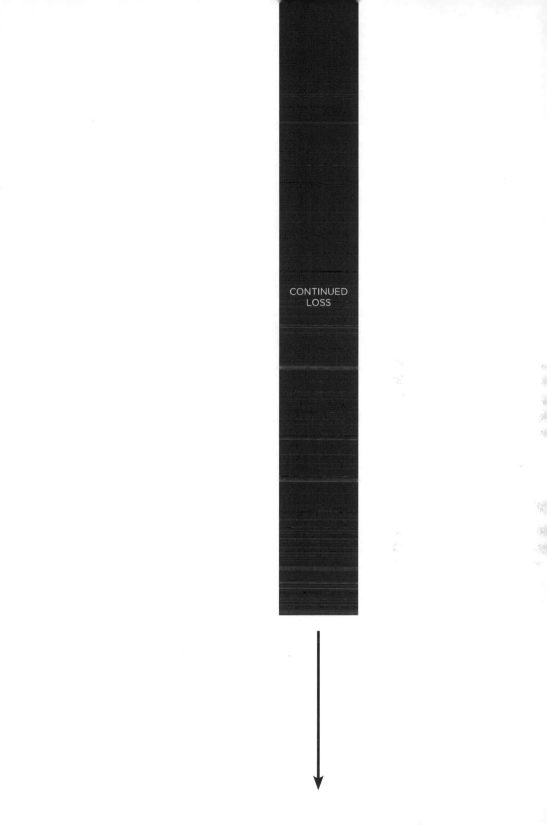

CONTINUED
LOSS

Schedules

Schedules help designers explain what will happen over the life of a project and when it will happen, including everything from project deliverables to required client feedback to launch dates. Missing delivery dates will damage your client relationship.

In order to create a schedule, a designer takes the final deadline for a project and works backward, outlining the steps required to achieve each deliverable. This is known as a work-back schedule.

Working backwards from the final deadline allows you to determine the following:

- Is every deliverable accounted for?
- Does everyone have enough time to complete the deliverables?
- Are extra resources required to complete the deliverables?
- Can we make a profit if this schedule is followed?

In most cases, the designer creates a test work-back schedule as part of any proposal, discusses it with her project team and any vendors, then generates a detailed work-back schedule for client approval after a proposal/contract has been signed.

You should provide schedules to your clients in a friendly and familiar way. You can outline areas in a monthly calendar view or generate a prioritized list. Many project management systems can automate this process.

How to create a work-back schedule

1. OUTLINE A CALENDAR WITH ALL CLIENT-REQUESTED DATES FOR DELIVERY

Due dates are drawn from your first conversations with the client. Be sure to ask if his suggested due dates are fixed or flexible, because you may discover in the estimating process that you can't meet them. If he doesn't have any dates in mind, be careful not to float theoretical dates without doing some research into their feasibility.

2. ADD EVERY STEP REQUIRED AND ASSIGN DATES

Clearly identify when critical deliverables will be provided for client review, as well as when feedback will be due from them. By including due dates for feedback on your shared schedule, you will reinforce how the client is contractually obligated to meet his deadlines, just as you are in providing the deliverables. Going to this level of detail will also help you determine if there are other crucial client interactions you might have missed, such as stakeholder interviews or weekly status calls. Place them all on the schedule so everyone understands how interactions impact deliverables.

3. ASSIGN INTERNAL MEETINGS AND REVIEWS TO REACH EACH DELIVERABLE

Your milestones should have enough space between them to accommodate the internal meetings required to support the project. If you don't have the appropriate space, consider moving out those delivery dates—as long as profitability isn't sacrificed. Do not remove steps from your internal business process in order to squeeze them into the schedule. As a precaution, assume that at least two things will go wrong over the life of the project.

4. REVIEW THE SCHEDULE WITH YOUR TEAM AND ADJUST

Run your schedule by your peers or internal stakeholders. When determining the appropriate amount of time for the project, you'll need to make space for overlapping projects, holidays and other important events. If someone is getting married or having surgery, you'll need to work that into the schedule.

If your team thinks the schedule doesn't seem feasible, see what is absolutely necessary to meet your client obligations. Can any deliverables be shifted or changed? Look for ways to begin earlier, combine meetings or anything else that the team can do to make the schedule easier for them. If all else fails, ask for additional monies or a change order to accomplish the schedule.

Do not use the weekends as part of the schedule unless your team agreed to the idea, and you have budgeted for it appropriately! At the tail end of a very tight schedule, nights and weekends may occur, but this should not be written into the schedule. Overtime is reserved for unusual or unavoidable circumstances only, not everyday business.

5. MARK ALL CLIENT INTERACTIONS

Design your schedule in a way that allows you to quickly focus your client's attention on the dates and times crucial responsibilities fall. It helps to use a different color or font weight.

WORRIED ABOUT MISSING A DEADLINE?

Deadlines are the heartbeat of design business work flow. Managing deadlines is a learned skill, and if conducted well over the life of a client project, can contribute value to your overall client relationship and increase the perceived value of your services.

What if I'm going to miss a scheduled deadline?

Deadlines can be moved, but they can't be missed. Ever! Be sure to inform the client ahead of time, so arrangements can be made to update the schedule. Remember: An approved schedule outlines your contractual obligations to your client. From a business perspective, it's better to renegotiate a schedule in advance than to beg for forgiveness after missing a deadline.

Is it a real deadline or an internal deadline?

Understand the rationale behind each deliverable deadline and the repercussions for not meeting that deadline. Gauge which are **real deadlines**, using some form of competitive advantage that can be quantified, and which are **internal deadlines,** which map to defined goals, implicit rewards, boss satisfaction and so forth. A product launch announcement at a major trade show may have different ramifications for your team than just sharing project progress at an internal staff meeting.

What if the client misses their deadline on our schedule?

Warn the client of any repercussions regarding a slipped schedule. Consider a day-to-day schedule slip for any missed deadline on their end. Some missed dates may also require a change order.

What should I put in my contract to protect deadlines?

If a provided contract to a client has a set start date, and the client signs the contract after the agreed-upon start date, you must have in your document a clause that allows you to shift the project end date or to adjust the project deliverables (via a zero-sum change order) to protect the project timeline. Don't put your project quality at risk.

What if my client goes dark for an extended period of time?

Inform him that you will be "pencils down" if you don't hear from him by a certain date. All deadlines will then move out, and the client should be assessed a fee (per your contract) to restart work.

6. CONFIRM DELIVERY DATES WITH EXTERNAL VENDORS

Before your client sees the draft schedule, run it by vendors or partners to make sure that any bids or services they have agreed to provide can be delivered within the timetable. Make sure your vendors agree in writing to your proposed schedule. If you skip this step, you can be liable for additional costs or changes to delivery dates.

7. SEND A CLIENT-FACING VERSION TO YOUR CLIENT FOR REVIEW

Information regarding your internal meetings and reviews are not for the client's eyes. Scrub internal information from your schedule, including your copywriter's surgery from Step 4, and then send this "client-facing" version to your client with a deadline for suggested changes. Ask her to confirm stakeholder availability for review dates.

8. INCORPORATE CLIENT CHANGES INTO SCHEDULE

The client will provide you with suggested changes. Run those changes by the appropriate people to confirm their feasibility. If necessary, talk with your client about other options. At this point, the schedule isn't fixed. There may be room to maneuver.

9. GET CLIENT SIGN-OFF ON SCHEDULE

Once you have the schedule finalized, send it to your client and ask them to approve it in writing. Once you have sign-off on your schedule, you and your client are obligated to fulfill the schedule to the best of your ability—and your team should get to work!

SCHEDULES SHOULD ACCOUNT FOR BACKLOG

Backlog is the amount of time that a studio is booked, running at full capacity. On average, a design business should always have a two to four week backlog. More than four weeks, and the studio may end up turning away opportunities from clients who want to start work immediately. Fewer than two weeks, and the studio may risk losing money due to inconsistent income.

Risk

On projects with hairpin-turn deadlines, high levels of technical complexity and large multidisciplinary teams that function across departments within a large organization ... well ... things can get tricky. Designers have to deal with risk sooner or later. This risk is often distilled into a series of assumptions or contingencies that serve as part of a proposal. They look something like this:

- Our firm will receive collated feedback from client within twenty-four hours of each provided deliverable
- Our firm will require access to the hosting environment at the start of the project
- Our firm will hold to the specified feature set provided in this estimate; any changes in the agreed-upon scope will have an impact upon timeline, budget or both

While these lists are great for defining client/designer boundaries, they don't do a good job of describing what happens when someone violates those boundaries. We rarely dive into the nitty-gritty details of how things can go wrong until we've signed the contract and started work, but you should take the time during a project kickoff to create a risk assessment.

For small-scale projects, creating a risk assessment doesn't have to be a formal affair. On much larger projects, however, plan at least one client meeting during which you can discuss the risks you'll face over the life of the work and how you can keep your project on the rails. When you show up for this meeting, you will need a risk-assessment document.

A risk-assessment document can be set up as a three-column chart designed to answer the following question:

If [something bad] happens, we're going to do [agreed-upon action].

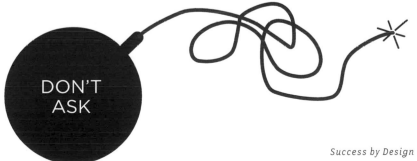

DON'T
ASK

In the first column, list all the possible things that can and sometimes do go wrong. For example:

- Missed milestones (both client and designer)
- Late payments from client, based on negotiated fee structure
- Additional feature requests, or removing existing features to replace with another feature at the eleventh hour (i.e., horse trading)
- Providing content too late in the process
- Receiving late or surprise stakeholder feedback on deliverables that have already been approved
- Approval chains that suddenly change or were unclear
- Failure of third-party vendors to respond in a timely fashion (server and/or IT vendors)
- Failure to deliver promised resources or information required to fulfill key deliverables such as research or metrics

In the second column, describe what you and the client will do as a team to surmount those problems. You can't always be specific, but you can posit some potential solutions.

The third column in your chart works with the established schedule. This is the place where you provide a list of the specific deliverables that will be most significantly affected by the hiccup in the initial event. Clients don't always realize the impact of small slips in the schedule, and this column can help them see it in black-and-white. From the clients' perspective, though, a risk-assessment chart also keeps your team honest.

Keep in mind that this document is a draft until the client provides her input and agrees to it (in writing). But you are in a much better position with her if you have thought through the best course of action before you get together to review it. Describe all of the possible things that can go wrong from a neutral perspective, which means that you'll detail risks from all sides, including your own team, third-party vendors and the client. This inclusive approach shows the client that you're acting in the best interest of the work, not trying to pave the way for pointing fingers.

Every project comes with risk. With this process, you can clarify those risks in advance and mitigate them throughout the project. Risk-assessment documents seem simple, but they have complex ramifications in implementation. The more risk assessments that you conduct, the easier it will be to pull one together for a similar project. You will keep improving your body of knowledge from project to project, based on any new problems or errors that slip through.

RISK TO PROJECT SUCCESS	HOW TO AVOID THE RISK	DELIVERABLES IMPACTED
Client provides feedback after agreed-upon deadline	Day-to-day slip on project schedule for late feedback and/or change order	All deliverables
Designer provides deliverable after agreed-upon deadline	Warn at least three days in advance, adjust schedule without any cost to client	All deliverables
Client does not deliver sample copy before wireframes are created	Designer stops work until copy is delivered, schedule slips, fee to start again	Wireframes, visual design comps, front- and back-end development
Client does not deliver all content before visual design phase	Designer stops work until copy is delivered, schedule slips, fee to start again	Visual design comps, front- and back-end development
Payment is not provided by client for final phase of work	Designer stops work until paid, schedule slips, all work to date invoiced	Front- and back-end development, testing, deployment
New feature requests received after sign-off on functional specifications	Change order is negotiated based on change in scope	Wireframes, visual design comps, front- and back-end development
Stakeholder responsible for approval of deliverables changes midproject	Change order is assessed for additional revisions on approved work	All deliverables
Vendors don't meet agreed deadlines for key deliverables	Adjust schedule without any cost to client; renegotiate with vendor	Front and back-end development
Technology platform requested for use by client is unproven	Have technology consultant on call to support team during development	Technical specifications, wireframes, front- and back-end development

An Example of a Risk-Assessment Chart

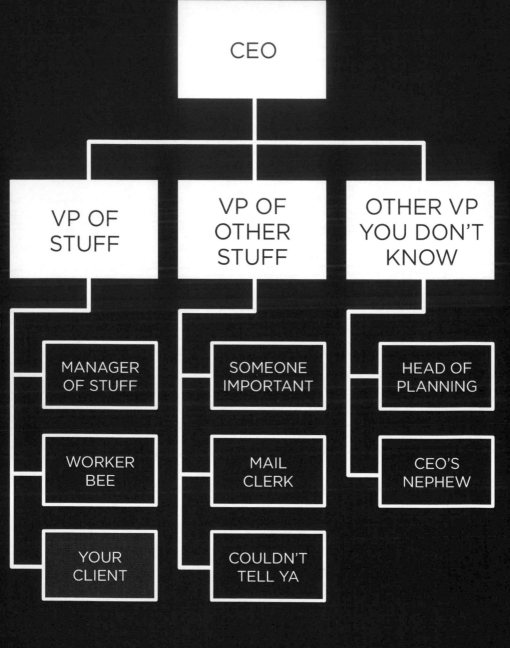

Stakeholders

When starting a design engagement with a new client organization, it's important to determine the people within that company—or outside it—who have the authority to influence your project. If you have more than one direct client who has approving authority, you should consider drawing up a quick RACI matrix to determine your stakeholders for the project. RACI stands for the following:

- **Responsible:** These stakeholders must negotiate with the rest of the people on this list to provide you with actionable feedback for specific project deliverables. Your day-to-day contact is often the person who is deemed responsible for all deliverables—but this is not always the case.
- **Approver**: The stakeholder within your client's organization who has the final say on a specific deliverable. Sometimes this is the manager or the director-level manager of your everyday client contact. Sometimes it's the CEO of the company.
- **Consulted:** Stakeholders who are shown your work and can offer a point of view to the people listed above. However, stakeholders who are consulted do not provide the final say on the project direction or the deliverable in question.
- **Informed:** Stakeholders who are shown your work but are not asked for a point of view. They generally care only that you finish the project or fulfill a stated milestone.

A RACI matrix is a simple matrix. It includes the project deliverables down the left-hand column, and all of the people involved with the project across the top row, whether they are on your design team or on the client side. The matrix is then filled with the appropriate code (R/A/C/I) based on that person's required level of involvement for each deliverable.

Roles can shift from deliverable to deliverable based on each stakeholder's domain of expertise. This is especially true when working on a large-scale website redesign or a web application that touches on multiple departments within a client organization.

Common issues that a RACI matrix can prevent

By creating a RACI matrix, you can better plan how you involve your clients throughout the life of a project. It can also help you identify the following common pitfalls when starting work on a project.

ASSIGNING MULTIPLE APPROVERS TO A PROJECT

Large client organizations will often identify multiple designated approvers. This forces you to design to a committee, which is something you should avoid at all costs. At the start of the project, whittle that team of approvers down to one key person who holds the final say over the project. Designate the other people as contributors.

PLACING APPROVERS LAST IN THE DECISION CHAIN

Ever had to present to group after group of contributors, never reaching the stakeholder who holds sway over whether your project lives or dies? Accountable stakeholders are often brought into a project so far down the path that the design in question is a shadow of the idea you'd originally presented. Be mindful of what deliverables require the highest levels of approval.

BEING UNAWARE OF AN APPROVER

Clients who claim responsibility over a deliverable might also say that they are the final approver for that deliverable—but it's not always the case. An investor, boss or co-worker might hold more sway over the approval of specific deliverables. Use your matrix: Responsible parties and approval parties should be clearly marked.

BEING BURIED BY CONTRIBUTORS

Everyone "helping out" with the high-profile project wants to "add value" to your design work. However, no one is sifting through those ideas and filtering them to ensure the final deliverable is focused and coherent. This is not wholly the designer's burden to bear—your client must also play an active role in sifting through input from her organization.

How to gather the information necessary to create a RACI matrix

Great project managers, as well as savvy designers, need to clearly state which stakeholders should provide approval and/or input with every design deliverable. If you have documented, in writing, the key approver for each deliverable, as well as the person within the client organization who's responsible for garnering that approval, you won't have to worry about simple miscommunications turning into major mishaps.

When starting a new project, tell your client that in order to expedite project execution, you'd like to establish who will be the key approver and other contributors. Then make sure those stakeholders provide their input and sign off on those key deliverables as part of the project process.

This approach can be a bit daunting when you're dealing with a very large client organization or complex office politics. In those cases, project managers and designers use some of the following tactics to glean the necessary information.

ASK YOUR CLIENT FOR AN ORGANIZATIONAL CHART
Take a look through the organizational chart and determine key managers, both laterally and higher up on the food chain. When you have conversations about project planning, try to determine whether those managers may be approvers, contributors or informed participants.

IF THEY WON'T GIVE YOU AN ORG CHART, LOOK UP THE RELEVANT INFORMATION ON THE INTERNET
Director-level positions are often a Google search away. Their names may never come up over the course of fulfilling your project work, but if they do, you'll have an inkling of what sway they hold over your project outcome, and you can dig deeper into their possible role as a shadow stakeholder. Extra research to determine who's really involved can also help soften the blow from the sudden arrival of the "surprise stakeholder," who shows up after they return from their vacation in Tahiti to derail your project.

DETERMINE AN EMERGENCY CONTACT, IF YOUR CLIENT BECOMES INDISPOSED
Your client may refer you to someone you haven't met before but might be involved in the process at a later point.

BE AWARE OF ALL PEOPLE CC'ED ON EMAILS AND INVITED TO MEETINGS, ESPECIALLY BEFORE THE WORK BEGINS
We often meet a whole swarm of people when courting a prospective client, but then end up fulfilling the work with a smaller team. However, don't assume that a stakeholder you met early on won't show up later. If a new name shows up on an email from your client contact, find out who that person is and adjust your RACI matrix to accommodate their influence.

NOTE WHO'S SIGNING THE CONTRACT AND THE CHECKS
If your contract was signed by the CEO, then she may also be the final approver on your work. And while those in accounting are always informed participants in your project—they need to know when you're done so they can pay you—they likely have zero input into your work.

What does a RACI matrix look like?

	CEO	Marketing Director	Marketing Manager	Director of IT
Research Brief	Informed	Approver	Responsible	Informed
Technical Spec	Informed	Consulted	Responsible	Approver
Research Findings	Approver	Consulted	Responsible	Informed
Creative Brief	Informed	Approver	Responsible	Informed
Content Strategy	Informed	Approver	Responsible	Consulted
Information Architecture	Informed	Approver	Responsible	Consulted
Visual Design Direction	Approver	Consulted	Responsible	Informed

Example of a RACI matrix.

A RACI matrix is an investment in long-term client relations

After you've built your RACI matrix, stick to it. Require the appropriate stakeholders to be present for your in-person presentations. Set up a formal approval process so you get the right input from the right stakeholders at the right time.

Making a RACI matrix may seem like a lot of effort to expend before you begin a new project. However, this tool will help you manage the implicit politics of any large client organization. If you end up retaining the client for multiple projects, the matrix can be worth its weight in gold.

Change Orders

A change order is when you ask for the client to pay you more money to fulfill a project in progress. This is due to any (or all of) the following situations:

- **Increase in scope:** The client asked for more changes, features or deliverables
- **Change in schedule:** The client has asked for deliverables within a shorter period of time
- **Schedule slippage:** The client has missed deadlines, so work has slipped and the schedule has grown longer
- **Work has to be redone:** The client has added key stakeholders, or the client has changed her mind regarding something already agreed upon: "I know I said I wanted the silver concept, but now we think it needs to be the one with the bananas ..."

Many designers are afraid to mention that a change in project scope will cost the client more money. But painting a clear picture of what deliverables and edits are included as part of your overall project is fundamental when running any service-oriented business. You need to aggressively interpret and manage client changes that veer outside that scope—especially when they have a far-reaching impact on your time and budget. You both have a responsibility to negotiate the appropriate outcome to make both parties satisfied with the results of your design efforts. If you spend all of your time working to please the client, you'll deliver exceptional client service, but if you aren't careful, you'll end up doing it for free.

How do I tell a client about the possibility of a change order?

In response to a client request that impacts project scope, say: "We'll be more than happy to make the changes that you've noted to this most recent round of [name of deliverable]. However, to accommodate your request, there will be an impact on the project schedule and overall scope, which may result in a change order. We'll get back to you within [X number of hours] with an idea of how these changes may affect the project."

Defer negotiating extra costs or schedule impacts until you have time to assess the situation without the client present. If you do need to negotiate a change order, you can soften the financial hit by saying you'll work with them to try to prevent further change orders. Some clients request that agencies forgo change orders. Don't do it; it's just too risky. Avoid "No Change Order" policies at all costs. (No pun intended.)

How do I create and negotiate a change order?

Change orders are not punitive. They are not meant to punish the client for changing his mind or altering the project. They are designed to protect your agency and your margin. Don't feel bad about initiating the process of requiring a change order for one of your projects. To quote Fiona Robertson Remley: "Change orders are part of the agency's negotiation tools. They are not positive or negative. They just are."

Write a change order the same way you wrote your estimate. Base it on your set hourly rates and consider the time required to fulfill the changes. Change orders are subject to the same agency markup but should be tightly managed and not too heavily padded.

Propose the change order to your client with full details on the new deliverables, their impact on the project and a new timeline. Be sure to negotiate the change order before the new work is done. Doing the work before the change order robs you of negotiation power and makes you look disorganized. It also devalues your time and effort.

Lastly, have the client sign the change order—consider it a mini contract that is appended to your original contract with the client.

YOU CAN'T EASILY NEGOTIATE A CHANGE ORDER WHEN:
- You write a proposal in a manner that doesn't clearly describe the amount of time, discrete deliverables or quantity of changes necessary to complete a project in an effective manner
- You have gone over budget for no client-based reason, i.e., "We didn't know how to do this properly when we started" is not a good reason
- You switch a resource for a more expensive one
- You have spent the budget and have nothing left
- You're attempting to make up for money lost on another project
- You just don't like working with the client... sorry!

Time Sheets

Time sheets are an important tool used to track project budgets. Team members need to fill out their time sheets daily and send them to the global team tracking system at the end of each week. They need to be as close to accurate as possible. Waiting until the end of the week to enter time can add up to 20 percent discrepancy.

Whoever oversees your projects should apply the reported hours against the hours allotted per team member in the budget. Variance of more than 20 percent from budget (more or less time spent) should be discussed with the team member as soon as possible.

Do you really need to keep time sheets? The answer is always yes—even if you work for yourself. If time is money, then time sheets are the receipt for the client money you're burning through on a project. If you don't track your time, you'll never know if you are improperly estimating your design work. And in a worst-case scenario, when your client disputes whether you put the appropriate time and effort into a project, you will be able to provide documentation that supports your story.

TRACKING TIME HELPS YOU BETTER UTILIZE YOUR EMPLOYEES

An employee who is not fully utilized can have a big impact on your bottom line, and the best way to identify an underutilized worker is to analyze the time sheets. Some people refer to these workers as marginal employees. Under the wrong conditions, you could be paying a marginal employee to sit at his desk and watch YouTube videos.

"In a small shop, the marginal employee can make a dramatic difference in the types of projects brought in and workload in general," says Nathan Peretic, cofounder of Full Stop Interactive in Pittsburgh. These employees can spend their extra time training, helping land new projects or plugging away on an internal project. Their "downtime" can be turned into an investment opportunity for your agency. But you'll never know if they're available if you can't track their time.

I like misteaks.

Proofreading

No one likes a typo. Even after you've finished the fourteenth round of revisions on the 128-page magazine and you're trying to send the files to the printer, it's inevitable that a typesetting error or grammatical mistake will still be lurking somewhere in the document. The same issues apply when completing content for a website and porting it into a CMS; gremlins always seem to hide in the corners of our code.

Proofreading and layout mistakes happen, but we can catch them!

Various grades of proofing can be applied to a document, so it's important that you know what you need. If you're conducting a light proof, you read through the material in search of any grammatical errors, typos and glaring inconsistencies. If you're working through multiple rounds of edits, highlight areas where the changes were made in a document and only reproof those areas after the edits had been made. On a full proofreading and fact-checking pass, you'll need to hunker down with the material and get uncomfortably close to it.

What should I do if I need to proofread my own design work?

If you're going to proof your design work yourself, use the following process, which I gleaned from an early career stint as an editor and proofer. This work can be time-consuming, but it's imperative to the quality of what you produce. Build the necessary time into your client estimates and charge for this activity.

1. GO LINE BY LINE THROUGH THE TEXT, PROOFING FOR TYPOS AND INCONSISTENCIES

It's best to proof the text before you typeset it, thereby minimizing the risk of errors that make it into the layout. Review each line, one after the other, in order, without distraction. Use a physical aid, such as an index card or sheet of paper, to block out all of the text except for a single line. By using this method, your brain can't default to its typical human reading behavior—where you read words by their shapes, instead of inspecting what letters on the page compose those shapes. This method of reading will also make you pay closer attention to typesetting issues such as widows, orphans and ladders.

Killing a tree with printouts is the least painful method to proof, especially from your eyes' perspective. Even if you're working on a one thousand-page website, you should consider this step. There are ways to manage how the content is printed out—duplex, lighter ink, recycled paper—to maximize the output and reduce the impact on the environment and on your physical printing supplies. This work can be carried out on screen, but you should double or triple-space the text in a story editor or text preview. If you're stuck proofing on screen, make sure you take a break every so often to rest your eyes.

Depending on the length of the piece and the type of information it contains, you may need to proof it in multiple passes.

2. AFTER YOU'VE READ THE TEXT, REREAD IT BACKWARD

This is one of the dirty secrets of most professional proofreaders. When they reach the end of a piece that they've proofed, they keep their index cards on the page and do the same process in reverse. It's a rare typo that escapes your notice on this second pass, as each word is now abstracted out of your regular reading flow.

3. HIGHLIGHT AND VERIFY ALL FACTUAL SOURCES—NO EXCEPTIONS

As you're reading through the text forward and backward, you should be indicating and verifying page content that you can cross-check against reputable sources. This can be the most time-consuming part of any large proofreading job, but it is the most important part as well. Even if the client says that everything in the document is correct, it's your duty to confirm their content whenever possible. If you can't verify something, you should query the client for their sources. This way, you are indemnified if they take their product to press with an error.

———

When the last line of a paragraph only has one word or part of a hyphenated word, we call it a **widow**. An **orphan** is the last line of a paragraph that's broken onto a new page, causing a single word to float "orphaned" in the air. A **ladder** is when three or more hyphens appear in sequence on the right edge of a paragraph.

———

4. FLAG MISSING INFORMATION SO IT CAN'T GO TO PRESS

When asked to show layout with fake calls to action, such as placeholder information like 1-800-123-4567, you need to do so in a manner that screams out "FPO!" (For Position Only.) Think yellow highlighting or bold red text—whatever stands out in a different color and weight.

5. CHECK YOUR WORK AFTER IT'S BEEN CORRECTED IN THE COMPUTER

After you've finished your hard proof, conduct a light reproof of all fixed changes to make sure new errors didn't slip in. Inevitably, one or two small typos or new errors sneak into layouts after a heavy proofreading pass. When changes have been made in separate documents and then flowed into your design, mistakes or re-ragging can occur. It never hurts to take another look. Adding a single letter to a single world can push the final line of a story off a page in a print file. When those problems aren't caught, there is often a hard cost associated with fixing the error in page proofs or HTML code. This can be less of an issue in proofing online content, but an extra carat or ampersand can cause mayhem.

6. AT THE FINAL PROOFING STAGE, REREAD ALL CONTENT FORWARD AND BACKWARD

You must be thinking, "No, please not again!" Sorry, this is the one area in which you can't afford to see a new mistake introduced. Even the best printers accidentally introduce errors at prepress, when the files are released. For a website, this would be the proofing that happens when content is flown into your CMS or coded into the system. Quality assurance should always happen at this testing stage!

When should I bring in outside proofreading help?

Outsourcing proofreading makes a lot of sense at critical milestones through the life of a project. A fresh pair of eyes can be invaluable. To quote Cynthia Fowler of Graves Fowler Creative: "Proofreading should not be done by the person who wrote the copy in the first place. The best eye is one that is fresh and objective."

Be aware that, even if you pay a professional to review your work, you are still ultimately responsible for any errors in the final, finished product. So it's always in your best interest to spend the necessary time fixing any errors that you're aware of before bringing in a professional.

Don't let the client say, "We don't need a proofer—I'll do it." Clients are rarely effective in catching proofing errors, unless they also happen to be trained proofreaders. In that final phase of a project, have someone from your firm, your client and a professional proofreader conduct the final proofreading work. The more eyes, the better.

———

Never deviate from your proofing protocol—and charge for it. Even if you're under a tight deadline, proofreading is one corner you should never choose to cut. Once you do, typos invariably happen. And if that error sneaks out into the wild—well, there goes your reputation.

———

What proofreading marks do I need to know?

This is only a small sample of the dozens of proofreading marks used by professionals. Some of your staff might have a lot of experience using these marks, but this may not be true for everyone. Query any marks that confuse you and encourage your team and your clients to do the same. As you can see below, there may be different marks in the margins versus in the text.

Errors are not so bad	℘ delete
Whatever do you mean?	⌣ close up
The trial is beginning.	℘ delete and close up
He demanded cheese. (had)	∧ add
(Giant Corgis) attacked!	ok/? query to author
paul Rand is upset.	(caps)/(lc) uppercase/lowercase
She said (y'all.)	(awk) awkward
They are fun onions. (#)	# insert space
said. What he meant... (¶)	¶ new paragraph
(So) very intense!	(rom)/(bf)/(ital) roman, bold, italic
Yes, you said it! Jan. 23–24.	M/N em dash, en dash
Heidelberg Presses rock.	(stet) stet

PRACTICE YOUR NEW PROOFREADING SKILLS ON
THE FOLLOWING ERROR-RIDDLED PARAGRAPH

When you assemb le a team to kick off a project, the leader in the room *will* often begin by Outlining what the client wantss at the team to deliver BUt after the team is fully briefed on what theyll need to create over the life of that project, the leader should explore what the team wants to gain from their participation yo.

Here's a great goalsetting exercise from Matt Conway, an Associate creative Director at frog. At the start of a project, give your team members five minutes to write answers to these questions on sticky notes:

- What would you like the client to gain from ths project?
- What would you like our company to gain from this project
- What would you like the team to gain from this project?
- What would youu, personally and **professionally,** like to gain from this project?

Have your team share what they've written, post it to a whiteboard and capture what themes have emerged. What new perspectives have been revealed? How does this change how the team will work together--or what you will deliver to the client? Share what you've learned by using this approach March 24-April 27 during Design collaboration Week.

Legend to errors in the above text. Paragraph 1: extra space, misplaced italics, wrong case, extra letter, wrong case, missing apostrophe, extra text. Paragraph 2: missing hyphen, wrong case for title. Bulleted list: missing letter, missing punctuation, extra letter, misplaced bold. Final paragraph: Missing em dash, missing en dash, wrong case.

```css
{
    text-decoration: none;
}


a:link { color:#FFFFFFUC
a:visited { color: #3c4490
a:hover { color: #5360D8;
a:active { color: #3c4490;


/* layout */


body
{
    margin: 0;
    color: #222222;
    background: #FFFFFF;
    font-family: Helvetica  A
```

Errors

Refreshed by your first eight hours of sleep in what feels like a decade, you stroll into your office only to be stopped cold by the message light blinking on your voicemail. It's your client, with a three-minute description of how his new shopping cart system—which you'd deployed late last night after months of slavish work—has been unable to process credit card purchases for hours. Thousands of dollars in sales have been lost.

Designers fail in the client-management process when errors slip through, and we can't explain to our client how we'll resolve those errors to his benefit. How will you resolve this issue, and how are you going to communicate your plan of action?

How should I resolve major errors on a project?

1. DETERMINE YOUR ROLE

To gauge an error's impact, start from the point that it manifested itself to you, then work backward. Where in your business process did the fruit of this error begin to flourish? Use root-cause analysis. Keep yourself from thinking, "In hindsight, I would have ..." and focus on the basic facts of what went wrong. Dig through your email, interview your colleagues, explore documentation and functional requirements, crack open design files, sift through code and otherwise reconstruct the path your project has taken through the design process. Document what you discover in writing. (There may be legal ramifications to what you've found, and a paper trail may be critical if you end up in court.)

Now is not the time to reprimand a co-worker or lay waste to a project team with harsh words. Until you know how your firm and the client may have contributed to the error, there is no room for blame.

If your team has the time to help, have them aid you in gathering the necessary information. They're probably going to feel just as bad as you until the problem is solved.

2. GAUGE THE IMPACT

Try to quantify in hard numbers what your client will suffer until the error is set right. Did they lose $10,000 in potential sales due to people clicking a button in an email and landing on a 404 page? Or did a thousand people receive a promotional email, and only two people clicked through a broken link to a nonexistent web page? You need to understand what repercussions the client has actually suffered as the result of the error. Using best-case math, calculate what you could provide that would help mitigate the impact of that error.

You do not have to fully disclose your in-depth assessment of financial impact to your client. This is an activity to guide your action plan.

If the root cause of your error is outside your control—such as working with technology your client requested that's in beta, or losing one of your contract employees or subcontractors due to extenuating circumstances—I hope that you outlined the risks and contingencies associated with their use or participation. *(See "Risk.")* Otherwise you're going to have to disclose those issues as swiftly as possible to the client as part of your action plan.

If the client had a substantial role in the error, you may want to describe the intimate details. In such cases, you will need a clear, rational argument as to why the client must partially or fully bear the onus of the error.

If the error is due to a subcontractor you suggested and hired, you are the one who falls on your sword. It's a sign of maturity to take responsibility when anything goes wrong on a project due to a subcontractor. If you hired the vendor, you have to manage their failures and work with them to make things right.

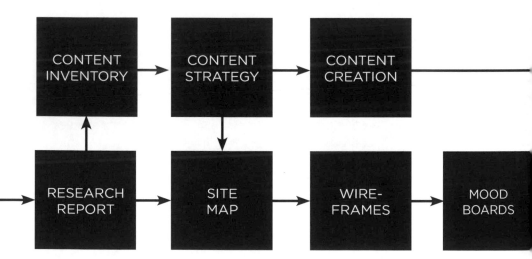

3. WRITE A PLAN

Now that you know how the error came to pass and determined what potential harm your client's business may have suffered, you need to write a plan of action. You need to address the following:

- Where did the error appear?
- When did the error happen?
- Who was involved in the error?
- Why did the error happen?
- What are we doing to fix the error?
- How are we sure the error will never happen again?
- What are the impacts on the project in terms of dollars, schedule and customer service?

You may need to outline more than one course of action to resolve the error, especially if there's a cost or schedule impact for the client. Advocate the best option for the situation that places the least burden on your client, unless they caused the error and need to help in resolving it.

The longer an error remains unaddressed, the more risk you assume from it. However, don't rush through your plan to place it in front of the client. Have it vetted by the highest levels within your firm. If necessary, take an extra few moments to run it by your lawyer.

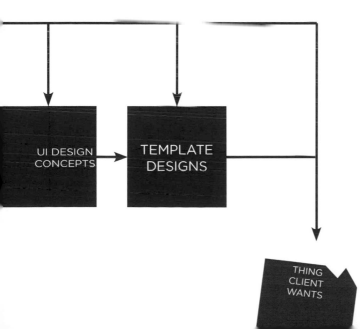

UI DESIGN CONCEPTS

TEMPLATE DESIGNS

THING CLIENT WANTS

4. HAVE A CONSTRUCTIVE CONVERSATION

You should not call the client unless you have the above plan, or you are able to pin yourself to a specific date and time that such plan can be finalized for discussion. If you do have client contact over the hours it'll take you to formulate your plan, keep it as simple as, "We're aware of the issue and are currently creating a plan that we will present to you on [date and time] to resolve it."

Don't put your firm at risk for taking on liability for something said in the heat of the moment. To avoid this kind of risk, you may need to say, "I wish I could answer that question, but I need to talk with [insert name of important person] before I can make an assessment. Can we talk later today, when I have the specifics?"

Set up a formal meeting with your client. Let her know you'll need a chunk of uninterrupted time to talk through your plan to mitigate the error. Use neutral language during the call or face-to-face meeting. (Face-to-face contact is always better for these conversations.) Be clear that this may be a difficult conversation, but phrase it in a meaningful way.

> This is hard for me to share with you. We care very deeply about the success of your project and want to outline what happened yesterday to the shopping cart on your website, and the actions that we're taking to resolve the situation ...

Take responsibility where appropriate, and provide a clear course of action that addresses the perceived problem. Transcend the issue and be clear as to how you've already begun resolving the problem with a defined solution. If there are multiple possible solutions to deal with the issue, outline each of them clearly before soliciting feedback.

After the discussion, send the client a copy of the error mitigation plan.

The error must be fixed before there is any discussion of compensation or barter to make up for lost uptime or revenue. Do not allow your client the opportunity to use the time in which you resolve the error as a period of negotiation. According to Fiona Robertson Remley, you should not offer a discount on contracted services in these situations unless:

- The client asks for one
- You can afford it
- All other options have failed

5. EXECUTE ON THE PLAN AS SWIFTLY AS YOU CAN

Hustle.

6. RECORD THE ERROR TO HELP YOU ASSESS FUTURE RISKS

While it might be tempting to sweep your errors under the rug, learning from them is the way you will come upon stable business processes for your firm. Project errors should teach you how to deliver better work for your current and future clients, and create better shared assumptions and implications for your estimating and proposal-writing process.

Start a simple wiki that outlines the process you take when working through different kinds of client engagements. In the wiki, write a brief paragraph describing what you've learned in various phases of the project. This material can then be referenced when you're writing up estimates for new projects. This living digital document could also be a good place to write a few notes after the project has ended. Conduct a project postmortem and detail what the team learned.

Will a major error ruin my client relationship?

Failure in delivery, when poorly managed, can be fatal for your livelihood. But keep in mind, no designer or developer has a perfect delivery record. In the midst of dealing with a project error—especially one caused by both client and designer—there is always a silver lining. It's not until things go wrong that you see the true personality of your client. And vice versa. Errors help your client understand the true depth of your character.

Your client will respect you even more if you can disclose and mitigate a mistake with grace and professionalism.

IF YOU DON'T FAIL, YOU WON'T SUCCEED

There are two types of businesspeople: those who have failed at some business venture, and those who haven't yet. (Kind of like motorcycle riders.)

The same logic applies to designers. Your projects will fail. Your companies will fail. You will find moments, if not months, where you will question if it made any sense to be in the design business in the first place.

Honor these moments, because you will only achieve success through experience gained through failure. Failure always yields some form of reward. But you have to take a risk to determine that reward and to understand how it shapes your path as a creative businessperson.

Paul Arden, former creative director for Saatchi and Saatchi, put it like this: "If you always make the right decision, the safe decision, the one most people make, you will be the same as everyone else."

Don't suffer this noncreative fate.

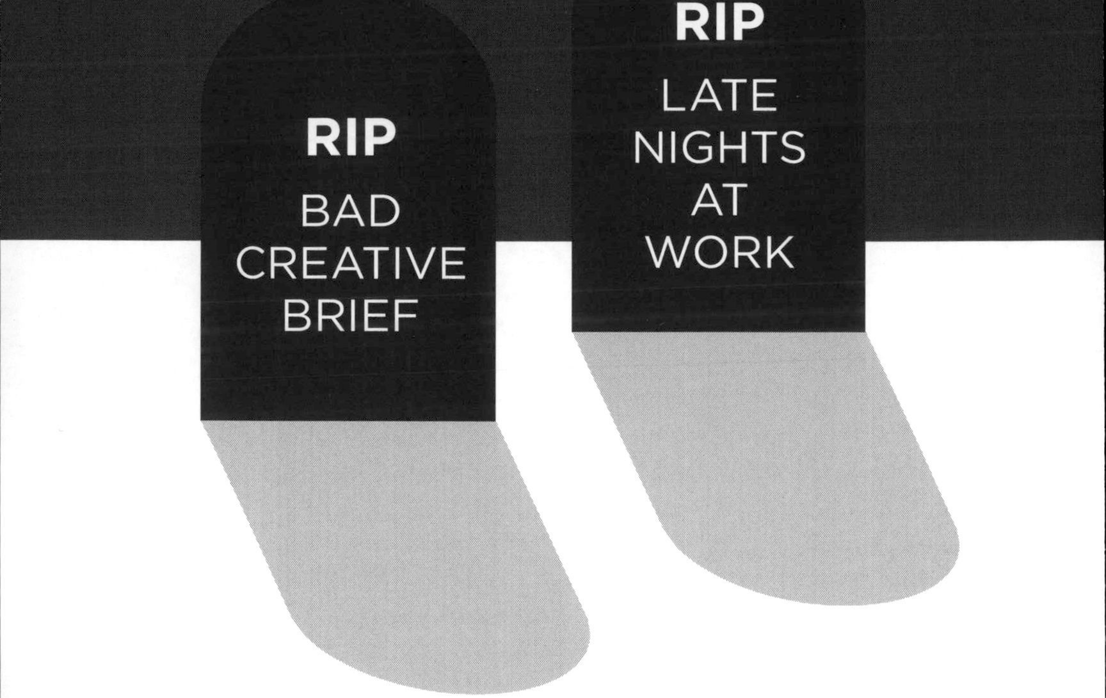
RIP
BAD
CREATIVE
BRIEF
RIP
LATE
NIGHTS
AT
WORK

Postmortems

The website went live last week, and the entire staff is throwing a party to celebrate! The developers are huddled in the corner with microbrews, plotting how they'll hack into the agency intranet to add a virtual dartboard. Designers are mingling with the copywriters and account people, clinking wineglasses and bonding over the ads they saw during *30 Rock*.

However, the job went way over budget, and the last thing your team wants to think about is who needs to take responsibility for it. It's not the best time to mention the postmortem you scheduled to talk about how the project *really* went. Tomorrow.

Was the estimate wrong to begin with? Did the designer spend too long tweaking those page comps? Why did the developer pull so many late nights wrangling with the content management system, when he said he knew how to code using the .NET Framework?

The reasons that a design business fails to make profit on a project boils down to a series of staff and client decisions that, while intended to contribute to project success, lead to cost overruns and errors. Isolating and clarifying those decisions, one by one and role by role, can be punishing if conducted incorrectly.

But if carried out in the right manner and in a safe group setting, a postmortem meeting can galvanize a team and bring them closer together. By being aware of everyone else's perspective, your team members can identify repeat problems in patterns of behavior and anticipate ways to prevent those problems from happening again. Plus, the ongoing learning that comes from open communication and active collaboration is what makes businesses more sustainable—especially on large multiphase projects that repeat year over year.

A "postmortem"? What a morbid term.

Some people are starting to call this meeting a "post future meeting" or a "lessons learned meeting," to avoid the negative connotations from the original term. Call it whatever you like. I prefer the term *postmortem* because ... well ... sometimes you need a dash of the macabre to keep everyone on their toes.

COMMON ISSUES THAT CROP UP DURING POSTMORTEMS:

- Did you fulfill what you promised in the proposal?
- Did the deliverables line up with what the agency actually created for the client? If not, why?
- Was the creative brief an accurate reflection of what is in the proposal and the strategic direction from your agency?
- Were there client requests that changed the project strategy from the approved brief while the project was in process? If not, did the agency absorb into the project cost getting the client to the right strategy? Were you paid for that extra time investment? What were the repercussions?
- Were there technical challenges that occurred during the life of the projects that were unexpected? Should they have been expected and factored into the schedule?
- Did the team have a thorough knowledge of what the project required?
- Were you penalized for the team verging outside their area of core expertise? Did you factor that time into the project budget to support the time they needed to gain the knowledge necessary to succeed? (Another way of phrasing this is: Did you bid the project for your best-case scenario, while knowing full well that best-case scenarios rarely occur if they are contingent on technologies or unique deliverables that are new to your team?)
- Did the team spend time scrambling to address client concerns without proper triage?
- Was the chain of command followed through each phase of the project? (Is there one?)
- Did your vendors fall in line with your agency process/timeline? Did your vendors contribute to your success or provide more hurdles to surmount?
- Did lack of communication or personality friction dictate staff behavior? (This is something that should be discussed candidly after the postmortem in a face-to-face conversation or relayed through the involved parties' manager.)

How do I run a postmortem for a project?

Here's a draft agenda for an hour-long postmortem meeting. Make sure you are meeting in a space that has a large whiteboard, so you can capture what everyone says as the meeting unfolds. When scheduling the meeting, think about what you can attach to the meeting request that will help ground people in what you'll accomplish during the meeting.

1. SET THE TONE FOR THE MEETING (THREE TO FIVE MINUTES)

The postmortem process requires the same deliberate care you would take for any form of client collaboration. Postmortems should always be constructive and be conducted in a manner that is professional and respectful. It often helps to have a meeting leader who wasn't on the project. This leader will be responsible for taking notes on the whiteboard.

Kick the meeting off by letting everyone know the goal for the meeting: understanding what went well and what could be improved about your recently completed project for the purpose of applying this information to future projects. There must be a clear balance between the good things and those that could be improved. Otherwise people in the room may use the whole hour to complain and the meeting will be neither pleasant nor productive.

Everyone in the room should be aware that nothing they say will go on their permanent record. Everyone is taking part in the postmortem to learn from each other. Nothing will be taken personally. If mistakes were made along the way, more respect will be given to those who own up to causing them. No finger pointing.

Let everyone know that if an issue warrants more than five minutes of group discussion, you promise to follow up with the team members individually to plan for similar situations in the future.

> **Dearest project team,**
>
> In our meeting on Tuesday, let's discuss how the server room caught on fire and destroyed nothing left but a burnt hulk of metal and deb The backups all failed as well. Since the team a client was not satisfied, seppuku is an option? Please let me know if you would like us to discu this next week when

2. DESCRIBE THE BUSINESS PROBLEM AND THE PROPOSED AGENCY APPROACH (FIVE TO TEN MINUTES)

Clearly describe what the client wanted to achieve from the project. Summarize the proposal the client signed, just in case anyone in the room wasn't aware of the agreed-upon terms. Ask your team to consider how the proposal did (or didn't) guide the team toward the final delivered project. Common questions during this part of the meeting may include:

- Were there challenges that could have been foreseen from previous agency projects that weren't factored into the proposal?
- Were there any issues with how the proposal was written?
- Were there any deviations that developed from poorly defined scope?
- Were promises made in business meetings or client conversations, but not put in writing, that influenced client expectations?

3. WALK THROUGH HOW THE AGENCY EXECUTED THE PROJECT (THIRTY MINUTES)

This portion of the postmortem is an intense exploration of what happened, and why, over the life of your project. Discuss the major milestones of the project and any key points at which you encountered items or situations that moved beyond your usual creative process. This doesn't have to be a linear process—the staff can skip around in time as appropriate.

If necessary, have on hand the artifacts that supported project completion: creative brief, technical and functional specifications, client communications, vendor input and the paper/digital trail of design work that occurred over the course of the project. You shouldn't be using the time to reproof or critique the minutiae of each deliverable. Simply use the artifacts to provoke your team's memory.

"DON'T PLAY THE BLAME GAME. NO ONE LIKES BEING THROWN UNDER THE BUS!"

4. SOLVE FOR PERCEIVED PROBLEMS (TEN MINUTES)

At the end of the previous phase, you should have a whiteboard list of your team's thoughts and impressions regarding what went well and what could have been improved. Now is your team's chance to be problem solvers and to suggest changes to agency process. Circle pain points and ask your team to brainstorm ways to keep them from happening in the future. When the brainstorming session is over, make a list of all the ideas and send them to the team after the meeting. Put the right people (including yourself) in charge of making sure that change gets implemented.

5. SHOW THE TEAM, IN A PLEASING VISUAL FORMAT, WHERE THE TIME AND MONEY WENT (FIVE MINUTES)

Your staff should have no illusion about how time equals money. There must be a balance between quality of work delivered and profit for your company. So, if you can, show your staff what your financial targets were and how the agency performed against them. Then ask your team (and yourself): Based on what we know now, how would we approach a project like this in the future? Was this project an investment in a new discipline for your agency, a great piece for your portfolio that came at extra expense or something you're never going to attempt again?

Such transparency and candor is rare for most agencies. But this kind of feedback can be worth millions to staff morale. I've worked at agencies where the final postmortem has even included detail regarding how each team member billed their hours. (This means your entire staff needs to keep accurate timesheets and can't lie if they go over their allocated hours on a project.)

Not all of your staffers run the business, so why should everyone know how profitable their project is for the owners or parent company of the agency? The answer is simple: If designers see how their behavior influences stability (and profit) for their employer, they can see how they fit into the grand scheme. These visuals show them how they are accountable for project success.

Did mismanaged client expectations burn up staff time and profit? Did the team suggest placing a few "bonus concepts" in front of the client, causing extra rounds of changes before the client selected the final direction? All of this comes out of the company's pocket and can be gauged in this closing postmortem discussion. Your staff will appreciate seeing exactly what this project meant to the agency—as long as it's delivered in a constructive manner. You can then fold this into the solutions you discussed earlier.

6. HIGHLIGHT THE MOST IMPORTANT THING EACH TEAM MEMBER LEARNED (FIVE MINUTES)

To close out your postmortem meeting, ask each person in the room to put two stars on the whiteboard. One star is drawn beside the most important positive thing to remember from the meeting. The second star is drawn next to the one thing that should be changed going forward. When everyone is done, the facilitator should ask any last clarifying questions regarding everyone's selections, then thank everyone for coming. Notes from the meeting should go out to everyone in a day or so.

What should I do if it's a really long project?

The postmortem gives your staff a chance to fully comprehend what challenges each member of the staff experienced and to create a dialogue about how each individual can be supported by agency peers. Think of it as a journey into exactly how your agency functions. But don't feel like you need to wait until the end of a project to reflect on your team's performance. You can hold a premortem, a midmortem, a retrospective, whatever you want to call it, whenever you want to have it. See how your team is doing, and start solving issues before the project comes to a close.

1 2 3 4 5

+ − * ÷ = $

OPERATING YOUR STUDIO

67890
¢#@%!

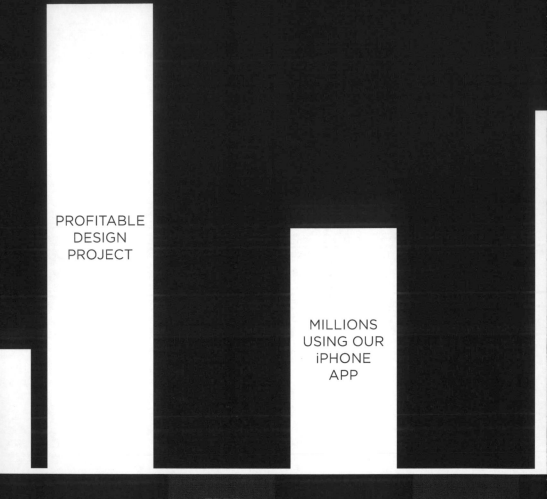

PROFITABLE
DESIGN
PROJECT

MILLIONS
USING OUR
iPHONE
APP

FREE
LATTES
FOR ALL
EMPLOYEES
DAILY

OPEN BAR
AT HOLIDAY
PARTY

Money

Every design business sells some kind of product, which earns money for the company. This revenue contributes to the ongoing operation of your business and the creation of profit. No revenue, no cash flow. No profit, no long-term stability for the business.

But selling products isn't the only way that design businesses stay afloat. Let's take a tour of the various ways design businesses make money, including billing for time, investing in real estate, selling physical products and licensing software or intellectual property (IP).

How do design businesses make money?

1. BILLING FOR TIME
Historically most design businesses have made their money from billing for time. If a design business is able to consistently bill the appropriate number of contracted hours per person on staff, their revenue year over year will yield profit. This falls in line with other professional services providers, such as lawyers, who bill their client for the hours worked towards a desired outcome. For lawyers, winning a case or striking a favorable plea bargain may be their product.

2. MARKING UP PASS-THROUGH SERVICES AND PRODUCTS
Few designers will have a Heidelberg offset printing press in their studio for printing a brochure or a server farm in their closet with a 99.999 percent uptime guarantee. Design businesses must pass through to their clients the costs of services or products required to yield a website or application, printed materials and other project outputs.

Revenue is earned on pass-through services and products via a markup on their total cost. Any markup must also account for the payment of local, state and federal taxes on those services and products, as appropriate. Here are examples of some pass-through services and expenses:

———

You may have altruistic reasons for being a designer, but some designers really do run their businesses because they want to make money.

———

- Purchasing media space on online and mobile properties, in print publications, billboards and out-of-home locations and television. A design business may earn a commission on the overall cost of a media buy that they facilitate or coordinate with a third-party firm.
- Purchasing printing services through a commercial printing firm. The overall cost of printing services, plus delivery, should be marked up if the design business is paying for the printing.
- Retaining a professional photographer or illustrator to generate assets that are then licensed to the client. When working with higher-end photographers and illustrators, you license to a client the rights to use the generated assets for a fixed period of time. If the client needs the rights for those assets after the time has elapsed, they are billed for additional rights usage (with a markup). Some clients seek to "buy out" the rights for assets generated, and it is possible to do so, but most photographers and illustrators will add a multiplier to their price to cover the future revenue they are forgoing.
- Hiring acting, modeling and voice-over talent. Don't forget to include time you'll need to bill for selecting the appropriate talent and directing them.
- Costs for catering, props and other materials used in the generation of photo or video assets.

DON'T RESELL YOUR PROJECTS

Contracting out small-scale specialized activities can make sense for a small studio. It can be cost prohibitive to have people on staff with solely niche skills. I will caution, however, that contracting out most or all of a client project is risky territory for any designer. A client hires us because we are the ones she expects to fulfill the work.

When working with any client, be clear what specific activities are to be handled by a contractor and what role you will play in ensuring they meet the quality standard of your studio. If you're not conducting the development in-house for a project, say so up front. If your studio is overwhelmed and you need the support of another to facilitate the completion of a project, say so before making the hiring call. It's better to be honest regarding these decisions, rather than begging for forgiveness if something goes wrong.

- Licensing the use of artwork and fonts from a stock provider or third party. A good baseline for markup on these items is 20 percent. Be aware that licensing agreements with many stock websites cannot be transferred to a client; in those cases, you may need to have the clients make the purchases as part of their own corporate account.

- Using professional copywriting, editing and proofreading services. Mark-ups on these services may need to be handled more like the billing cost of a staffer: One and a half to three times the hourly rate of the contractor.

- Working with a professional photo retouching service or color-correction artist. The same markup rules apply here as for writing services.

- Helping to coordinate or manage website/application hosting. You may need to negotiate with your hosting provider to secure a wholesale/reseller agreement, which will allow you to resell their services without charging the client more than the market cost for commodity services.

- Purchasing domain names and online services that support the creation of online products, services and properties. Your markup for these services should reflect the time and energy required to secure and transfer those services and the associated rights to your client.

- Travel expenses related to project activities, including plane and train tickets, mileage and gasoline costs, food and beverage per diem, and related costs the client agrees to bear in the signed contract. Travel expenses are usually not marked up.

Additionally, design businesses may retain the support of subcontractors, such as freelance talent or another design or development studio, if the work outstrips resources available in the studio or requires a skill set that may not exist in the studio. This may include front- and back-end development, usability testing, testing and quality assurance on websites, and motion graphics and animation.

3. MAKING CAPITAL INVESTMENTS
Money spent on a studio space is often the largest expenditure, independent of paying for staff revenue. Why not make that money an investment in your business? You can turn an overhead expense into a long-term investment vehicle—especially if the space is in a neighborhood or location that adds value over time. Design businesses also hold smaller-scale assets: computers, furniture, peripherals, artwork, automobiles and other tangible items. These are then depreciated as part of the studio's balance sheet and can be sold to earn revenue as necessary.

4. LEASING AVAILABLE SPACE AND RESOURCES

A design business may have resources at its disposal that may be leased or purchased by clients or by customers at large. By leasing part of an office building, home or other physical location to another business, for example, a design business may pay its own mortgage. If a design business has seats open on its studio floor, it may lease these spaces to other designers or freelancers.

Additionally, design businesses may lease their "public" spaces to other businesses or third parties for the purposes of conducting meetings and events. For example, pinch/zoom, a design studio in the Fremont neighborhood of Seattle, has a rentable space called the Watercooler that can host small workshops, seated events and mixers.

Many design businesses have galleries built into their work spaces that contribute to the business's operating revenue. Such galleries help cover overhead and expenses, as well as contribute to the overall studio culture. If the studio is open to the public, the open space may also be used to sell or promote products, artwork and other resalable items.

5. PRODUCING AND SELLING PRODUCTS AND SERVICES

People at design businesses generate ideas at a prodigious rate. Some of these ideas may apply to client projects, while others may inspire anything from artworks to online subscription services.

Physical products

Design businesses can design, produce and sell physical products. This is often in partnership with other companies or vendors that can help facilitate the production and shipping of those products.

LET YOUR CLIENTS TEACH YOU

Looking for some tips on how to create your own products? David Conrad, from Design Commission, suggests that you internalize market intelligence and insight gleaned from your clients.

> They are educating you while they are paying you.
> You absorb their expertise—while you are helping them—
> and you can use that knowledge to design your own
> products more effectively.

Examples of physical products created by Design Commission. UIStencils.com and LuxePlates.com currently account for over 40 percent of studio revenue each year.

Design Commission, for instance, came up with an idea for UI Stencils (www.UIStencils.com). These stencils are pieces of metal that have been chemically etched with the appropriate icons for drawing user interfaces for websites, iPhones, iPads, Android phones and many others. The stencils are produced on demand, avoiding the need to make a capital investment in a few hundred stencils before opening for business. Based on the success of this initial product, the studio has diversified from stencils into pads of grid paper and small whiteboards with markers. The sales of these products now account for a portion of the overall studio revenue. Another of Design Commission's ventures, LuxePlates.com, was developed with the same revenue-generating philosophy.

Design studios can receive more than revenue from selling products. Full Stop Interactive created a line of design-related T-shirts called United

———

When creating products, aim for unsolved problems. "Money is only an outcome of being able to intelligently design and develop a solution that creates real value," says Matthew May, author of *The Laws of Subtraction*. David Conrad puts it another way: "Find more valuable problems, make more money."

———

Pixelworkers. The studio's cofounder, Nathan Peretic, says: "Selling T-shirts to designers has enabled us to more than pay the rent and expenses on our office every month, and best of all, it's created a number of connections within the industry. Those connections have an inestimable value."

Software as a service

Thousands of individual designers and studios worldwide currently earn money by generating software. Studios can design and develop software products and online services for a variety of devices and platforms. A business can earn revenue from these products and services through a variety of revenue models: a single cost for an application, an ongoing subscription fee for use, by offering an application for free and selling advertising, by selling reports generated from metadata collected from product use, just to name a few.

Jackson Fish Market created an application called A Story Before Bed that people can use online or download for their iPhone or iPad. The application lets its users record reading the book, then play it back with the book. Jackson Fish Market offers this functionality through a variety of annual subscription models. The company has also taken a unique approach to how they deliver the children's books available within the application. On their blog, they say:

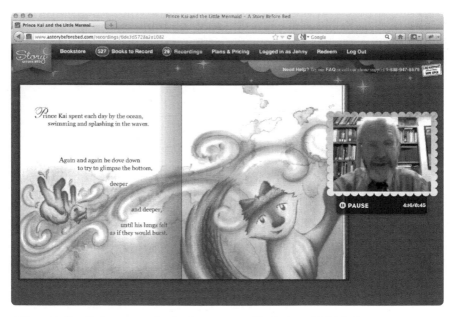

A Story Before Bed, an example of software created by Jackson Fish Market.

ADVICE ON BOOTSTRAPPING FROM JENNY LAM AT JACKSON FISH MARKET

Jenny Lam, chief designer and cofounder of Jackson Fish Market in Seattle, has launched multiple successful products through her design business. She shared the following with me via email:

There are so many incredible things about owning and creating your own products. Sure, there's the financial risk and I've heard designers claim they might get bored with focusing on just one product/service. To me, the upsides outweigh the negatives. Creating our own future, shipping stuff regularly and often, owning our successes and, most importantly, owning our failures has been one of the most rewarding, enjoyable and uplifting work experiences I've ever had. For those interested in going down this path (and I hope you do!) here are some insights I've learned over the years:

Partner with people who have mutual respect for you and your discipline

For me, this is the most essential component to making Jackson Fish Market what it is. The three of us balance each other and really value our disciplines (design, business and engineering).

Do design consulting on the side to bootstrap your product

For us, we figured out that it took about three hours of engineering for each hour of design work I did. So I used the rest of the time to consult on design projects, which in turn helped bootstrap our products.

Have patience and passion

Patience: Invariably when you ask the people who are overnight successes how it went, they will confide in you that they worked hard for years and years before their product made it over the hump. It took us two years of tweaking, learning from our customers and experimenting with different designs and business models before we started seeing real results.

Passion: We made A Story Before Bed so that parents at our company could read to our kids. We made the Thrilled For You Video Guestbook for my wedding. Making something for yourself that solves a real problem not only ensures your commitment, but ensures that you'll have fun making it in the process.

To make sure we had a nice starter collection of books beyond those we got from our excellent launch partners, Jenny Lam led a heroic effort to produce all the Jackson Fish Market titles you see in the bookshelf. *The Frog Prince*, *The Emperor's New Clothes* and others were all produced by our crack team of authors and illustrators. Jenny led the whole effort. If Disney can create a great business based on public domain children's fairy tales, then so can we.

By holding exclusive rights to this content, Jackson Fish Market created a vertically integrated publishing platform in which they can fully control how revenue is generated both for their firm and for the authors that they represent.

Still other examples show how designers can disrupt or reinvent industries with their design savvy. Design studio 37signals transitioned from billing for time to fully supporting a range of productivity-geared software products, such as the project management tool Basecamp and the group chat tool Campfire. Their success in this area emerged from software products they created for their own needs, which they discovered other businesses also needed and would willingly pay to use.

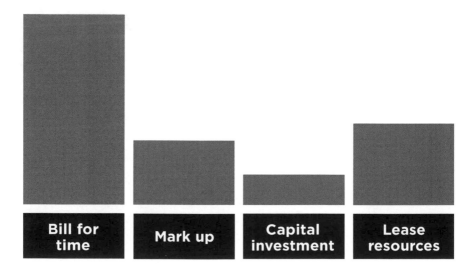

Bill for time **Mark up** **Capital investment** **Lease resources**

Monetizing design news and thought leadership

Some design businesses generate thought leadership, such as blog posts, e-books and other digital products that can be sold online, through subscription or be supported by online advertising on their sites, applications and through RSS feeds. Many popular design blogs partially support themselves through this model.

Tina Roth Eisenberg's Swiss Miss blog (www.swiss-miss.com) started in 2005 as her personal visual archive. It has since grown into one of the world's most popular design journals. Swiss Miss is supported by revenues from site advertising via The Deck, an exclusive advertising network started by Coudal Partners, and RSS feed sponsorship. The revenues from Swiss Miss help support Tina's other business efforts.

Educational events and training

Design businesses can provide training as a service to help designers and businesses do their jobs better. This takes the form of hourly or daily consulting, prerecorded or live webcasts, or producing and hosting live events. Studio members can write, blog, teach, speak or facilitate events as part of how they earn revenue, either for their business or as individuals.

———

Your revenue streams will change organically, based on how your studio revenue diversifies. This can carry risk, acting as a drag on operational revenue and profit from other products you provide.

———

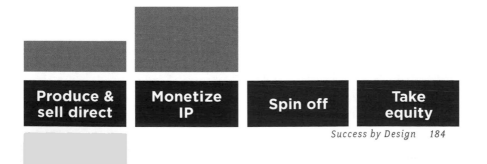

| Produce & sell direct | Monetize IP | Spin off | Take equity |

Adaptive Path, a user experience firm headquartered in San Francisco, holds regular events such as UX Week and UX Intensive. These events are a chance to share tools and techniques that the firm uses in its project work to earn revenue independent of client work and to attract new clients.

6. MONETIZE INTELLECTUAL PROPERTY

A design business can produce novel ideas or inventions that can be patented or trademarked, then licensed to customers or per-project clients. The generation of these patents and trademarks occur as part of delivering products and services (as discussed above) or in the process of fulfilling client work. Depending on how a design business structures its contracts with the client, it could negotiate co-ownership of any unique inventions spawned from client work.

7. SUPPORT OF A SPIN-OFF LINE OF BUSINESS

Some studios support side businesses that have little to no association with traditional design services or the generation of design-related products and services. Running these side businesses can require dedicated staff with skill sets that can't be billed by the design business if extra resources are required for project work.

———

The dream of most business owners: Reaching the right time to sell their business and utilize the money they've earned to make personal investments or launch grand endeavors.

———

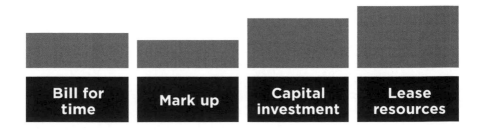

| Bill for time | Mark up | Capital investment | Lease resources |

Christian Helms, designer and founder of the studio Helms Workshop, is also a cofounder of Frank, a hot dog joint in downtown Austin. Christian was able to bring his design sensibilities to the holistic restaurant experience, as he noted in an interview: "I always joke that the design strategy was 'circus comes to town, broadsides hot dog cart.'" However, Christian still works with design clients and other projects as opposed to exclusively running Frank. Read more about Christian's work and the thinking behind Frank at methodandcraft.com/interviews/christian-helms/

8. TAKE EQUITY IN A CLIENT BUSINESS

When working with start-ups or other young businesses, designers can be offered stock or partial ownership in return for their services. In some cases, this is in lieu of cash payment. In others, the design business may have intentionally asked for equity alongside payment for design services or the provision of unique intellectual property or services.

If you are considering taking equity in a client business, be thoughtful about the amount of time (and direct revenue) you can forgo to aid that client with her needs. The value of your investment may never be realized; the

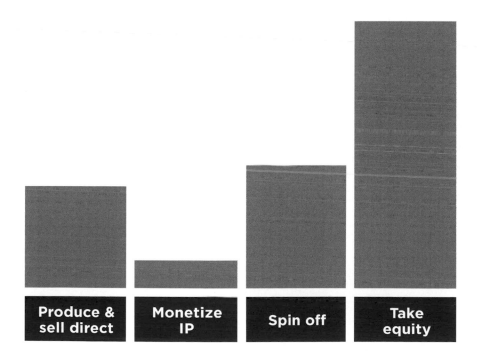

Produce & sell direct | Monetize IP | Spin off | Take equity

An inspired spin-off business: Frank, cofounded by designer Christian Helms and Geoff Peveto.

company could go bankrupt or the shares could become diluted after future rounds of investment. If you choose to go down this path, consult with an accountant. You need to know how any tax liabilities would impact your business if you decide to sell your equity stake or if your share grows in value year over year.

9. SELLING A LINE OF BUSINESS, OR THE ENTIRE BUSINESS

Designers can earn revenues by selling a line of business for their firm or by selling their entire share in their design business.

When first starting a design business, design partners may not want to discuss the fact that there will be an eventual point in time—whether it's years away or decades—that they will need to exit. Be as honest as possible with your business partners regarding your long-term plans before you enter any venture. By setting clear expectations regarding what each person wants from the business from a personal and a monetary perspective, the partners can openly discuss and adjust their goals as business conditions change.

SO YOU WANT TO CREATE A SOFTWARE START-UP?

In the past decade, there has been an explosion of both small boutique studios and large-scale design businesses that have found ways to earn revenue outside of billing for professional services and associated revenue streams. In some cases, they do it to diversify their revenue sources and protect their business in case of drought. In others, designers and studios have sought to become their own clients, producing products and services and selling them directly to customers.

If you're considering creating a new revenue stream for your design business from software, remember: It takes more than a compelling idea to create a profitable business. You need to balance the business model of your software (how it makes money over time) with your technology choices (how it will be constructed and maintained over time). If you solely focus on creating a great experience for your users, you may be able to ship your product, but it's unlikely you'll be able to sustain it.

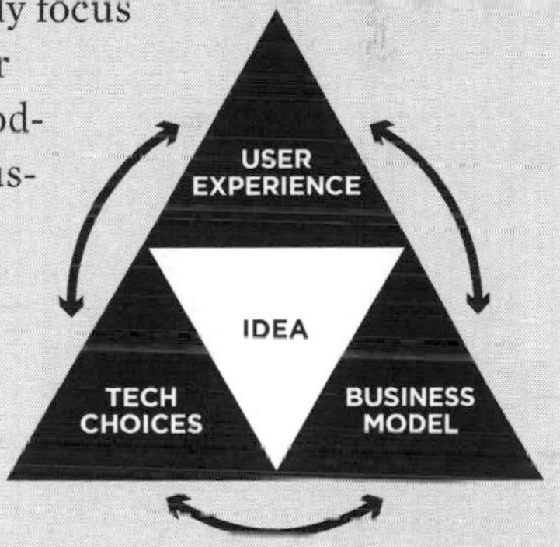

For more on this, go to imprint. printmag.com/web-design/ designbiz-the-tipsy-triangle- of-software-startupdom/

USER EXPERIENCE

IDEA

TECH CHOICES

BUSINESS MODEL

FOR YOU, THIS WILL COST:

$1/hr $1k/hr

Hourly Rates

How much should you bill for your work? More than you believe your client can afford? A price set according to the value you provide for your client?

In order to answer these questions, you should make sure your hourly rate accurately reflects your studio expenses and profit margin. This is a crucial part of ensuring studio stability and profitability.

Sharpen your No. 2 pencil and get ready to generate your baseline hourly rate.

Hourly rate generation

Over the following pages, you'll find what you need to fill in the blanks for the following equation:

Total Labor Cost:	$ _____	+
Total Overhead:	$ _____	+
Total Studio Debt:	$ _____	+
Total Taxes:	$ _____	=
Total Cost:	$ _____	x
Profit Margin:	_____ %	=
Total Profit:	$ _____	
Total Cost + Profit:	$ _____	÷
Hours Per Year:	_____	=
Base Hourly Rate: (Per Employee)	$ _____	

Total labor cost

Paying your employees is never an optional expense. Even if times are hard, payroll is like clockwork. It happens at the same time, every time. This includes your own paycheck!

Total Labor Cost: $ _____

Total overhead

These are the bare essentials you need to run any service business.

SUPPORTING YOUR EMPLOYEES

Health insurance: $ _____

Dental insurance $ _____

Retirement (401k) $ _____

PROTECTING YOUR BUSINESS OPERATIONS

Payroll service $ _____

Property insurance $ _____

Workers' comp $ _____

RUNNING YOUR PHYSICAL OFFICE SPACE

Rent $ _____

Utilities $ _____

Office furniture $ _____

Computers $ _____

Software $ _____

Peripherals $ _____

Mobile phone $ _____

Phone $ _____

Internet $ _____

Fax $ _____

Office supplies $ _____

Postage $ _____

MANAGING YOUR FINANCES

Accounting fees $ _____

Bookkeeping $ _____

Lawyer $ _____

PAYING YOUR TAXES

Local taxes $ _____

State taxes $ _____

Federal taxes $ _____

TRAVELING TO AND FROM CLIENT MEETINGS

Transit & parking $ _____

Car loan $ _____

Car insurance $ _____

Gas $ _____

Upkeep $ _____

KEEPING EVERYONE INSPIRED

Office snacks $ _____

Subscriptions $ _____

Training/conferences $ _____

Office parties $ _____

PROMOTING YOUR STUDIO AND SERVICES

Association dues $ _____

Advertising costs $ _____

Marketing expenses $ _____

Fees for awards $ _____

PURSUING SALES OPPORTUNITIES

Travel $ _____

Meals with prospects $ _____

Networking events $ _____

Total Overhead: $ _____

Total studio debt

Most design businesses carry some measure of debt in loans, revolving lines of credit and credit cards. Paying down your debt is a critical part of your hourly rate. Otherwise your business will be suffocated by never-ending interest payments.

You should have at least three to six months of overhead and salary costs in the bank before opening a design business. If you're just out of school, balance your debt obligations against what the market can bear for your design services, per your level of experience.

Total Studio Debt: $ _____

Taxes on earnings and salaries

A design business is taxed in multiple ways: on the earnings of the business on a local, state and federal level, and then per individual employee, according to their salaries. For the purposes of calculating an hourly rate, write your estimate of your total taxes on the earnings of your business, but be aware you will also have to factor in payroll taxes.

Total Taxes: $ _____

The profit margin you're seeking year over year

Profit should always be included in your hourly rate. Otherwise you would have to bill above and beyond forty hours a week to meet your margin.

    Your profit margin is calculated against the sum of all the expenses listed so far: Labor costs, fixed overhead, debt and your taxes. Here's an example from David Conrad, targeting 20 percent profit across three employees:

Total Labor Cost:	$ 150,000 ($50,000/year for three people)	+
Total Overhead:	$ 270,000	+
Total Studio Debt:	$ 0 (Wow, you're lucky!)	+
Total Taxes:	$ 23,700 (Minus 15.8% of $150,000 salary)	=
Total Cost:	$ 443,700 per year to employ three people	x
Profit Margin:	20 %	=
Total Profit:	$ 88,740	
Total Cost + Profit:	$ 532,440	

Moving from total costs to your hourly rate

How do you get from costs and profits to generating your base hourly rate? Calculate how many hours you'll be utilizing your employees, based on their role in your business. Then determine what benefits they'll receive for their personal time off. Start plugging in numbers on the following worksheet. There's a completed example on the next page, as well.

Weeks per year:	52 weeks	-
Weeks of sick leave:		-
Weeks of holiday:		=
Weeks per year:		x
Hours a week:	40 hours	=
Hours/year:		x
Utilization rate:		=
Hours Per Year:		

GENERATING UTILIZATION RATES

The industry average is 75 to 80 percent per individual contributor creating the work. The amount of billable time decreases the further the person is up in the management hierarchy, and not all of your employees at your business will be fully billable to client work. Your overhead will need to accommodate activities such as bookkeeping and marketing, which cannot be charged back to clients. David Conrad generated the following utilization rates for his company's staff:

80% Creative direction
80% Design
80% Production
80% Project Management
30% Marketing
10% Administration
65% Overall blended rate

With this information, we can determine the number of hours that can be billed to clients over a calendar year:

Weeks per year:	52 weeks	-
Weeks of sick leave:	2 weeks	-
Weeks of holiday:	3 weeks	=
Weeks per year:	45 weeks	x
Hours a week:	40 hours	=
Hours/year:	1,800 hours	x
Utilization rate:	65% rate	=
Hours Per Year:	1,170 hours you can charge your clients	

Your hourly rate is only a starting point for generating quality estimates

At this point, you should have the numbers you need to calculate your base hourly rate. But an accurate hourly rate is not a silver bullet for ensuring profitability. If you don't estimate your time properly as part of your client proposals and then run your projects effectively against those estimates, an hourly rate will do little to keep you in business.

LOW UTILIZATION RATES CAN LEAD TO LOW STAFF MORALE
You may be tempted to adjust utilization rates downwards to create more "thinking time" outside of projects for your employees. However, Ted Leonhardt advises:

> Creative shops are happiest when there is slightly more work than what the numbers say you should take. You can calculate how many hours to expect from a billable employee—thirty-five hours a week times fifty weeks—to determine your revenue target and workload. Then focus your sales effort on achieving five to ten percent more sales than that. Creative people like to be busy. The worst thing for a studio is to not have enough to do. It's demoralizing. It can also destroy your budgets, because people expand their project workload to fit their free time. Happiness comes from being busy but not overwhelmed—a delicate balance.

Insurance

When running a business, you need to support your staff and protect your company from situations that you can't predict: Disasters, lawsuits, on-the-job injuries and potential interruptions in how you deliver your products and services. To ensure this protection, you need to carry insurance and maintain an up-to-date disaster plan.

You should research your insurance needs intensively before purchasing policies for your business. You will need to consider purchasing insurance from the following categories:

- **Automobile insurance:** A commercial policy that protects your vehicle when you and your staff use it for work
- **Business interruption:** Coverage in case your design business is unable to provide its services to your clients (overlaps with casualty and property insurance)
- **Casualty and property insurance:** Covering your business locations and what they contain from a specified range of risks (earthquake, fire, flood, tornado or tsunami)
- **Health insurance:** Never run a business without offering this
- **Liability insurance:** Protects you from lawsuits in cases of possible negligence
- **Life and disability insurance:** Critical for you and your employees, especially if you or one of your business partners dies
- **Workers' compensation:** Protection for your workers from injuries they might sustain on the job

In addition to insurance, a business owner needs to maintain a disaster plan. The plan helps you and your staffers know how to respond in the case of an emergency that may cripple a business location, destroy critical infrastructure or potentially harm employees. If don't have a disaster plan, create one. That way, if someone steals your computer, the pipes burst in your server room or an earthquake destroys your studio, you will have instructions regarding what to do.

Be sure everyone in your company is aware of the plan and understands what they should do in case of emergency. Doing so will protect the lives of your staff and the future of your business.

Sustainability

Much of this book has focused on ensuring that your business is sustainable—that it will endure over time. But it is critical to also think about the social and ecological impacts of your business, and how those impacts will be felt by society.

This isn't just about using 100 percent postconsumer waste recycled paper, soy inks and wind power to print your client's business cards or using solar power to power the server for your client's web application. Factoring sustainability into your work product is just one layer you'll need to consider in running a world-changing business.

How do I hold my business accountable to the world at large?

The extent to which you consider sustainability a part of how you run your design business resides on three basic levels: within the work that you create for your clients, within the clients you choose to work with and within your collective efforts to contribute to people and the planet.

Many businesses now cleave to "triple bottom line" (TBL) accounting practices, which require managers and leaders to consider the health of their business not as a personal profit-generating scene, but as an organism that lives within an ecosystem full of interdependencies. Read through the following and consider how these factors might apply to how you run your business.

PEOPLE (HUMAN CAPITAL)

TBL businesses carefully consider what labor is required for work, by whom, and where—and whether those laborers are treated fairly within an equitable work environment and their local community. A TBL business would go beyond selecting vendors that match a series of baseline standards (such as avoiding use of child labor or limiting overtime practices) and devise ways to materially give back to their communities in a manner that could support social and educational services. Tracking compliance and efficacy in this area, especially when working with vendors and partners overseas, may require working with third-party independent auditors.

PLANET (NATURAL CAPITAL)

In this area, the ecologic footprint of any products or services is considered, with the ideal outcome that any products or services have been produced with a "cradle to grave" lifecycle in mind. This means that, wherever possible, the business is considering how to reduce, reuse or recycle what is tangibly produced—and eliminate dangerous chemicals and toxins, as well as wasteful materials as by-products of any form of manufacture. Such a mind-set can also be applied to energy use from renewable sources.

PROFIT (ECONOMIC BENEFIT FOR ALL)

Without some form of ongoing revenue in excess of expenses, most businesses fail to thrive—even nonprofits! But take a moment to consider how the people around you profit as well. What fiscal benefits do your clients, their customers, your customers, partners and suppliers, and other businesses and organizations receive as a result of how you run your business? Are they supporting you, while you may not be supporting them? Is there mutual benefit that could be provided back to the world?

I want my business to be more sustainable ... Where do I start?

If you're about to start a design business, consider what decisions you can make early on that support how you want to contribute to people, the planet and profit. Make those decisions visible to everyone in your business, as well as your clients, so all parties involved can be held accountable.

In order to understand how to do this, I spoke with Corbet Curfman, creative director and principal at Riverbed, a graphic design firm that specializes in brand strategy and sustainable design practices.

HOW DID YOU MAKE YOUR BUSINESS MORE SUSTAINABLE?

When I first started, I created policies to describe how I wanted to go about conducting my business in a sustainable way (purchasing program, general operations, that sort of thing). The easiest part for me was understanding who I wanted to work for and the work I wanted to do for them: I wanted to help good companies be successful at doing good work. That was the entire reason for the existence of my company in the first place.

I turn down work that doesn't meet my company's standards. I need to have a good understanding of how the work I do potentially will impact others. The B Corp certification has a good model for this, and it closely matches the kind of organization I want to have.

The harder thing to tackle was my company's environmental impact. I knew most of the right things to do and was doing most of them, but I did not know how to set up metrics to track them. I had a professional work with me to create an Environmental Management System (EMS). This centered on greenhouse gases and my company's carbon footprint.

The EMS covers several aspects. Aspect 1: Direct use for the company, Aspect 2: Purchase of the embodied use for the company, and Aspect 3: Downstream effects by our projects for a client. This is broken down into three main components: transportation, energy and materials.

I'm still working on ways of tightening my system and improving it. That is the whole point, after all. No company has all the answers and does all of this perfectly. We are all constantly working on it. That is why you set up metrics, so you can understand how you're progressing and keep working toward your goals.

WHAT WERE SOME WAYS YOU TIGHTENED YOUR SYSTEM?

The materials are the easiest things to tackle. It is a matter of reduction, reuse and recycling. I track my exact expenses, so I can see how much I'm buying or not buying. I set up guidelines for things I do buy in my purchasing program: avoiding toxins, buying free trade and carbon free. When I'm stumped by a new product, I refer to the handy iPhone app Good Guide.

We are lucky in Washington state that most of our energy is produced through hydroelectric power, but it still is important to reduce as much as you can. This has a twofold benefit. The more you reduce your energy and help the planet, the less you are spending on it. I can track this right on my energy bill each month. I can also decide to pay a certain fee to offset my carbon. This might seem a little like greenwashing, and to some degree it

CHOOSE WHERE YOU DRAW THE LINE, AND STICK TO IT
"Stop designing for the symptom," says Designers Accord founder Valerie Casey. "A lot of design work focuses on making the problem easier to stomach, rather than tackling its problematic source." Valerie recommends experiencing your business's own by-products. As an example, she suggests carrying around all your noncompostable trash collected in one week. Read more about this at www.fastcompany.com/1595167/designers-accord-seven-principles-for-interactive-action/

is, but this money goes directly to building renewable energy sources. The more people who participate in the program, the more options we will have. Then there's a better chance for building greater amounts of renewable energy in the future.

The crux is transportation. My car is my biggest habit to conquer. I track my miles in the car and track my time spent traveling in all methods: automobile, public transportation, biking and walking. After working hard at it, three years after my business started, I find the majority of my travel is through public transportation. I'm creating a new habit. My traveling time has increased significantly, but I think it's actually helped my business. The extra time has become dedicated to thinking, reading or researching.

So far, all of this refers back to my own company's environmental and social impact. These are all of the things that I have the most control over, but in the grand scheme of things, they make less of a dent.

WHY IS THAT?

I think that a designer's best chance at making a difference is in his selection of the clients he works for.

In order to look at the influence I can have with my clients, I created a report card. It tracks most of the things I do for a client project I'm working on from a resources perspective. The report covers:

The goals for the project: Purpose, audience, restrictions, life span, requirements and social impact or benefit

Operations: Travel, resources and time

Life cycle: Media, materials, sourcing, end use, size, awareness and innovation

Specifications: Printing, paper, ink, coatings and bindery

Each of these sections has a scoring system. This way, I can tell how it relates to other projects that are similar. In some ways, the scoring system becomes less important than process itself. The report card forces me to consider these details for every project and to look at ways of improvement and innovation. It also creates an opportunity to talk to my clients about ways to improve the thinking behind the project.

The more I can relate to my clients what factors are involved, the better they can understand the choices to make. This is an ongoing tool to bring awareness and education to my clients and to keep myself on track.

Legal

What should a designer know about legal issues?

While it may seem like we are defying the laws of nature when brainstorming compelling design solutions, when it comes to running a design business, we do have to consider the legal implications of our actions. What follows is a list from Steve Baty, a principal at Meld Studios in Sydney, Australia, of the things a studio owner should consider from a legal perspective.

SUPPLIER AGREEMENTS WITH YOUR CLIENTS AND VENDORS

Anytime a client signs a contract with your firm, you are legally obligated to follow it to the letter. If you need to change the terms of the contract, you must document those changes and seek their approval with a change order. The same rules apply for how your vendors work with you. *(See "Contracts" and "Change Orders.")*

EMPLOYMENT AGREEMENTS

When you hire a new employee, they should agree to a set of rules and conditions that govern their employment and provide you with the appropriate rights to terminate their position based on nonperformance. Your agreement should be reviewed by a lawyer to ensure you are following all applicable local, state and federal laws. Anytime you hire a freelancer, they will need to sign a similar agreement. In the United States, certain states allow employment "at will," meaning that it's pretty painless to terminate an employee. But be aware that laws in some places, especially overseas, require extraordinary measures to fire an employee for nonperformance, so extra care in the hiring process must be taken to ensure that employee will be a good fit.

———

"It's worth having the same lawyer review your client agreements, insurance policies and your employment/contractor agreements to ensure they're all aligned," Steve Baty says. "You don't want to agree to a clause with a client that effectively voids your insurance or isn't being met by your own staff."

———

INSURANCE

Businesses are required by law to carry certain types of insurance. *(See "Insurance.")*

COPYRIGHT AND INTELLECTUAL PROPERTY RIGHTS

Clients will often want to negotiate what rights they—and the design studio—hold over work created during a project. Design studios should avoid work-for-hire agreements, which force a designer to assign her authorship of a copyright to the client. Instead a designer should license the appropriate rights to use the work to the client when payment is made in full.

"There are a few other points I would note here," says Steve Baty. "Be clear about the use of preexisting copyright, intellectual property (IP) and materials you bring to the table, and your ability to continue using them. Try to avoid agreements that would allow your copyright to transfer into the hands of a competing design studio for their own use. Finally, it is usually the designer's responsibility to ensure that her work does not infringe on the copyright of another party—whether or not it's explicitly stated in any contract."

PAYMENT SCHEDULES

Any payment schedule outlined in a signed client contract is a legal obligation. If they don't keep to that payment schedule, there are legal ramifications that should be included in the contract, such as an interest charge on the amount due or stopping work on other projects for that client. *(See "Accounting.")*

EXCLUSIVITY AND NON-COMPETE AGREEMENTS

Clients often want you to sign noncompete agreements. You should have a lawyer on call to help negotiate the thickets of legalese that may accompany a client-provided agreement. Additionally, a studio principal may request that their employees sign an exclusivity or noncompete agreement to make sure they don't poach clients when moving to a new employer.

TAXES

You're legally obligated to track and pay local, state and federal taxes. *(See "Accounting.")*

WHAT SHOULD I LOOK FOR IN A LAWYER FOR MY STUDIO?

I asked Steve Baty for details on how his studio handles their legal counsel. This is what their studio does.

Does Meld have a lawyer on call?

We have a lawyer on call to help us draft agreements and review the longer or more problematic agreements we receive from others.

How frequently do you ask for his help?

We find we don't need to call on our lawyer all that frequently, maybe one or twice a quarter. We're more likely to need help when we're beginning an engagement with a new client or in response to changes in government legislation. I've had enough experience with contracts over the last six or eight years that I can catch most of the unbalanced clauses, but it's still good to have backup. It helps to have a very clear understanding of what you need in areas such as indemnity, warranties, copyright, intellectual property and termination. It's worth talking these through with a lawyer before having anything drafted and certainly before signing any agreements.

What should a design studio owner look for in a legal resource?

I worked with a law firm a few years ago, as a director at another studio. The firm was very knowledgeable, but overly aggressive. Contract negotiations would drag out, delay the start of engagements and place the client relationship—which had been excited and positive with the winning of the contract—onto very sour footing.

When choosing a lawyer for Meld Studios I looked for someone who was balanced, pragmatic and not 'out to win.' Someone with general knowledge of commercial law, as well as access to expertise (through colleagues) on industrial relations and intellectual property law.

Dear John,

The new project about   is going famously.

Do you think the   should still be confidential?

Let me know before we tell anyone about the   police.

Thanks, David

Confidentiality

Client confidentiality and intellectual property rights must be respected. Even if you haven't inked a formal agreement with a client, be very cautious about the information you disclose, even over coffee with a close friend. There's nothing worse than watching years of effort evaporate in a single post on Gizmodo.

I saw what happened when a fellow designer let slip a seemingly inconsequential detail. His whole world came crashing down.

Roger worked at a printing firm, where he created packaging for software products. As a course of creating the packaging, he was working with products that had not been announced to the public yet. The press releases for these new products would be accompanied by the luscious graphics he created.

He was very excited about one particular design. While playing video games with a friend, Roger mentioned the name of the software product and when it would be released. He also said that it was confidential information and shouldn't be shared until it was publicly announced.

In such situations, we often feel like there is a strong social contract for friends and family members to keep within the "cone of silence." Roger's friend, however, betrayed his confidence and wrote about their conversation on his public blog. This quickly snowballed into worldwide knowledge of the release, including posts on leading technology sites. The client's lawyers descended like vultures. The situation constituted a violation of his nondisclosure agreement (NDA) and confidentiality agreement, due to that single mention of his work to a single person. The client felt that the leak had cost them their competitive advantage.

And Roger? It cost him his job.

You could argue that such leaks really aren't that damaging. Press releases can be fired off in a matter of hours and advertising campaigns spun to dispel market perceptions within a week, but to change course on

———

In today's hyperconnected internet culture, where unprotected computers and servers are regularly hacked, confidentiality is critical.

———

a multiyear project is often impossible without taking a huge fiscal loss. When hundreds of thousands of people subscribe to TechCrunch feeds and a single tweet can cause Oprah to respond, you want to be sure that what you say in the market puts your best foot forward, not into your mouth.

Stick to the following rules when considering what can be shared outside of your immediate work team.

How do I know what information I can share?

Different types of disclosure can be written into your contracts with your clients. Review your confidentiality agreements with your clients and agree to clear rules about who may have access to:

- Names of companies you've worked with in the past
- Names of companies you are working with now
- Names of companies you are discussing working with in the future, as part of your new business process
- The names of people working at your business (aka "recruiter bait")
- The types of projects you are fulfilling and in which media
- Discrete design examples, from raw process work to fully executed designs

Be crystal clear about what those rules are, and don't diverge from them. They may create a host of oblique, uncomfortable conversations at dinner parties, but you'll be secure in protecting your client's interests. I make up strange code names to refer to projects when I talk to my wife about work. It makes the confidentiality issue slightly more entertaining, at least for her, and it prevents me from slipping up when we're out.

Joanne works at a company where employees can disclose what clients they work with and what kinds of projects they are working on, but they are not allowed to share any work in progress—concepts, detailed designs, prototypes—until the projects go live. Since many of their projects run two

to three years, this allows them to openly discuss what they're working on with prospective new clients.

Contrast this with another designer I know, Laurie. She can't tell anyone outside her firm about her clients, her project work, the types of work they create and so forth. None of her work can be displayed in her portfolio, if she were to interview for a new job, unless the client has given her employer explicit approval.

Remember: Even if you didn't sign an NDA/confidentiality agreement, be careful about what you do share. If a client asks you to keep something they tell you in strict confidence, treat it like confidential information until they say otherwise. Be a businessperson of your word.

And prepare for your boundaries to be tested. People from outside your company and/or client organization might be aware of the project you're working on. At one point in my career, I was stunned when a friend who worked for one of my clients revealed over coffee several details about my own project for them. She was in a completely different department than the one working with my firm, and she had no idea that I was involved with the project. And yet, she knew things that had been discussed in boardrooms where I knew that very clear rules regarding confidentiality had been established. In that situation—and I'm sad to say that it's happened a number of times since then—I followed the confidentiality rules established with my client, friend or not. No cup of coffee is worth it.

How should my contractors and vendors comply with my confidentiality rules?

When working with vendors or subcontractors that have to handle confidential information, make sure they're bound by the same agreements you are. Stories abound of printed material, fresh off a printing press and sitting in pallets for shipment, then photographed with a camera phone and posted to the internet. Such behavior should not be tolerated. The same

GH

rules apply for an interactive project in beta. Keep your sites or applications password protected until the client approves the project to go live.

The same rules apply for any freelance or contract talent that may help you on a client project, even after they've moved on to another company. No posting of the work on Cargo Collective. No Tumblr posts. No sharing of the work of any kind.

Can I vent about my ongoing project in public or on my social networks?

When out with co-workers decompressing after a long day, don't mention client names or characteristics. After a few cold ones, it may not seem like a big deal, but you never know who's sitting in the booth behind you.

The same rules apply for anything that you say or do on the internet, especially social media. It doesn't matter if your Twitter feed is locked and your privacy settings for Facebook are at DEFCON 1. Inevitably your client will see what you say and do—even if there's no way you think they can access it. Remember Roger! Information can be copied and reposted in a matter of seconds. If it's tantalizing, it will be shared.

Even if I have no confidentiality agreement, do I need to ask clients before promoting a project?

Ask for permission to promote projects postlaunch. This is a good business practice that eliminates embarrassing conversations where a client asks you to pull a project from your website. Even better, work these details into your contracts so there are no surprises.

What should I do to keep material on my computer safe?

Compartmentalize your work on your computer. Don't risk exposing critical information about your clients and your business. Don't leave a client's

———

During the new business process, treat everything a client shares with you as confidential—even if you are only discussing a hypothetical project or negotiating a handshake agreement.

———

job up on your screen when you have to step away from your desk at work, and don't leave it on a computer desktop in public or in client meetings. Place client work in folders that do not appear on your desktop. Close your email before delivering client presentations from your machine.

Always lock down your mobile phone and/or tablet with a password if you're receiving client calls, texts or email on them. Set up your phone to "self-destruct" after a set number of failed password attempts, and make sure it has a remote wipe capability in case it's stolen. (This happens more than you think.)

How should I protect intellectual property that I pass back and forth with my client?

When working with highly confidential information, be very aware of what is passed via email and by what types of email accounts. Forwarding files via email can increase your risk of exposing confidential information to an outside party. Try not to use third-party email services for critical client information—instead use secure servers and encrypted file transfer protocol (FTP) services, which require users to log in with a user name and password that can be tracked. Most corporations will require you to use secure servers that are accessible whether you're utilizing an office network or you're accessing a virtual private network (VPN), which encrypts information transferred between your computer and the server if you're using Wi-Fi on the go. An email can be forwarded without any way to easily track it once it leaves your business, while every download from a server can be logged.

For any email or log-in, use strong passwords with numbers, special characters and caps/lowercase digits. If you're using password protection on documents, don't send them in the same emails. Instead communicate them separately to ensure that if an email account is hacked, the files can't be utilized. If you're posting your work on secure cloud services, be vigilant regarding whom has access to that shared information. Tidy up when projects are completed.

Delete files that you pass between computers from storage media. Don't leave around USB keys, off-board hard drives or memory cards from digital cameras that may contain sensitive material. Lock them away in a secure location. Some companies don't even allow portable storage devices.

Names and identifying characteristics have been altered to protect the confidentiality of the individuals and companies mentioned in this chapter.

DO NOT
DISTURB

Culture

Culture is everything people in a design business do that supports the process of making work happen. Culture can create joy for designers, while improvements in process can facilitate profit.

A studio's culture is not created solely by the business owner. For a design business, culture is generated from ongoing contributions and discoveries from both studio owners and employees. With this in mind, the following pages cover the building blocks of design studio culture—some of which the business owner can invest in, and others that staff can generate in order to create their ideal working environment. A healthy studio culture draws equally from both sides.

These building blocks are divided into two groups: hard building blocks and soft building blocks. Hard blocks are realized through a budget, meaning that you can allocate money and time for them as part of business overhead. The soft blocks can be created through the decisions employees make over the course of their daily work, life and play (with less material investment by the owners).

Both types of building blocks provide emotional and material stability to employees in the face of ongoing work challenges, and often clients, family and the general public perceive them as ingredients of the company's brand.

What are the "hard" building blocks of design studio culture?

TYPE OF WORK
Type of work is one of the largest cultural building blocks of any studio, as the majority of the time in any studio is spent immersed in the work.

The kinds of customers selected by the business owner, the design disciplines practiced by the staff and the way projects are delivered by the

------

Design studio culture is critical for employee happiness, for recruiting the right people to join your team and even for defining your brand. Don't discount its importance in the face of just getting the work done.

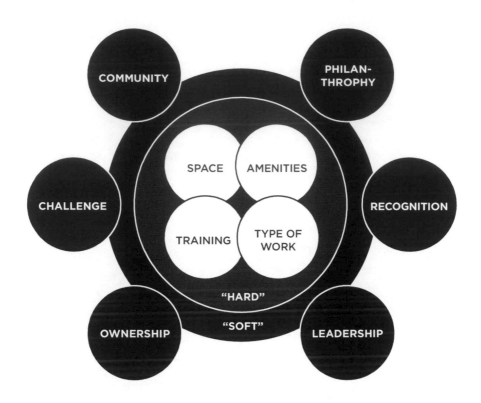

The Building Blocks of Design Studio Culture. Great studios are able to balance all of these factors as part of their day-to-day operations.

team all contribute to the excitement that motivates employees and owners when they start work every morning.

What follows are the questions you should be asking yourself before the phone rings and prospective clients ask you if you'd like to take on a project. Your answers, and how they may overlap (or not) with your staff's answers, will help you better understand where you can take your studio portfolio.

Customer types
- What industries do you want to work with? As an example: Health care or consumer electronics?
- What size of client do you prefer? Working with small companies or only the Fortune 100?

- Are you working with for-profit companies? Are you focusing on opportunities from the nonprofit sector? Or are you interested in working with start-up firms?
- How deeply are you entrenched in helping shape your client's business? Are you a strategic partner, or does the client see you more as an executional vendor?
- What types of brands are you seeking to work with? Small, hip local companies? Or older, established international firms?
- What ethical stance do you take on certain types of clients? For example, working with a religious organization may not be considered appropriate for some studios, while others would jump at the chance.

Discipline and practices of design

- What types of design does your studio want to practice? Print design? Interactive? Industrial? Environmental? Service?
- What tangible things do you want to generate? One of the benefits of designing products, environments and brand systems is that every project generates physical evidence of your efforts. When creating interactive products or online advertising, that may not be the case. You may blink and miss it.
- On what scale do you want to operate? For example: If your firm focuses on branding, do you want to create simple identity systems or the kind with hundreds of moving parts?
- What other disciplines would you like to partner with? For instance, an interior designer may work with an architecture firm to design a retail space.

Style of delivery

- What size projects do you seek? Do you prefer short-term projects, or would you enjoy working on an engagement that lasts years?
- Are there specific delivery processes you prefer over others? Some designers like to work in a controlled waterfall-style project process, while others like the close collaboration and constant change that emerges from an agile or scrum-based project process. *(See "Process.")*
- Where are the clients located? Are you comfortable working with clients in a completely virtual manner, or do you prefer face-to-face interaction?
- What level of security do you want as part of the client relationship? For example, do you desire a client retainer, which guarantees revenue at

the cost of freedom? Or do you generate revenues from flat fees, causing the staff to regularly propose and secure new work as part of their work life? This can influence the studio atmosphere.

SPACE

Once you know what kind of work you'd like to create, you'll need a space where you can make the magic happen. Studio owners must carefully consider the placement of their work space, the studio layout, the use of the studio environment and whether a formal space is even necessary to get the design work done.

Placement

You may be tempted to lease or purchase space in a far away, yet "up and coming" neighborhood that is great for your budget. However, getting to work shouldn't be hard work for your employees or your clients. Otherwise you are implicitly charging your employees time that they could be using to take care of their wants and needs. Well-placed studios can help support those needs, by being near local coffee shops and restaurants, gyms and yoga studios, public transit or the freeway.

Layout

The layout of a studio helps facilitate the flow of conversation and the style of work taking place. Studio layouts can be open, closed or some combination of open and closed elements.

Closed environments are manifested through cube farms, closed-door offices and conference rooms—areas where people can seal themselves off from others and focus on their work. My first years as a designer took place in studio environments where each designer had his own cubicle, and any ongoing conversations required us to peek our heads over walls. At one point, we joked about sawing holes in the cubicle walls so we could see each other's faces without having to stand up. (This was before video chat, mind you.) The layout of the space was a direct reflection of the kind of work that was taking place: production-heavy print deliverables.

On the other end of the spectrum, I have been working the past six

———

A great studio environment has its own soundtrack: the buzz of engaged conversation between designers at their desks, music pumping from shared speakers or the thrum of a lunchtime debate about what local coffeehouse has the best espresso.

———

Use of Environment. Design Commission's studio space doubles as an art gallery. The above photograph shows "The Modern Bird," an exhibit of one-of-a-kind birdhouses on display in 2007.

years in entirely open studios, with little to no privacy possible unless I exit the studio floor. The complexity of the work product—much of it rooted in designing and developing interactive products and services—requires constant collaboration. An open studio plan encourages ad hoc conversation and a cross-pollination of ideas that otherwise would never see the light of day. However, an open plan also requires pockets of privacy, whether via conference rooms or closed-door "war rooms" where the staff can work without distraction. Noise-canceling headphones also are handy. Some designers consider them the new "do not disturb" sign.

Use of environment

Decisions about the use of studio space can have a major impact on culture for both employees and visitors to your studio.

Design Commission leases an affordable studio space within the Tashiro Kaplan Artist Lofts. As a requirement in the lease, part of the design studio must be run as an art gallery. Every first Thursday of the month, the employees have to put on a show as part of a community art walk. Year after year, they have exhibited work from a range of international artists as well as created their own interactive art installations. This activity is also reflected online through a gallery website.

Other examples come from design studios that intentionally preserve a portion of their space for bringing in visiting artists and fellows, running a small retail store or subletting office space to like-minded businesses.

Co-location via virtual spaces

Some businesses choose to forgo a leased office space and work virtually, using by-the-meeting office spaces for face-to-face meetings with clients. In these situations, design teams work from home or from a local coffee shop, connecting regularly through email, IM, phone calls, video chat and online collaboration tools such as Basecamp, Campfire and WebEx.

With the recent increase in drop-in and shared spaces, you can have the benefits of a studio environment on demand—providing the needed infra-structure at a fraction of the cost of leasing a full-time space. Plus, you also get the benefit of having some office mates to chat with.

AMENITIES

Amenities help create an atmosphere that supports staff as they go about their business. These amenities can help satisfy creature comforts—such as the daily caffeine fix—or encourage the staff to stick around the office, whether to socialize or to stay at work a little longer. (Sometimes both.)

Free food and drink. Whether it's locally sourced fruits and vegetables as a daily late after-noon snack or ice cream sundaes with chocolate chip cookie dough on the side after a hard week, what does your studio provide to keep your staff well-fed and happy?

Amenities are factored into the studio overhead as part of the benefits provided to all employees. They may be as simple as free soda and juice in the fridge, or a studio iTunes account stocked with thousands of tunes. They may also include side benefits, such as subsidized gym memberships, a weekly on-site masseuse or free dining for those who choose to work past 7 P.M. Be aware that these perks can say a lot about your firm to potential employees. If you offer free cab rides home after 9 P.M., you might be broadcasting that working there requires staying late.

TRAINING

Training is a line item struck from studio budgets when cash flow is meager. But both on-site and off-site training opportunities help foster a culture of continual learning. Designers are refreshed and revitalized by information and inspiration from outside their daily purview at work. This can happen in person or virtually, whether by attending conferences and events or taking classes in new techniques or technologies.

Strapped for cash but want to satisfy your staff? Rotate the staffers who attend important events and require them to summarize and share what they learned with the studio.

What are the "soft" building blocks of design studio culture?

COMMUNITY

All work and no play can make a design team wear away. For this reason, design business owners should carve out dedicated time where studio staff can decompress and grow closer on a personal level.

Community-building activities and social outlets may be designed into the workday by studio management and staff, but ideally they should be realized and enlivened by the staff. Whether movie nights, Friday afternoon cheese tastings or ad-hoc happy hours, semiregular social outlets are often the highlight of a busy week. They become rituals ingrained in the company operations.

When I lived on the East Coast, Wednesday lunch meant Tex-Mex. It was our ritual for decompression. The studio principal would take the last few minutes of lunch to encourage staffers

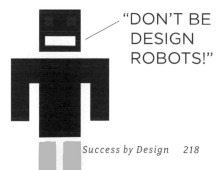

"DON'T BE DESIGN ROBOTS!"

to talk about what was happening in their work and to tap into the creativity of the other designers to help them solve any problems they might be having. (It also made the lunch billable!)

The larger the business, the more these connection opportunities will help define the culture and inspire your staff. "The details, rituals and the camaraderie are an important part of frog culture," says Doreen Lorenzo, president of frog, a global innovation firm. "For example, coffee time is at 4 P.M. every day at every office. It is a time to pause, maybe grab a bite to eat, talk to someone you haven't spoken to, even play a friendly but competitive game of foosball. I often thought that if we took coffee time away we would have the highest attrition frog has ever seen. These small details make it an important reason why people choose to work at frog."

PHILANTHROPY

While earning money is obviously important for running a stable business, many studios also donate staff time or money toward passion projects related to nonprofit, educational and philanthropic causes. Studios can provide staffers with charity days that they can use individually or in groups. Some studios donate their space or evening hours toward supporting local educational or fundraising events. The costs of these efforts are included in studio overhead and can influence the type of work that a studio receives.

RECOGNITION

Design business owners set the tone regarding how the performance of studio staff and their work should be recognized. The best recognition for your efforts should come from your client's customers. Studio staffers, however, may desire additional praise from their peers, the press or the blogosphere. Some studios take pains to enter competitions, though such efforts can be costly and steal time and attention away from other endeavors.

Also, recognition doesn't have to be solely about the work. The personal passions of studio staff can be shared with the world, as long as you continue to support your studio culture and properly represent your brand.

LEADERSHIP

How the studio owners lead a team, as well as how staff are properly trained and supported in taking leadership roles, can have major cultural implications for staff happiness. Not enough leadership, and your core staff may feel adrift. Too much active leadership, and your staff can feel like there's no space in the work (or the studio) for their vision. *(See "Leadership.")*

CHALLENGE

A high level of challenge in client projects can supercharge a studio environment. Smaller-scale, more tactical projects may exercise the staff's skills and craft sensibilities. Tackling larger-scale projects and design problems can provide the studio with new perspectives on persistent issues in the world and give your staff the chance to make a difference.

Additionally studio owners and staff can take on internal projects and initiatives to stay nimble and challenged when the project work isn't as stimulating as they would like. Regular critique of ongoing projects should also challenge designers and studio owners to realize their best work.

OWNERSHIP

Ownership is the one of the best indicators of healthy leadership. Ownership is when the staff feels like they have control over their time and their work product. It emerges when business leaders provide their designers with the necessary space to ideate and create appropriate design solutions. It can also arise when a designer is able to imprint her unique perspectives and expertise on any of the cultural building blocks, such as the design of her office space, securing the right type of work, gaining a leadership role, receiving recognition or even coordinating a guest speaker series for the office.

Some design businesses provide incentives for demonstrating ownership around growing studio accounts, such as profit sharing. Staff can also gain an ownership stake in the studio if they stay with the studio for a substantial period of time. However, such monetary carrots might not appeal to everyone, and they should never preclude your staff receiving regular opportunities that align with their evolving passions.

———

Don't assume that your studio's culture will grow organically over time. Leave spaces for your team to tailor the studio's physical space and workday to their own interests. Otherwise they won't be able to fully express themselves at work—and over time, they'll be punching the clock with frustration.

———

**FOLLOW THE
LEADER**

**CREATE MORE
LEADERS**

Leadership

What does it mean to lead a design business? Design leaders guide organizations in planning and fulfilling desired outcomes for their clients—and they grow their designers in the process.

The real definition of design leadership, however, is quite blunt: **Design leaders make awesome shit happen.**

Leaders at a design business may not be the ones in charge of the day-to-day client management, project management, accounting, bookkeeping and other activities that require deep focus on operational management, but they will always touch those facets of the business, ensuring they support the quality of the creative product.

Hartmut Esslinger, founder of frog, put it best: "When we have a 'concept' and people smile, we take the next step. When there are questions, we go back and try harder."

What traits does a design leader need to succeed?

A design leader is not the same as a design manager. While managing people may be the most important thing that any design leader does, it isn't the only thing that a leader needs to worry about.

There are a series of traits that define every design leader. How these traits manifest in the day-to-day work flow of a design organization govern the ways in which the organization develops over time. If design leaders aren't fully aware of these traits, they can wreak havoc in a smoothly functioning organization.

HAS AN UNQUANTIFIABLE "SECRET SAUCE," WITH VISION AS ITS BASE INGREDIENT

There are many flavors of design leader, but vision is the most important ingredient in how they work with others. Along with vision, a delicious mixture of a leader's innate character, education, talent, hobbies, passions and loves oozes from his every interaction with others. This secret sauce can often be powerful enough to help ensure the quality of the company's day-to-day creative work, as well as the overall strategic direction of their firm and its client businesses.

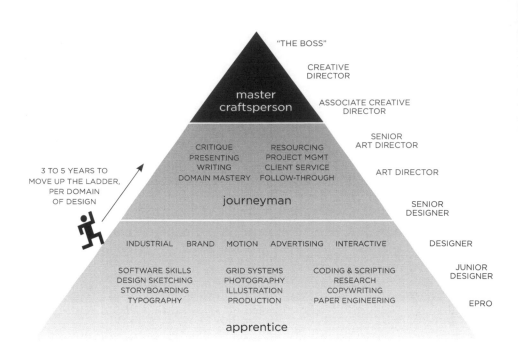

Being a design leader requires you to become a master craftsperson in your domain of practice. During this journey, you'll gain hard skills as an apprentice designer (such as use of software) and soft skills as a journeyman (such as presenting).

CONNECTS HER VISION TO AMAZING IDEAS FROM HER TEAM

Evidence of a design leader's secret sauce is most present in how she expresses and encourages ideas from her team. A design leader can, within a few seconds at a whiteboard or at a computer, powerfully articulate why these ideas are connected to a stated vision—no matter who suggested that vision. To quote Pelle Sjoenell: "No one works for a creative director. Everyone works for the idea. The idea hires us and we go to work."

ENJOYS WORKING WITH DESIGNERS AND CLIENTS—AS PEOPLE

A design leader must love working with his clients and staff as people first. In many ways, the people are the leader's work. Leaders must nurture relationships and stoke passions that often live outside the day-to-day work. If you don't help your colleagues realize their potential as people, you may just be a manager of projects.

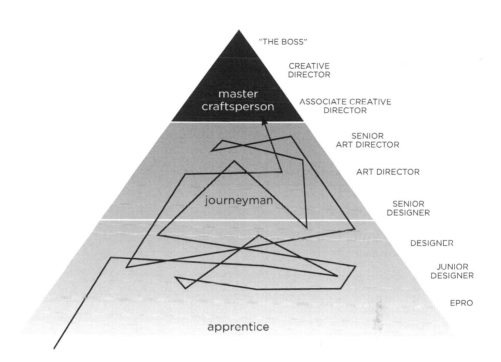

"THE BOSS"

CREATIVE
DIRECTOR

master
craftsperson

ASSOCIATE CREATIVE
DIRECTOR

SENIOR
ART DIRECTOR

ART DIRECTOR

journeyman

SENIOR
DESIGNER

DESIGNER

JUNIOR
DESIGNER

EPRO

apprentice

But during your career, you may gain mastery over several domains. A versatile leader doesn't necessarily follow a linear path. You may need to return to the apprenticeship position in order to acquire new skills. I did this when I moved from print design to interactive.

FUNCTIONS DAILY AS A BEHAVIORAL PSYCHOLOGIST

As you hire talent and grow a firm, you need the full range of people, from planner to visionary, to force the necessary creative friction that leads to great work without pissed-off employees. To encourage this sort of atmosphere, leaders need a strong "emotional quotient." This means you are able to perceive the emotions of yourself and others around you. This aids you both in understanding what motivates people's behavior and also in using that information to better support them. A true design leader helps everyone care about their work and feel like they have a reason for being there.

UNDERSTANDS HER OWN CREATIVE DISPOSITION AND THOSE OF HER TEAMMATES

Does a designer's creativity emerge from the right side of the brain, where lightning continually strikes to create an inspired design solution? Or does the creativity move methodically from the left side of the brain, where beautiful design solutions are honed until the designer achieves a polished sheen? Design leaders know how to adjust their language and approach to interact with these different dispositions, facilitating the appropriate level of discussion and creating the necessary space for success.

SEES FROM MILES TO MICRONS
A great design leader travels from the 50,000-foot view, with a full understanding of where projects and clients should be traveling, all the way into the tactical nuances, such as poorly kerned type or a missed detail in a design comp. Along the way, she distills what she sees into effective, actionable perspectives for her clients and teams.

ABLE TO FIGURE OUT WHY, OR TRIES
A strong design leader must be able to frame his creative vision in the context of sound business strategy—or collaborate with a client to reshape that strategy. This requires an understanding of how design activities (and vision) can delight customers and earn a profit in the process. *(See "Strategy.")*

COMMUNICATES UP, DOWN AND SIDEWAYS
A design leader does not need to be present for the creation of every design deliverable. However, she needs to communicate upwards, to her bosses and her clients. She also communicates sideways, to leaders and managers on her level and to their peers in project management, client service, development and other domains. And, of course, she needs to clearly communicate down to the people she manages.

FOSTERS PROJECT OWNERSHIP AMONG PEERS AND CLIENTS
If a design leader doesn't give his team enough space, the members of the team won't grow. A strong design leader will calculate ways in which his staff can own key pieces of projects without oversight. He'll also be cautious in how he delivers feedback, careful not to train a generation of order takers. To quote the businessman Tom Peters: "Leaders don't create followers, they create more leaders."

———

Reach outside of your organization for growth. Ask leaders you admire if they can mentor you or suggest someone who might be a good fit.

———

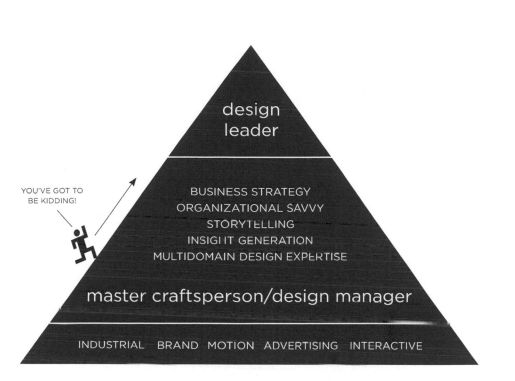

A design leader has another mountain to climb, beyond mastery of craft. Leaders must balance both creative vision and their fellow creatives' talent.

APPLIES STEADY, CONSTANT PRESSURE

A good design leader is invested in outcomes for everyone in her organization. She applies pressure at the right points in a project to propel the team forward. She is willing to tell everyone that the work isn't good enough (yet), and in worst-case scenarios, how to rethink the entire approach. A design leader should be honest regarding trade-offs, compromises and other elements of a given design direction that seem illogical or less than ideal. At the same time, she should use those moments of honesty to help identify what new opportunities may exist that could lead to excellent work. If a leader isn't direct about these issues early enough in a project, she will ruin her own credibility and risk mutiny.

IS BRAVE AND ALWAYS WILLING TO TAKE RISKS

In our lightning-fast culture, many great ideas can be realized in a matter of weeks. Taking risks is the only way to assure that your idea reaches the world first. As Andy Rutledge said: "Risk takers get first choice. All others can pick through the scraps."

However, risks should be taken with the proper information at hand. What sacrifices may be required of your team? What sacrifices might you have to make as well? And can you be an effective leader if you make them? All of this should be assessed before sprinting for the prize.

How can I learn to be a design leader?

There's no "one true path" to becoming a design leader, no clear checklist you can follow to become one in ninety days or less. But when I coach other designers on how to acquire stronger leadership skills, I ask them the following questions, which help them begin designing their journey:

What hard skills do you still need to learn?
Is your growth path hobbled because you haven't mastered a basic skill? Can you not sketch an idea on a whiteboard or build a competent slide deck for a client presentation because you don't know how to use PowerPoint? These are everyday skills that need to be in your arsenal, no matter what.

Who will help you gain those skills?
Do you work with people that have the skills that you need? Can they teach them to you? If you can't teach yourself, don't be afraid to reach out to those around you for help.

What domains of design do I need to add to my portfolio?
While it's important to have a deep competency in at least one domain of design—whether it be brand, interactive design, industrial design, or advertising—design leaders need a view across a wide range of domains. What domains are adjacent to what you enjoy and would help you have a more holistic understanding of design?

What "soft skills" do you need to acquire?
Soft skills are what differentiate designers from design leaders. Business writing, public speaking, the ability to read a room, compelling storytelling—these skills come from practice and active mentorship from other leaders.

What ingrained behaviors might stand in my way?
If you hate standing up in front of people and speaking, you can't go to Toastmasters and improve instantly. As people, our behaviors are very slow to change. It takes constant attention to adapt, but in time, we will be rewarded.

THE SIX C'S OF CREATIVE LEADERSHIP

Much like a kung fu disciple, who must climb the tall mountain peaks in order to find the secret dojo where he can learn a particularly rare fighting style, many design leaders must mature in their craft before they can realize their leadership skills under the right mentor. Some of these skills are not easily teachable. They are behaviors that a design leader must infuse into his daily work habits.

At the same time, a design leader must be aware of the same skills and behaviors she is trying to grow in the people that she manages. These behaviors, which serve as a concise summary of what we've discussed in this chapter, are as follows:

Leaders **conjure** compelling design work in their own right, when pressed into service.

Leaders **communicate** actively, with rational and emotional intelligence. As a result, co-workers and clients want to communicate with them.

Leaders **coax** stellar work out of their teams by creating space for creativity to flourish. This space is protected, so incursions by clients or organizational politics do no harm.

Leaders **compel** their teams to realize a vision, no matter who suggested or informed that vision. The best leaders know how to suss out internal motivations as encouragement, rather than external pressures.

Leaders **cajole** through critique, by asking the right open-ended questions at the correct time to encourage the flourishing of great ideas. The leader can also choose to hold her tongue, allowing other people to lead.

Leaders **cheer** their teams on, both within a design organization and publicly by promoting their work. Leaders should inspire through endless enthusiasm and engagement. To quote designer Brian LaRossa, "Earnest interest and excitement can be a contagious remedy for low morale."

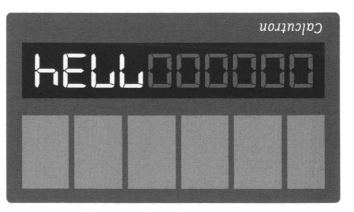

Accounting

When considering the most critical functions of a creative business, cash flow often falls by the wayside. With a looming deadline, our minds focus on what's right in front of us: The design work that needs to be completed. *Get it done, pronto!*

But if you want your daily efforts to support a design business, you'll have to do more than make the work sing. Satisfying the needs of your clients and their customers is a must. "If design isn't profitable, then it's art," says Henrik Fisker.

For this reason, the practices of accounting and bookkeeping, while not part of your day-to-day design duties, are critical business functions that you need to accommodate. Accounting activities should be scheduled like clockwork as part of your weekly, monthly, quarterly and yearly business activities. If you're responsible for your studio's finances, then you need to be aware of the assets, liabilities, cash flow and profitability of your business on an ongoing basis. Otherwise you may be putting the stability of your business at risk.

Do I really need to conduct the accounting for my business?

The owner of a design business doesn't have to do all of the bookkeeping work. But she must be aware of how her books are being maintained. The owner of the business is liable for what's listed on the balance sheet.

Every design business that I've worked at has had either an accountant on staff or one hired outside of the company to aid the owners in managing their books. But that doesn't mean those designers fully delegated all accounting activities and knowledge about their business cash flow to an outside party. To quote Nancy McClelland, an accountant in Chicago who specializes in helping out small and medium-size businesses:

> Starting off right means finding a good accountant to be part of the team. That person should be able to set up your company and your books in a way most appropriate for your industry and your plans for growth. And they can do more than just set things up; they can train you or your staff to handle the books in-house, if that's appropriate. They should check in every month at first, and eventually

every quarter to calculate your estimated tax payments and to assist with things like sales taxes, licenses, operating agreements and payroll.

Having someone as a go-to source for questions after everything is set up is essential. But there's no reason that most small businesses can't handle their own day-to-day bookkeeping and more, with proper setup and training.

In talking with many owners of design businesses, I found that Nancy's advice holds true. What follows emerged from a series of interviews and co-presentations with David Conrad, studio director of Design Commission, an interactive design studio in Seattle. David and his accountant gave me a guided tour of the activities and tools he uses to manage the high-level finances for his ten-person studio.

What weekly accounting activities should a design business conduct?

The owner of a design business should be reviewing the following financial information on a weekly basis and taking action where appropriate. This is likely to be facilitated through bookkeeping software such as QuickBooks, which can generate a majority of the reports and views described here.

INDIVIDUAL PROJECT REPORTS

An individual project report describes the budget for a project in both time and materials. By comparing the budget to actual expenses, you can see the "burn rate" on an ongoing project, i.e., a measure of how much work has been completed on a project per staff member, plotted against the timeline provided in the estimate.

"Burn down" is most frequently visualized in chart form, so the design team can see trends in time utilization at a glance. A burn down chart can help studio owners identify if a project's time budget is going to run out

———

The information provided here is for reference only and should not be substituted for the advice of a trained accounting professional.

———

before the project ends—a key indicator that the team is working too hard, the project scope and deliverables are not being controlled or the agreed-upon project estimate was not accurate. These charts can also help managers gauge which staffers are "burning hot," i.e., they are using overtime hours for their current tasks and need support.

Of course, all of this project reporting is for naught if staffers don't fill out their time sheets accurately. And be aware of the true margin that you're protecting beyond meeting hourly estimates. "I'm always careful to make sure that I'm taking our padding, or contingency amounts, in account here as well," says David Conrad. "If a project is 'on budget,' make sure you're conscious of whether that's the internal estimated effort, or if it's eating into your contingency."

AGING SUMMARY

You can't just send an invoice to your client and expect a paycheck back a few days later. There are specific actions you should take as a business owner to make sure you can pay your employees, keep the power on and cover the amount you paid out of pocket for that expensive client lunch.

Individual Project Reports. Some agencies use project management or time-tracking software to generate these reports. Others have internal systems they've devised, from low to high tech. The above screenshot is an example of a project report from the online time-tracking tool called Harvest.

You can track the ebb and flow of accounts paid and received through an aging summary. This is a simple tool in which you list which clients have outstanding accounts in monthly increments called "buckets."

An aging summary may seem like common sense, but many freelancers and studios neglect to manage incoming receivables at this level of detail and keep it "all in their head." If you've never used an aging summary, it's good to start using one immediately, and make sure it's in a place that you can refer to regularly. In this example, created by David Conrad, he's highlighted in red the key areas where a story has emerged from patterns in past-due payments:

Client Name	0–30 Days	31–60 Days	61–90 Days	Over 90 Days
MegaCorp	$100	$500	$1,000	
LittleCo, LLC	$50	$50		
Mom-n-Pop	$25	$25		$500
Total	**$175**	**$575**	**$1,000**	**$500**

Aging Summary

Are you allowing invoices to go unpaid past sixty days?

"The longer it takes a client to pay, the less likely you are to actually get paid," says Conrad. "Also, getting even a little bit of money out of a client can be helpful if you need to bring in a collection agency at a later point. A collection agency is more likely to collect if there has been past payment from that client."

———

"You have to be a little careful here because you need to schedule out those projected payments from clients based on either past experiences with payments from them or gut instinct about when you'll get paid," says David Conrad. "Just because one client is at ninety days and another is at thirty days, it doesn't mean that you'll receive the later payment first."

———

Additionally you have to be religious about sending your invoices on time. You should send your invoices no later than the Friday following the completion of a project. If the project is delayed, then invoice the client for the amount due per your contract after forty-five days.

Are you withholding credit if the client has a poor payment history?

How did you end up doing new work for MegaCorp or Mom-n-Pop when they both have an outstanding invoice that's almost three months past due? In such a situation, try to bring the client into a payment plan. Include as part of the terms and conditions in your contract that any past due invoices will freeze new work until all invoices are paid in full.

Are you providing a discount if the client pays early, within the first thirty days of receipt of invoice?

Cost cutting has become so ingrained at some companies, they may have policies that require early payment if they can receive a discount. This can work to your benefit if you set your rates appropriately and it helps limit the overall aging of client invoices on the books.

Are you keeping in contact even over small sums?

LittleCo, LLC may have only $100 on the books with you, but sending a client letter at the start of every new thirty-day period can be the prod that facilitates a faster payment for any outstanding invoice. These client letters or statements can be sent directly from software like QuickBooks.

Have you communicated to your client that nonpayment is unacceptable?

In the case of Mom-n-Pop, you're in a bad position because you've agreed to do work even after you haven't been paid for three months. You must notify your client in writing repeatedly (and politely) that payment is due, and what happens if it's not received. (More about this on the next page.)

Are you asking for payment up front?

Should you extend a client credit for small sums or ask them for payment in advance of getting started? "Always ask for something up front," says Conrad. "If nothing else, it will serve as an indication of that client's relationship with money and an indicator of things to come."

How you handle up-front payment is important, as you haven't really earned it until you've delivered the corresponding contracted services. Nancy McClelland suggests two ways of handling it:
negative accounts receivable or client deposits. She says: "It's not income until it's earned!"

WHAT SHOULD I DO IF A CLIENT DOESN'T PAY ME?

If a client doesn't pay you for services rendered, communicate before you litigate. You have options.

Be sure they've approved everything in writing

The proof is in your trail of records. You should ask for appropriate signatures on everything that could be considered legally binding: Your design contract, change orders and approvals for design deliverables that are directly associated with payment. Both my firm and the client countersign contracts and change orders. I'm old fashioned about requesting most approvals in writing.

If there are minor changes in scope or in your payment schedule that are discussed via email, ask your client to formally say, "I approve this change" via email before committing to the new scope or schedule. And speaking of email: Keep all emails between you and your client. You should document any installment payments received from your client. Along with notes taken during client conversations, these details are your protection if a client declines or withholds payment at any time. If you don't have these records, it's your word against theirs.

Be consistent in how you provide invoices to your clients

Clearly label an invoice overdue. If your client hasn't responded to your invoices, call him. Ask him when payment will arrive for your services. If he hedges, discuss some payment options he may consider. These may include:

- A longer-term payment plan (with interest)
- Taking out a loan to pay for your services (with interest)
- Payment via credit card, rather than cash (mindful of any processing fees that come with this route)

Be persistent in reaching the people responsible for payment

If a client isn't immediately responsive, being creative can help inspire a response. This may mean reaching out to accounts receivable or to your client's boss directly. Send a reminder fax, with a letter outlining where their business is in the payment process. If you're close by, see if you can schedule a face-to-face meeting on a range of topics—your payment among them.

Be able to negotiate fair compensation if they lack cash

If you reach your client and he simply can't compensate you monetarily for the services you've provided, are you willing to forgo cash payment for things of similar value? Will he consider a trade? Will he let you take equity in his company in return for what they owe?

Be clear about the consequences for nonpayment

If the above fails, or the client completely stops communicating with you, your next step is to hire a collection agent. An agent may be able to claim a fraction of your fees on your behalf. If she can't, your lawyer can craft a simple letter that outlines how the client is in breach of your contract. If you've gone this far down the path, however, it's possible your client is filing for bankruptcy protection. If you're lucky, you may receive pennies on the dollars owed to you, as designers are often one of the last creditors in line.

Be willing to mediate before you litigate

To protect yourself from having to take anyone to court, consider including a mediation clause in your contracts. If the amount owed to you is more than what would qualify for small claims court, this will save you from serious legal fees. But if you're asking for hundreds of thousands of dollars in fees, mediation or binding arbitration may not be as effective as dislodging the money owed to you through a discussion between your lawyer and theirs.

If you're lucky, such a situation will never come to pass.

Pennies on the dollar. This is a bankruptcy claim distribution check from Entellium, a client of David Conrad's design firm. Entellium filed for bankruptcy protection after completing a major project, but only paid a small portion of the design fees after the filing.

CASH FLOW PROJECTIONS

It's not enough to simply track the cash you are expecting from your clients. A cash flow projection will allow you to understand how much money you will have banked for your business to use over the coming months. Any cash flow projection should include at least the following information, listed on a week-by-week basis:

Total Income

- How much cash you have in the bank right now
- Your total accounts receivable, including what's been invoiced to your customers and is listed on your aging summary

Total Expenses

- Accounts payable, such as payroll and associated expenses, health insurance, retirement account contributions, payroll taxes, workers' compensation and other benefits and subsidies required by local, state and federal law
- Fixed overhead costs, which may include rent and utilities for your work space
- Debts payable, inclusive of any lines of credit or credit cards being utilized for business expenses
- Miscellaneous expenses that weren't budgeted for, but may be considered necessary, for running your business
- Your profit margin—make sure you always account for profit in your fees and expenses!

Subtracting your total expenses from your total income will tell you how much cash you will have in the bank on a weekly basis. Projecting this information across a few months will give you a sobering indication of your overall business health, and it will allow you to adjust your business tactics to pursue outstanding accounts or new business opportunities.

Be aware, though, that the method you choose for tracking your income and expenses can influence your projections.

If you choose to use the **cash** accounting method, you will not record any income in your books until you've received the money. You'll withhold from recording expenses until you've paid them.

If you decide on the **accrual** accounting method, you will record income when you provide services to your clients, not when you receive payment for those services. The same holds true for recording expenses— you record them upon receipt of the service or product, not when you have paid for them.

	Jan 1–2	Jan 3–9	Jan 10–16	Jan 17–23	Jan 24–30	Jan 31– Feb 6
INCOME						
Opening Cash	$45,000	$38,485	$35,410	$1,145	–$7,380	–$28,370
Accounts Receivable						
Total Accounts Receivable	$8,000	$12,000	$5,000	$6,500	$12,500	$10,500
Total Income	**$53,000**	**$50,485**	**$40,410**	**$7,645**	**$4,620**	**–$18,370**
EXPENSES						
Payroll						
Salary	$0	$0	$16,793	$0	$16,793	$0
Taxes/Labor Costs	$0	$0	$904	$0	$904	$0
IRA Contribution	$0	$0	$293	$0	$293	$0
Health Insurance	$2,300	$0	$0	$0	$0	$2,300
Dental Insurance	$450	$0	$0	$0	$0	$450
Employee Transportation	$1,300	$0	$0	$0	$0	$1,300
Total Payroll	$4,050	$0	$17,990	$0	$17,990	$4,050
Fixed Overhead						
Total Fixed Overhead	$5,165	$0	$4,275	$0	$0	$5,165
Debts Payable						
Line of Credit	$500	$0	$0	$0	$0	$500
Credit Card	$0	$0	$2,000	$0	$0	$0
Total Debts Payable	$500	$0	$2,000	$0	$0	$500
Miscellaneous Expenses	$0	$75	$0	$25	$0	$0
20% Profit	$4,800	$15,000	$15,000	$15,000	$15,000	$15,000
Total Expenses	**$14,515**	**$15,075**	**$39,265**	**$15,025**	**$32,990**	**$24,715**
Closing Cash	**$38,485**	**$35,410**	**$10,145**	**–$7,380**	**–$28,370**	**–$43,085**

Example Cash Flow Worksheet. Cash flow describes how money moves into and out of a design business. A studio owner needs to track cash flow on many levels, including as a measure of overall business health and how each client project is fulfilled, invoiced and paid on time. On paper, a design business can look like it is performing well, while in reality no actual cash is available due to late payments from clients, poorly managed capital expenditures coming close to foreclosure or the bartering of design services for nonmonetary goods and services—per the worksheet above.

	Date	Status	Amount	Description
Bid #1				
	02/01/2013	Accepted	$17,500	Design
Bid #2				
	02/16/2013	Pending	$4,373	Redesign
Bid #3				
	02/16/2013	Pending	$4,373	Web Application
Bid #4				
Phase 1	02/05/2013	Accepted	$4,500	Email Campaign
Phase 2	03/12/2013	Accepted	$8,100	Email Campaign
Phase 3	04/12/2013	Accepted	$1,950	Email Campaign
Total			**$14,550**	

Work-in-Progress Worksheet

Client Name	Projected Revenue
New project for MegaCorp	$2,000
Updates to last year's LittleCo project	$800
Total	**$2,800**

Opportunities Worksheet

You should ask your accountant/bookkeeper which method is most appropriate for your business, as each has advantages and disadvantages. (While you're at it, have her walk you through how to incorporate noncash expenses, such as depreciation of office equipment.)

WORK-IN-PROGRESS (WIP) WORKSHEET
Unlike an aging summary, which describes what has been invoiced, a work-in-progress worksheet includes work that your firm has contracted but not yet billed to your client.

As you begin to fulfill this work, its progress will be summarized on an individual project report. And as you invoice the project, any contribution to agency revenues will be projected as part of your cash flow. "This is helpful because it's a way to make sure you don't miss invoicing something," says David Conrad.

OPPORTUNITIES WORKSHEET

An opportunities worksheet is where a studio owner keeps track of future revenue that may be earned from new business efforts, including proposals currently being reviewed by existing clients and possible new clients.

Remember that anything you list on your opportunities worksheet is theoretical revenue! You won't close every opportunity presented to you. This is also called a "pipeline report," as studios must nurture a steady flow of potential opportunities to keep their business running.

"For Design Commission, I like for the value of opportunities to be somewhere around four to five months of operating income," says David Conrad. "Since half of those opportunities won't materialize, and some will likely shrink in billings by the time they are contracted, you want to make sure you are filling your pipeline with enough opportunities to support future expenses."

What monthly accounting activities should a design business conduct?

Every month, a studio owner must step back and take a longer-term view regarding her studio's performance against her financial goals. Some of the activities every design business owner must conduct follow.

REVIEW AND SEND CLIENT STATEMENTS

What happens if a client doesn't pay their invoice on time? They receive a client statement, which consists of the following:

- What invoices have been sent to the client
- When those invoices were sent to the client
- When the balance of the original invoice was due
- How late the payment is, in thirty-day increments
- The overall amount owed to you, as well as which previous invoices have been paid and when they were paid

Sending out client statements is important, as they provide your client with the necessary impetus to pay a past-due invoice. If you ever enter into

Dear MegaCorp,

For your records, below you will find a current account statement.

Account Balance	Invoice	Project	Due Date	Amount Due
31–60 Days Past Due 1/1/2013	Invoice 724	Website	1/31/2013	$100
61–90 Days Past Due 12/1/2012	Invoice 721	Branding	2/4/2013	$100
			Outstanding Balance	**$200**

Sample Client Statement

mediation, court or collections because of a client who won't pay you, the client statement is a critical document to prove that you gave them every opportunity to pay for your contracted and fulfilled services.

The processing and sending of client statements can be automated based on the bookkeeping software you use. Sometimes your direct client isn't the one paying the bill, so a client statement serves as a great reminder for them to speak with their accounts receivable department.

PROFIT AND LOSS STATEMENT

A profit and loss statement represents the finances of a business over a given period of time, most typically year to year. In the sample profit and loss statement shown here, many of the same expenses and income details from the weekly cash flow projection are shown. The critical difference is that instead of looking forward, a profit and loss statement provides a recap of how your business's finances have performed over time. It also goes into more granular depth about the types of revenue and income gathered over time. (Remember: This varies based on whether you've chosen cash or accrual accounting methods. Your software can help you keep track.)

The most important number for any studio owner is net income, which is the bottom line of this statement. The net income is divided among business partners/shareholders of the organization and will be taxed.

BALANCE SHEET

A balance sheet represents the overall value of a design business. There are two primary areas listed on a balance sheet: assets and liabilities/equity. The assets and liabilities/equity should always be equal. "One of the best

Profit and Loss, January–December 2012

	Total
INCOME	
Total Income (AGI)	$775,000.00
EXPENSES	
Direct Business Expenses	
Project Costs	$12,000.00
Hosting	$3,600.00
Total Direct Business Expenses	$15,600.00
Employee & Staff Expenses	
Total Insurance	$33,000
Payroll Service Fees	$900
Company 401k Match	$7051.20
Staff Meetings and Functions	$44,331.20
Total Payroll Taxes	$21,710.08
Total Salaries and Wages	$235,040.00
Total Employee and Staff Expenses	$342,042.48
General and Administrative Expenses	
Advertising and Marketing	$1,800.00
Business and Professional Development	$7,200.00
Dues and Memberships	$2,400.00
Business Liability Insurance	$600.00
Travel, Meals and Entertainment	$6,000.00
Postage and Delivery	$3,000.00
Total Professional Fees	$3,300.00
Rent	$24,000.00
Repairs and Maintenance	$4,200.00
Supplies and Equipment	$41,400.00
Taxes	$6,000.00
Utilities	$8,880.00
Total General and Administrative Expenses	$108,780.00
Total Expenses	$450,822.08
Net Income	**$324,177.92**

Profit and Loss Statement

Balance Sheet as of December 31, 2012

	Total
ASSETS	
Current Assets	
Bank Accounts	
Checking Accounts	$30,000
Saving Accounts	$15,000
Tax Savings	$5,000
Petty Cash	$525
Total Bank Accounts	$50,525
Accounts Receivable	
Total Accounts Receivable	$38,650
Fixed Assets	
Accumulated Depreciation	–$75,000
Computer Equipment	$65,000
Furniture	$8,000
Leasehold Improvements	$6,000
Software	$10,000
Total Fixed Assets	$14,000
Total Assets	**$103,175**
LIABILITIES AND EQUITY	
Liabilities	
Credit Cards	$2,000
Bank Premium Credit Line	$10,000
Total Liabilities	$12,000
Equity	
Capital Stock	$1,000
Retained Earnings	$128,535
Partner Distributions	–$387,898
Net Income	$349,538
Total Equity	$91,175
Total Liabilities and Equity	**$103,175**

Balance Sheet. In the above chart, the Total Liabilities must equal the Total Assets— that's the basis of what makes it a "balance" sheet.

things about accounting software is that it forces your balance sheet to balance," says Nancy McClelland. "Doing this manually is almost impossible."

Studio assets

Total assets represent the current strength of a business. The more money a company has on hand, the better off it should be.

The assets section of a balance sheet describes the total amount of cash that a design business has on hand as accounts receivable, as well as the depreciated value of any material or fixed assets the firm owns, such as computers, furniture, software and other items. (If you make and sell products as part of your design business, your inventory will be included here as well.)

Liabilities and equities

This portion of a balance sheet outlines liabilities, which consist of credit cards and credit lines that have been extended on behalf of a design business, and equity, which is measured in retained earnings and distributions to owners/shareholders.

Equities "represent the profitability of a business over its lifetime," says David Conrad. "You are looking for big, positive numbers." Distributions "represent the amount of cash the partners have drawn from the business. This does not include payroll figures, just the distributions taken." The methods of distribution change depending on whether you're running a sole proprietorship, a partnership, an S-corporation or other type of business.

LOOK AT YOUR BUDGET

Once a design business owner has had a chance to review the above statements and a balance sheet, she should review both her year-over-year and month-to-month financial picture, gauging whether the business has been meeting its goals. This will allow the studio owner and her staff to make minor or major adjustments in their current business activities.

———

It can help to summarize your goals: "Next year we want to grow the studio by X number of people, increase revenue by XX percent, and add X benefits ..."

———

What yearly accounting activities should a design business conduct?

The primary year-over-year activity every studio owner should conduct, without fail, is to set realistic goals. Goals can take a number of forms, all of which have some impact on your financial performance. Here are a few goals that may be part of your arsenal:

- An overall increase in profitability
- An overall increase in yearly revenue
- Change in overall composition of work (i.e., "client mix")
- Increasing client retention
- Improving staff retention
- Adding additional benefits
- Reconsidering utilization rates for the studio and individual employees
- Adding new staff or capabilities in order to reach the above goals

When should I pay my taxes?

As part of your accounting business responsibilities, you will have to pay taxes to the federal government, your state government and in many cases your local government. Your taxes will vary by where you live, how you choose to account for your income and a host of other factors. As a rough estimate, plan to put aside at least 20 to 30 percent of your revenue for tax payments.

Don't ever pay taxes late or leave calculating what you owe until the last minute. In the former situation, you risk penalties, and in the latter situation, you might not have the cash on hand to pay the taxes.

———

Keep six years of tax records on hand in case you are audited. Don't include the current year when you count to six.

———

Is this all I need to know about accounting?

That's probably more than you ever wanted to know about accounting—and it was only a quick peek into what you'll need to know if you want to run your own design business.

If this seems a bit over your head, go out there and find that professional who can take care of your accounting needs. Select the appropriate bookkeeping software and an accountant to support your business. You won't be sorry.

And if you already know everything there is to know about accounting, it never hurts to have a professional on call in case your finances don't add up.

LOGO-MATIC

$

← INSERT
TALENT
HERE

Hiring

If you're looking to hire people for your design business, these are words you should remember every time you interview a candidate:

OWNERSHIP
The number one reason people will come to work at your design business? They can lay claim to a piece of it. If you can't offer a prospective employee an area they can own, then you won't retain them over the long haul.

TITLE
Many people are motivated by title more than a huge salary increase. The value of that title, both in terms of potential experience to be gained and its role as resume fodder, must be weighed in the negotiation.

FORTUNE
Earning a good salary is important, but the value of a paycheck may be subordinate to ownership and title. The sweetest deal you can provide any designer is the ability to maximize potential earnings through increased ownership and title. "Would you rather be a war-tested senior designer earning $85,000 a year or a newly minted creative director starting at $80,000 a year?"

SKILL
Perusing candidates' design portfolios is one way to gauge their skill. Another is to carefully screen your candidates through in-depth conversations with their previous co-workers or managers. For certain disciplines of design, however, you may need to provide your job candidate with a chance to show how he thinks through and solves problems. One way to do this is asking the candidate to work through how he'd solve a design problem in the interview. "For me, it is the only way to hire, especially in Germany, where it is next to impossible to fire people," says Sebastian Scholz, leader of the Munich office of Ergosign, a usability agency.

GROWTH
Is there potential for growth in the role you are offering? Will mentorship or training be provided? Will the employee acquire skills on the job to further grow his talent? And will roles be available for him to grow into as a potential long-term reward?

DESIRE

At different points in their careers, designers will have unique motivations. A junior designer may just want to get her foot in the door, no matter what. A senior design leader might want to understand you and your business in great detail before negotiating whether she would be a good fit. But if you're sitting in an interview explaining to a candidate why he will love working at your company, you may be deluding yourself. The candidate should have the desire to work at your company and the ability to explain why.

PERSONALITY

Portfolio is an important consideration, but quality of execution won't matter if your work style and personality don't mesh with the talent you hire. You want to recruit people who don't think exactly like you, who are passionate about their work, who are equally passionate about preserving space for their personal life pursuits, whose skills exceed yours in crucial areas where you need support and whose personality type is compatible with those in your studio. "Though it may sound like we're hippies, in small agencies applicants have to be approved by all existing staff," says Sebastian Scholz. Not sure if someone is a good personality fit after a few interviews? Ask them to take a personality test. You won't be sorry.

———

Ego is bad for business. It can negatively influence your studio culture. If you detect a whiff of ego from a candidate, carefully measure if you should hire that person. Like perfume, ego can diffuse itself into your business and make everything stinky.

———

SHOULD YOU OFFER BENEFITS?

If you're a business owner, read this:

Don't complain about the ballooning costs of health care premiums, or how many billable hours you're sacrificing in order to provide sick leave. Find a way to manage these costs as part of your studio overhead. If you don't, you may fail to retain your best employees or attract new hires.

Whether you like it or not, it's your responsibility to provide your staff with benefits that will help keep them healthy and safe. You aren't the only one who needs to plan for retirement. If you avoid these responsibilities, you need to ask yourself: What kind of business are you trying to sustain in the long term? One without people?

If you are a hired gun, read this:

See above. Even if you are not provided benefits as part of your current employment contract, you should include the cost of health insurance premiums in your operating overhead. If you were ever to have a catastrophic health issue, you will need a net in place to protect yourself and your business.*

If you are an employee of a design business, read this:

Demand the best benefits to support you and your family's health and happiness: Health care, a health savings account, a flexible spending account, the appropriate amount of sick leave, a 401(k) retirement plan and so on. Bolster your argument by pointing out which benefits map to the type of culture the studio owners are trying to cultivate.

---

* If you live in a country where health care is provided to all citizens, this may not apply. Lucky you.

Freelance

I heard this from a friend who wanted to leave his full-time job as a graphic designer: "I want to work as a freelance designer, so I won't have to do any of this design business stuff."

Wrong! Being a freelance designer means that you are a design business consisting of one person—an agency of one. This has been confirmed by the designers I know who are successful in running their own studio practices, including Luke Mysse of CrossGrain Studio.

What follows are excerpts from a conversation I had with Luke about the unique challenges and opportunities that designers face when they choose to work as a sole proprietor of a studio.

BEING A FREELANCER IS NOT JUST ABOUT BEING CREATIVE

Twenty percent is creative work, eighty percent is the business side of it. Managing clients and managing their expectations. Many freelancers lean toward the creative, but you have to push through and learn about the business side of things. That's the difference between someone who is good at freelance work and someone who just scrapes by. It's about how you deal with the client, find work and sell yourself—it's not just about creating the work. You need to decide if you do creative work or if you are in the business of selling creative services.

POSITION YOURSELF BASED ON YOUR STRENGTHS AND WHAT YOU LOVE TO DO

Know who you are. What excites you? What's your bent: artistic and creative, business and strategy, or your marketing side? Consider using the *StrengthsFinder 2.0* book by Tom Rath. Schools support the artistic creative, but they should be focusing on your strengths as a person first, then as a designer. "Everyone can be the next Saul Bass," the design schools say, but the truth is most people aren't going to be that good, and you need to find your place in the market. If you have an artistic bent, you may be better as a hired gun.

DON'T FEEL LIKE YOU HAVE TO BE GOOD AT EVERYTHING

For me, the less I know and the more I can lean on others to do stuff, awesome!

SHOULD YOU GET A JOB BEFORE YOU FREELANCE?

I tell people if they're thinking about working on their own, they should spend five years working for someone else. They should pay attention to how the boss runs the business side of things, how they sell the work, how they manage their clients. This is the stuff you likely didn't learn in design school.

KNOW WHAT EXCITES YOU

As a freelancer, if you figure out what excites you, the creativity takes care of itself. The more I get excited about the clients I'm working with, the better I am at creating things visually for them. Then the design is really easy. Otherwise it's brutally hard. I don't have an understanding of why we're doing it.

I don't create something just for the sake of creating it. I have to have an understanding of why we're doing it. That's why I'm spending more time as a business consultant. Before, whether they'd paid me for learning about their business and clientele or not, I had to do it. Now I tell them I have to be paid for it.

MATURE INTO WHAT YOU'RE BEST AT, THEN FOCUS ON IT

Three years ago, my studio lost 85 percent of its revenue. It was the second time around, and it stung a lot more because it created a situation where I had to figure out what was wrong. It was the only time in my career where I said, "I need to do something with my business model." I took three months off and met with my mentors. In the process, I discovered that sitting in my office doing design work wasn't the best use of my ability. Rather, [the best use of my ability] was when I was talking with clients and the people that I work with. Other people reflected that my business thinking was what was best in our relationship and that was why I was hired.

This sent my studio in a whole different direction. Design was sucking the life out of me, and I didn't know there was anything else I could be really good at. Now my focus is more on knowing about my clients' businesses and desired outcomes. I don't care about perfecting a design to get it into a magazine. If my work makes my client money or grows their business, then I get excited.

KNOW THE WHAT AND THE WHEN

To run a creative business, you have to conduct the following four activities: planning, administrative, marketing and creative. As a freelancer, you're not going to fulfill just marketing and creative activities. You have to plan your year. No one should look back at how much the client was able to spend in the past and forecast the same or more for their next year.

With regard to operations, you have to do the billing, keep track of your hours, organize your week so you have time to focus on work and meet with clients. Save a full day to focus just on your business stuff. I tend to only meet with clients on Tuesdays and Thursdays.

CREATE AN ADVISORY BOARD FOR YOUR BUSINESS

I have an advisory board that I meet with every quarter. The board consists of another designer, a friend, a salesperson, a guy with another company I'm part of, and an ex-CFO, who's my main mentor. They are there to support me. I lay out my personal finances, business finances, pipeline and what I'm doing with my marketing. I think every freelancer should have some people they talk with once a month or a quarter. A group setting is better than a one-on-one situation, because if there's only one other person, I can talk my way out of things. If I gather all of my advisors in a room, there's nothing I can do but listen. A lot of my financial planning and advising for my business happens in that setting.

If it's a round of uncomfortable squirming in a chair that gets you to do what you need to do, then it's worth it. One of the reasons I'm exercising and eating better is because my advisory board wouldn't let me continue discussing my business issues until I had a physical and worked out some ongoing health issues. These last few years have been amazing, thanks to their input.

DON'T BECOME TOO ATTACHED TO YOUR IDEAS

If you're not willing to let your ideas die, you're always going to be butting heads with clients. You're not going to make it as a businessperson if you're not willing to say, "I did my best, and I'm moving on ..."

Clients can shoot down ideas or be difficult to work with. As a freelancer, that rejection can destroy some of your creativity. You have to figure out a way to separate yourself from it. If you don't want to live with some of these situations, you should consider being an artist and getting a corporate job. I'm good at my job, and I'll state my case of why I designed something a certain way. I will argue with a client to a point, but at the end of the day, I have to ask "for the sake of what?"

It makes you ask, "Why do I work?" It's so I can be home with my family, work on fun side projects and ride my bike more. So, find good clients who you can do great work for, and don't get too emotional when they kill an idea.

Vacation

When should I go on vacation?

The question should be: When should you *not* go on vacation?

Take a recent trip I took to Oahu, Hawaii: Standing in hip-deep salt-water, the cloud-streaked sky forms a wheel over my head that the sun pierces through. This cove is protected enough that I can see my feet clearly, toes sinking into coarse white sand. As I listen to my breath, colorful fish swirl between my legs, their bodies turquoise marbled into orange. Light refracts upon the ocean floor, undulating like cellular life pulsing inside a microscope.

By degrees, I continue to inch my way outward until the perceived chill tickles my belly button, tenses my shoulder blades. This is the only way I know to acclimate myself to the cold Pacific, beyond plunging my head below the waves and absorbing the immediate shock. Looking back toward shore, I can see my friends in the shadow of a hotel—we've poached a few feet of sand. Cleverly they had designed an improvement on the beach towel by pulling taut a fitted bed sheet, then filling the corners with sand to keep it in place.

Bobbing in the ocean, calm and fully unplugged for the first time in almost a year, my body begins to remember what it felt like before the past few months of solid design work. Yes, so much was accomplished in those late nights, those turn-and-burn trips. And yet here, illuminated by the sun, little of it seems important now. In the ever-overlapping jigsaw puzzle of project work, I had forgotten what made me ... me.

"The most important thing is to be able to enjoy your life without being fooled by things," Zen Master Shunryu Suzuki said. And yet we are fooled so easily. In the heat of our daily work, seeking to maximize every hour invested in the act of making things, hoping to treat our clients and our employees with respect, we lose ourselves. Perspective vanishes. Sleep is cheated. Food is wolfed down between emails and client meetings. Social and family engagements are rearranged due to last-minute emergencies that spring up like those perky pests in a Whack-A-Mole game.

The life we bring to the things we make vanishes in the summer heat. You bought your ticket to Burnout City, and you didn't even know how much it would cost until you arrived. Now, what will it take to leave?

Yes, your business is part of your life—and it is what you make of it. But don't let it make you. You are not putting yourself into it. You are letting it become what it needs to be, like a bonsai tree that you cultivate because you enjoy encouraging its growth. The tree is not you, and you are not the tree. But you are shaping each other's lives equally.

But this is only one tree, whether your business is your life or a thousand livelihoods. If you are responsible in how you cultivate it, then you also cultivate yourself.

The sun sneaks out from behind a cloud. Its reflection in the water is dazzling. I plunge a hand in, let it spill through my fingers. My wife looks up at me from her book, smiles and waves, beckoning me back to shore.

———

If you take your work everywhere you go, you won't got anywhere. Set clear boundaries around your time when you're off the clock.

———

● LATE NIGHTS

● WEEKENDS

★ BURNOUT CITY

● UNPROFITABLE

● UNDER-
STAFFED

BRINGING IT
TOGETHER

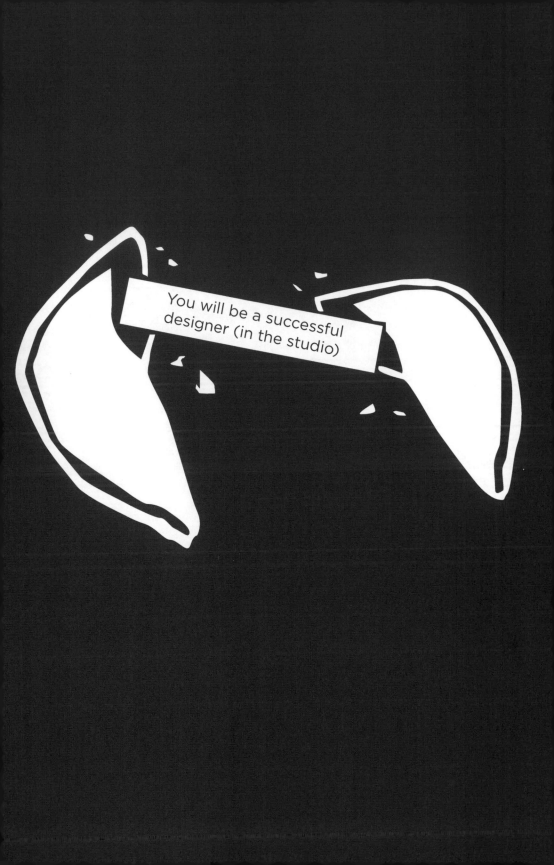

Bringing It Together

As you've seen throughout these pages, there is a constant tension between the demands of your business—receiving monetary reward for your level of effort—and the knowledge that what you make has some form of meaningful impact. As design business owners and leaders, we wrestle with certain fundamental questions: What if I can't earn a living running a design business? Am I going down the right path? Does this work make me happy?

Exactly how do you balance the competing demands of sustaining a profitable business with a joyful design practice? Use the worksheets on the following pages to determine what your ideal design studio experience should be like. David Conrad and I devised them, and we hope you can use them to better structure your design business to support what you love. Profitably. *(Download the worksheets at www.SBDBook.com)*

PROFIT: Design studio as a business

JOY: Design studio as a practice

PRODUCT

MARKET NEED & CAPABILITIES

PROCESS & CULTURE

CUSTOMERS & STAFF

PHILOSOPHY

The Elements of Design Studio Experience

THE ELEMENTS OF DESIGN STUDIO EXPERIENCE

Design studio as a practice

PRODUCT: What impact will our work have on the world?

CAPABILITIES: What skills do we need to achieve our goals?

CULTURE: How will we enjoy working together successfully?

STAFF: Which employees will strive to create our best work?

PHILOSOPHY: What values drive our daily practice?

Joy-oriented (time)

FULFILLMENT

TANGIBLE

PRODUCT		
MARKET NEED	CAPA-BILITIES	
PROCESS	CULTURE	
CUSTO-MERS	STAFF	
PHILOSOPHY		

DESIRE

INTANGIBLE

Design studio as a business

PRODUCT: What impact will our work have on the world?

MARKET NEED: What skills do we need to be hired?

PROCESS: How will we fulfill work profitably?

CUSTOMER: How will we work together to make products?

PHILOSOPHY: What values drive our daily business?

Profit-oriented ($$$)

THE ELEMENTS OF **DESIGN STUDIO EXPERIENCE**

Design studio as a practice

Design studio as a business

TANGIBLE

FULFILLMENT

PRODUCT

MARKET NEED	CAPA-BILITIES
PROCESS	CULTURE
CUSTO-MERS	STAFF

PHILOSOPHY

INTANGIBLE

DESIRE

Profit-oriented ($$$)

Joy-oriented (time)

Download this worksheet at www.SBDBook.com

The elements of design studio experience

There are five key elements that are necessary to create a stable design business. By working your way from the bottom up, you'll better understand how structure your design business to support your goals. Fill in the chart on page 262 with the elements that will help define your studio. There isn't much space to write on the worksheet, so strive to be concise.

ACTIVITY: DETERMINING YOUR DESIGN STUDIO PHILOSOPHY

If you don't know where to start in forming your design studio philosophy, try this exercise. It's okay if it takes a few days to work through this—you'll know when it's right. When you make important personal or financial decisions, it will serve as your North Star.

1. Write down what you do now as a designer. Sort those tasks into two categories: what you enjoy doing and what you don't like to do. Then, create a new category for things you want to do as a designer in the future. These can be your professional and personal aims, as well as new areas of interest you'd like to explore. (You can organize this information similarly to the chart on page 270.)

2. On sticky notes, write down the major themes and values that you see emerging from the content of this chart.

3. Distill the major themes and values into a philosophy for your creative business. Try to keep this to a few words—e.g., "Design to guide a better society"—not a manifesto.

PHILOSOPHY

One of the definitions of philosophy is: "The rational investigation of the truths and principles of being, knowledge or conduct." A designer's studio should have an underlying philosophy that dictates the day-to-day values of your business practice. Many designers make intutive decisions regarding how they earn their money (their design studio as a business) and decisions regarding how they spend their time (their design studio as a practice). But when they aren't able to describe this philosophy clearly to their peers and co-workers, they put their studio at risk. These shared values are the critical foundation that encourages long-term success.

CUSTOMERS AND STAFF

Once you understand your philosophy for your business, you'll need to consider who will support it. This includes the customers who will work with you to realize products that they desire, as well as employees or partners who will strive alongside you to create their best work.

When you're considering adding partners or hiring employees, try to foster the right overlaps for philosophy and goals for your business. However, make sure your skill sets don't overlap too much. That way, you'll get traction on studio growth and create your own spheres of influence.

When hiring customers—yes, we hire them, just as much as they hire us—you should always consider how their goals and needs match the philosophy of your business. If you spend too much time generating work that isn't aligned with your business philosophy, there will be little joy in the work.

WHAT ORGANIZATIONAL MODEL SHOULD MY STUDIO USE?

An organizational model describes how your studio employees work together: how tasks are delegated to people, how people collaborate to complete projects and who supervises the work to make sure it's great. It should be a reflection of how your studio earns revenue—the mix of types of work and products created for your customers—and of your studio philosophy.

What follows are some of the more common organizational models for design studios, and some new ones that are emerging. *(For examples of these models, go to www.SBDBook.com)*

Chain of Command Model: At the top of the pyramid, the boss. The rest runs more like an assembly line.

Coaching Model: The principal stands back and lets the studio teams drive the client work and the business.

Associate Model: Staff can take a stake in the business and its long-term growth.

Incubator Model: The business revenue is split between project work and creating products/services to sell to customers.

Hybrid Model: The studio can mix, match and experiment with different projects and products, emulating different models as needed.

Culture can create **joy.**

Process can create **profit.**

ACTIVITY: WHAT STUDIO CULTURE WOULD YOU LIKE TO CREATE?

The activity on the next few pages will help you answer the following questions: What can your staff do to create their ideal studio culture? And how can that culture align with everyone's desired working environment?

Here are the rules:

1. On the next spread, list what cultural building blocks you currently have in place as part of your studio.

2. Consider, based on what you (and your staff) want to do in the future, what new building blocks might increase joy. Add them to the worksheet.

3. Highlight which cultural building blocks you could give to others to increase their sense of ownership.

4. Have other team members do the same thing.

5. Merge all of your ideas together and implement what the majority of the staff want. Delegate ownership to those who want it.

CULTURE AND PROCESS

Culture and process are joined at the hip. Studio culture is everything people in a design studio do that supports the process of making work. Process is a shared awareness of how to conduct a design project as a team—staff, clients and vendors working in concert to fulfill the right activities, at the right time, to create the right desired outcome without burning through the entire budget.

Process is a beast that slays many a project budget, leaving design teams at odds with their studio management masters. To know where and when to employ the appropriate business process for a client request, and then to collaborate with a design team to define the right project approach to yield design awesomeness, requires mindful effort on the part of all parties in a design studio.

While process can aid a design studio in gaining profit, a dynamic studio culture can create joy for staffers and help provide stability in the face of ongoing work challenges.

STUDIO CULTURE WORKSHEET

HARD ATTRIBUTES

SPACE

Is your space large or small? Open or intimate? Minimalist or crowded?

AMENITIES

Do you have the latest technology? Free snacks? Season tickets to the game?

TRAINING

Do you support ongoing technical training or offer training workshops?

TYPE OF WORK

CUSTOMER

What industries do you work in? What is the size of a typical client?

DOMAIN

What type of design do you provide? (e.g., industrial, branding or interactive)?

PROJECT STYLE

Short-term projects or long-term projects? Waterfall processes, or agile and scrum processes?

SOFT ATTRIBUTES

COMMUNITY
How do people mingle in the studio? Craft nights? Happy hour?

PHILANTHROPY
What opportunities do employees have to "give back" to the world?

CHALLENGE
Do employees feel challenged to do good work? How are they challenged?

OWNERSHIP
How does the studio provide employees with a feeling of ownership?

LEADERSHIP
Who are the leaders in the studio? Are they managers or staffers?

RECOGNITION
How are great work and passionate effort recognized? Awards or contests?
Are employees publicly recognized?

Download this worksheet at www.SBDBook.com

DethStar

Your world. Destroyed.™

QUESTION: DOES THE MARKET NEED
THIS NEW CAPABILITY?

MARKET NEED AND CAPABILITIES

Clients may hire designers to create beautiful design work, but it takes specific capabilities for studios to be able to generate that work effectively. This can go far beyond hiring another designer, developer or a client services professional. If a design business is looking to expand capabilities, they will need to add new forms of talent and unique third-party partnerships to their overall set of studio resources.

Conversely, whether you love designing greeting cards or hot-air balloons or websites built on Ruby on Rails, you need to consider the market need for your services. Many designers have found their niche by focusing their attention on a specialized domain, such as creating book covers or conducting user research on how people are using mobile applications. The Holy Grail for any design business is a defensible niche paired with an endless market need.

WHAT I CAN DO	WHAT I WANT TO DO	WHAT I DON'T DO
Concept Development	Content Strategy	Resource Allocation
Information Architecture	Copywriting	Technical Specification
	Content Editing	Database Design
Visual Design		Coding and Scripting
Asset Preparation		Code Debugging
Project Commission		Search Engine Optimization
Content Population		
Functional Specification		Compatibility Testing
Usability Testing		Acceptance Testing
Accessibility		Launch Project
Business Analysis		Accounting
		Maintenance and Improvement

Creating a task inventory. In the example above, an interactive designer began to itemize tasks as part of his skill set. These skills were then organized according to project life cycle in the chart on the next page. Red type denotes the designer's current "sweet spot" in his skill set. For more on this activity, turn the page.

STUDIO CAPABILITIES MAP: INTERACTIVE DESIGN STUDIO

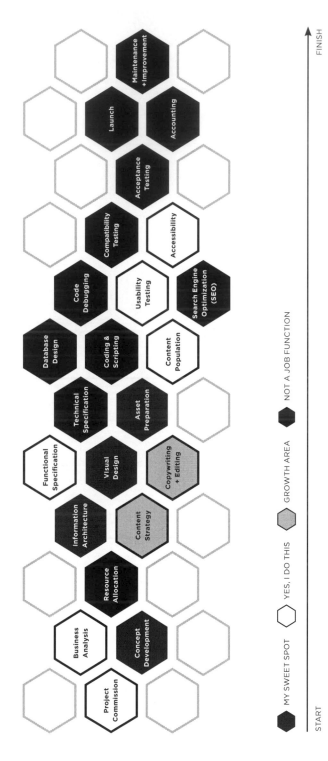

START

FINISH

◢ MY SWEET SPOT   ⬡ YES, I DO THIS   ⬣ GROWTH AREA   ⬣ NOT A JOB FUNCTION

Project Commission

Business Analysis

Concept Development

Resource Allocation

Information Architecture

Content Strategy

Functional Specification

Visual Design

Copywriting + Editing

Technical Specification

Asset Preparation

Database Design

Coding & Scripting

Content Population

Code Debugging

Usability Testing

Search Engine Optimization (SEO)

Compatibility Testing

Accessibility

Acceptance Testing

Launch

Accounting

Maintenance + Improvement

Mapping skills for a design studio. This chart shows the various skills an interactive design studio may use when fulfilling projects. The color coding indicates what skills have been most utilized and most lacking, per the capabilities mapping activity outlined on the previous page. (Adapted from Skillset.org.)

ACTIVITY: HOW DO I ASSESS MY STUDIO CAPABILITIES?

Any design business must assess on a regular basis whether the services and products they offer remain attractive to their customer base, and they must potentially shift the core capabilities of their organization—as well as their partnerships and vendor relationships—to meet new and emerging demands aligned with their philosophy. Here's an activity to help you determine what skills and roles you may need to hire for your business in the future. It functions as a studio capabilities map:

1. On a sheet of paper, write down all the tasks you can fulfill with your current skill set—from soliciting new business to closing out a design project. If you're doing this for an entire staff, do the same thing for each of your employees. *(See an example of this on the previous page spread.)*

2. Note what you (and your staff) are really good at. Highlight it as a "sweet spot" for a particular skill.

3. Add to the list a second column with the skills you haven't acquired yet but want to in the future.

4. Add a third column with all the skills that others currently do, either in your studio or as an outsourced task.

5. Map the skills on a chart, organized by the life cycle of your current studio process. The process of how you fulfill projects from a skill-based perspective progresses from left to right. In the example shown on the following page, the hexagons on the left are activities associated with commissioning interactive projects. The hexagons in the middle and to the right flow through the design and development process.

6. If more than one person in the studio has a skill, mark it as such in the corner of the hexagon. If no one in the studio has a particular skill, but there is a hexagon present, this may be an area to grow skills or continue to outsource.

Redo your studio capabilities map every three months to assess growth in your current studio skill set against what specific skills your projects and secondary lines of business may require. Look at examples of the output from this activity on the following pages.

STUDIO CAPABILITIES MAP: STAFFING FORECAST 2009

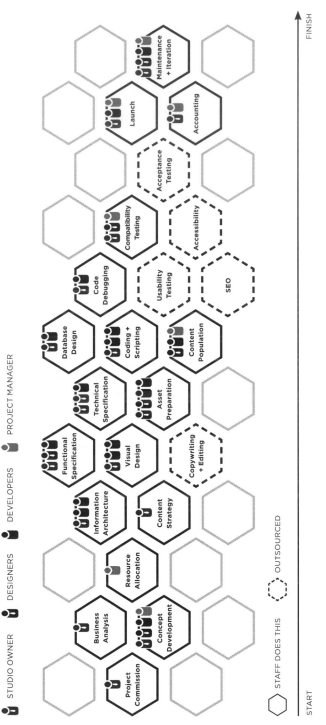

STUDIO OWNER DESIGNERS DEVELOPERS PROJECT MANAGER

START FINISH

○ STAFF DOES THIS ⬡ OUTSOURCED

Mapping capabilities for Design Commission. The capabilities map above shows how an interactive design studio forecasted—based on their 2009 staffing—what specific tasks their current mix of employees supported. They also used this assessment to identify gaps for future staffing needs. The map on the page below shows how the company increased their studio revenues through two new lines of business (a physical product and a licenseable software product), and how the overall composition of capabilities provided by their staff and third-party vendors needed to evolve. A need to ensure quality control required greater oversight by full-time staff, which pointed to hiring another designer.

STUDIO CAPABILITIES MAP: STAFFING FORECAST 2010

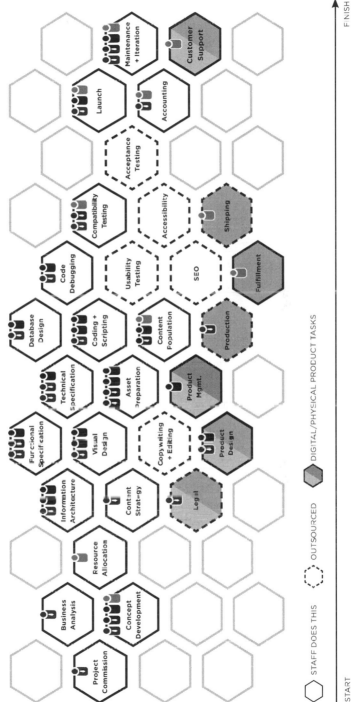

STUDIO OWNER   DESIGNERS   DEVELOPERS   PROJECT MANAGER

Project Commission

Business Analysis

Concept Development

Resource Allocation

Information Architecture

Content Strategy

Functional Specification

Visual Design

Copywriting + Editing

Legal

Technical Specification

Asset Preparation

Product Mgmt.

Product Design

Database Design

Coding + Scripting

Content Population

Production

Code Debugging

Usability Testing

SEO

Fulfillment

Compatibility Testing

Accessibility

Shipping

Acceptance Testing

Launch

Accounting

Maintenance + Iteration

Customer Support

STAFF DOES THIS   OUTSOURCED   DIGITAL/PHYSICAL PRODUCT TASKS

START   FINISH

STUDIO CAPABILITIES MAP
PEOPLE:

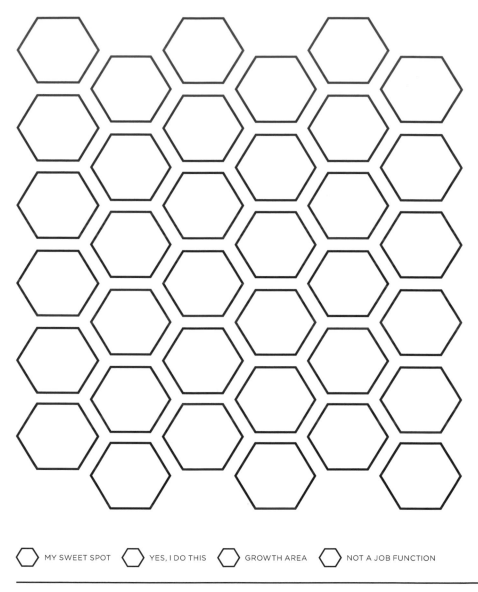

 MY SWEET SPOT   YES, I DO THIS   GROWTH AREA   NOT A JOB FUNCTION

START

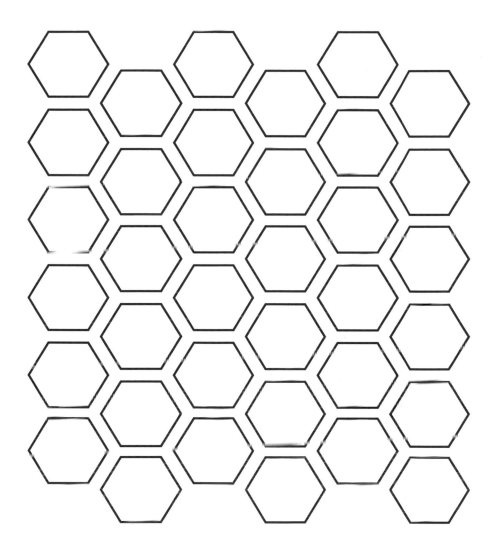

FINISH

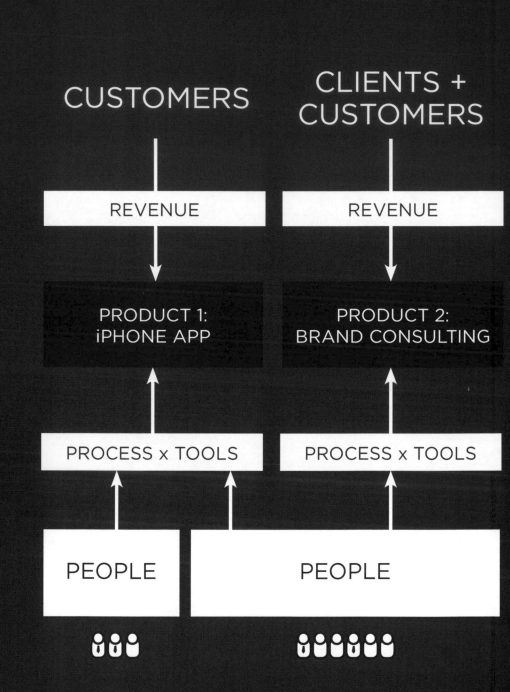

PRODUCT

Whether you're providing traditional design services or bootstrapping your own products and services for direct sale to customers, you are making products for customers. This product is the end result of the services that designers provide. Whenever I show our company's design portfolio to someone else, whether designer or nondesigner, I make sure our philosophy is evident in the work. We should be proud not only of the product we create, but also the process by which we created it, the profit we generated along the way and the impact our work has had on the world. Otherwise we're left wondering what we might have sacrificed along the way.

One important way to ensure quality of product is through regular, rigorous critique. Critique is a language that every design studio leader must master—the ability to explore through word, sketch and action the various qualities of a series of design compositions. Well-employed critique can add immense value to ongoing project work and serve as a potent differentiator for design studio output. When poorly considered, however, sloppy critique can demoralize a creative team, sending a creative idea into an tailspin. Ideally critique should be about focusing, shepherding and protecting potent ideas. To quote Pelle Sjoenell, executive creative director of BBH LA:

> The creative director's relationship with the idea is unique. It's a combination of three professions—a politician, a farmer and an assassin. The politician handles the multiple stakeholders of the idea, traditionally pursuing different agendas. The farmer's part is to nurture the idea so it can grow from interesting to awesome. This means identifying which add-ons, or fertilizers, will make the idea better and which will hurt the crops. Lastly, the creative director needs to be able to shape-shift into an assassin ..., isolating any threat against the fragile idea and putting that threat to sleep forever.
> http://bbh-labs.com/creative-direction-vs-creative-selection

PURSUING NEW PRODUCTS CAN DEMAND NEW STAFF
Be aware that the composition of your studio's staff, technology infrastructure and partnerships with other firms and vendors may change radically as you diversify your business from a professional services model. Regularly reevaluate what staff are necessary to support new products and their long-term growth.

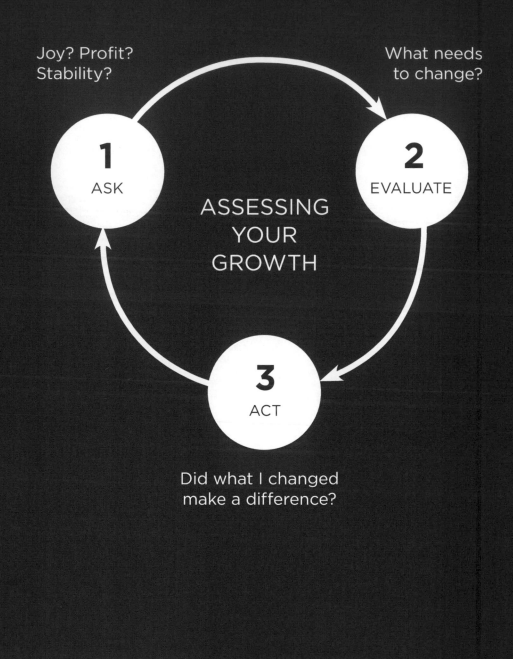

Joy? Profit?
Stability?

What needs
to change?

1
ASK

2
EVALUATE

ASSESSING
YOUR
GROWTH

3
ACT

Did what I changed
make a difference?

ACTIVITY: ARE YOU STAYING ON TRACK?

After you've determined the elements of your design studio experience, make sure you conduct the following assessment every three months:

1. Ask

For each activity that you're conducting as part of your design business, ask yourself:

- How does this activity bring me joy as a designer?
- What profit do I yield from conducting this activity?
- What stable structures have I devised to support the creation of joy and profit through this activity?

Rate each activity on a scale of one to three. A rating of three means you are doing great in that category, while one means you aren't. You can also enter in new activities that you might want to add to your business, but there will be little to no profit or stability associated with it at first.

2. Evaluate

Based on your ratings, determine whether you have a desire to maintain each activity you've outlined. Write the reasons why. Consider what would need to change if you were going to try to increase the amount of joy, profit or stability for activities that you want to continue maintaining. This is also where you can plan how new activities fit into the mix.

3. Act

Over the next month, make changes based on your reflections above. Then monitor their impact on your business and adjust over the next two months. After three months, you'll be ready to go back and start this process over again.

Use the scorecard on the following page spread.

———

Going through this process may require you to make some tough choices, including scaling down or even closing your business for other opportunities. Don't let the pain of change stand in the way of a much better future for you, both personally and professionally.

———

PROGRESS EVALUATION WORKSHEET

ACTIVITY/MARKET SERVED: _____

JOY	1	2	3	DESIRE TO MAINTAIN? Y / N
PROFIT	1	2	3	WHY? _____
STABILITY	1	2	3	_____
NEW ACTIVITY?	Y	/	N	_____

ACTIVITY/MARKET SERVED: _____

JOY	1	2	3	DESIRE TO MAINTAIN? Y / N
PROFIT	1	2	3	WHY? _____
STABILITY	1	2	3	_____
NEW ACTIVITY?	Y	/	N	_____

ACTIVITY/MARKET SERVED: _____

JOY	1	2	3	DESIRE TO MAINTAIN? Y / N
PROFIT	1	2	3	WHY? _____
STABILITY	1	2	3	_____
NEW ACTIVITY?	Y	/	N	_____

ACTIVITY/MARKET SERVED: _____

JOY	1	2	3	DESIRE TO MAINTAIN? Y / N
PROFIT	1	2	3	WHY? _____
STABILITY	1	2	3	_____
NEW ACTIVITY?	Y	/	N	_____

ACTIVITY/MARKET SERVED: _____

JOY   1   2   3   DESIRE TO MAINTAIN?   Y / N

PROFIT   1   2   3   WHY? _____

STABILITY   1   2   3   _____

NEW ACTIVITY?   Y / N   _____

ACTIVITY/MARKET SERVED: _____

JOY   1   2   3   DESIRE TO MAINTAIN?   Y / N

PROFIT   1   2   3   WHY? _____

STABILITY   1   2   3   _____

NEW ACTIVITY?   Y / N   _____

ACTIVITY/MARKET SERVED: _____

JOY   1   2   3   DESIRE TO MAINTAIN?   Y / N

PROFIT   1   2   3   WHY? _____

STABILITY   1   2   3   _____

NEW ACTIVITY?   Y / N   _____

ACTIVITY/MARKET SERVED: _____

JOY   1   2   3   DESIRE TO MAINTAIN?   Y / N

PROFIT   1   2   3   WHY? _____

STABILITY   1   2   3   _____

NEW ACTIVITY?   Y / N   _____

Download this worksheet at www.SBDBook.com

REMEMBER
THESE

5

THINGS

Look for **joy**
in what you do.

Find a way to
get **paid** for it.

Make your
income **reliable.**

Monitor your
growth.

Don't be afraid
of **change.**

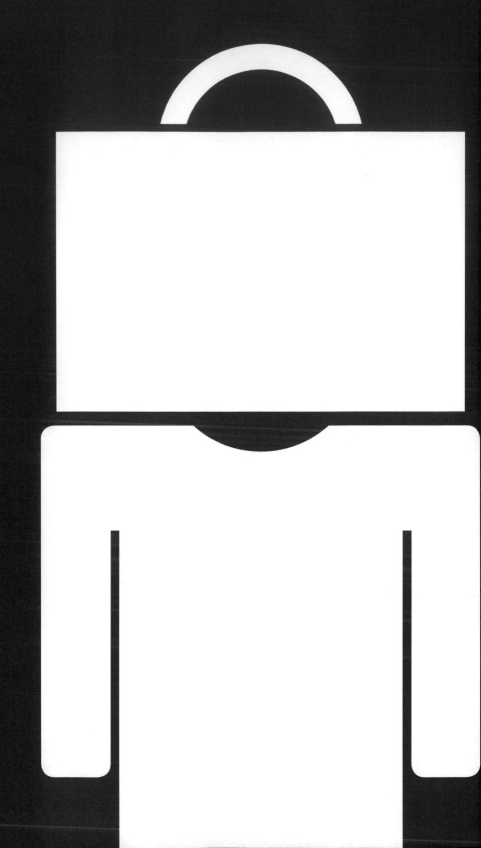

Resources

If you want to learn more about the topics addressed in this book, the following resources will continue you on your journey into design business.

Benun, Ilise and Peleg Top. *The Designer's Guide to Marketing and Pricing: How to Win Clients and What to Charge Them*. Cincinnati: HOW Books, 2008.

Berkun, Scott. *Making Things Happen: Mastering Project Management (Revised Edition)*. Sebastopol, California: O'Reilly Media, 2008.

Carnegie, Dale. *How to Win Friends and Influence People*. New York: Simon and Schuster, 2009.

Cialdini, Robert B. *Influence: The Psychology of Persuasion (Revised Edition)*. New York: HarperBusiness, 2006.

Crawford, Tad. *AIGA Professional Practices in Graphic Design, 2nd Edition*. New York: Allworth Press, 2008.

Faimon, Peg. *The Designer's Guide to Business and Careers: How to Succeed on the Job or on Your Own*. Cincinnati: HOW Books, 2009.

Fisher, Roger, William Ury and Bruce Patton. *Getting to Yes: Negotiating Agreement Without Giving In (Revised Edition)*. New York: Penguin, 2011.

Foote, Cameron S. *The Creative Business Guide to Running a Graphic Design Business (Updated Edition)*. New York: W.W. Norton and Company, 2009.

Fried, Jason, and David Heinemeier Hansson. *Rework*. New York: Crown Business, 2010.

Granet, Keith. *The Business of Design*. New York: Princeton Architectural Press, 2011.

Graphic Artists Guild. *Graphic Artist's Guild Handbook of Pricing and Ethical Guidelines*. New York: Graphic Artists Guild. 2010.

Holson, David. *The Strategic Designer: Tools & Techniques for Managing the Design Process*. Cincinnati: HOW Books, 2011.

Maeda, John and Rebecca J. Bermont. *Redesigning Leadership*. Cambridge, Massachusetts: The MIT Press, 2011.

Martin, Roger L. *The Design of Business: Why Design Thinking Is the Next Competitive Advantage*. Boston, Massachusetts: Harvard Business School Press, 2009.

Mintzberg, Henry, Joseph Lampel and Bruce Ahlstrand. *Strategy Safari: A Guided Tour Through the Wilds of Strategic Management*. New York: Free Press, 2005.

Neumeier, Marty. *The Designful Company: How to Build a Culture of Nonstop Innovation*. Berkeley, California: Peachpit Press, 2008.

Osterwalder, Alexander and Yves Pigneur. *Business Model Generation: A Handbook for Visionaries, Game Changers, and Challengers*. Hoboken, New Jersey: Wiley, 2010.

Perkins, Shel. *Talent Is Not Enough: Business Secrets for Designers (2nd Edition)*. Berkeley, California: New Riders Press, 2010.

Rath, Tom. *StrengthsFinder 2.0*. New York: Gallup Press, 2007.

Ries, Eric. *The Lean Startup: How Today's Entrepreneurs Use Continuous Innovation to Create Radically Successful Businesses*. New York: Crown Business, 2011.

Solomon, Robert. *The Art of Client Service: 58 Things Every Advertising & Marketing Professional Should Know (Revised and Updated Edition)*. New York: Kaplan Publishing, 2008.

Suzuki, Shunryu. *Zen Mind, Beginner's Mind*. Boston: Shambhala, 2006.

Stone, Douglas, Bruce Patton and Sheila Heen. *Difficult Conversations: How to Discuss What Matters Most (Revised Edition)*. New York: Penguin, 2010.

Ury, William. *Getting Past No*. New York: Bantam, 1993.

About the Author

David Sherwin is an interaction designer and creative director with a depth of expertise in developing compelling solutions for challenging business problems. His first book was *Creative Workshop: 80 Challenges to Sharpen Your Design Skills*, also from HOW.

David is currently a principal designer at frog, a global innovation firm, where he helps to guide the research, strategy and design of novel products and services for some of today's leading companies and nonprofit organizations. He is also a senior lecturer in the BFA in Interaction Design program at California College of the Arts.

He has spoken and conducted workshops at events such as SxSW, Interaction 11, HOW Design Live, as well as at several design schools. His writing has appeared in TheAtlantic.com/Life, *A List Apart*, PSFK.com, *HOW* and many other periodicals.

He lives in the San Francisco Bay Area with his wife, the poet and writer Mary Paynter Sherwin. In his free time, he maintains the blog ChangeOrder at www.changeorderblog.com.

Online Resources

Visit www.SBDBook.com to download the worksheets and other materials referenced in chapters throughout this book. All worksheets are covered under Creative Commons Attribution-NonCommercial-ShareAlike 3.0 Unported License. For details on this license, please visit www.creative-commons.org/licenses/by-nc-sa/3.0/.

Permissions

All photos and illustrations are by the author, with the exception of:

p. v: Photo ©2011 Design Commission, Inc.

p. v: Photo provided by Erica Goldsmith, ©2012 by Mike Perkowitz.

p. v: Photo provided by Fiona Robertson Remley, ©2012 by Scott Areman.

p. 20: Photo by Max Halberstadt from the LIFE Photo Archive, now in the public domain.

p. 94: Illustration created by David Sherwin from a sketch by Gabriel Post. ©2012 Gabriel Post.

p. 180: ©2011 Design Commission, Inc.

p. 181: AStoryBeforeBed.com ©2012 Jackson Fish Market.

p. 187: Photo ©2012 Frank.

p. 216: ©2011 Design Commission, Inc.

p. 217: ©2012 Eric Oesterle.

p. 233–243: Accounting spreadsheets created with David Conrad at Design Commission. ©2011 Design Commission, Inc. and David Sherwin. Check photograph ©2011 Design Commission, Inc.

p. 260-282: Charts and templates created in collaboration with David Conrad at Design Commission. ©2011 David Sherwin and Design Commission, Inc.

p. 288: ©2010 Mary Paynter Sherwin.

Index

coaching organizational model, 264
collaborative decision-making, 52
collaborators, designer network of, 87
communication, 10-11, 24, 108
    accounts receivables and, 234
competition, 21, 88
    estimating and, 122-123
confidentiality, 206-210
confidentiality agreement, 206, 207, 208
confidentiality rules, third-party vendors
    and, 208-209
Conrad, David, 33, 179, 180, 193, 194, 231,
    232, 233, 234, 236, 240, 244, 260
contact, client service and, 10-11
content strategy, 90, 96
contingency fee, 125
contracts, 42-45, 68, 202, 209
    critical terms, 43-45
    deadlines, 140
    designer protection and, 42-43
    fluctuating scope and, 113, 114
Conway, Matt, 158
Cooper, Kyle, 47
copyright, 203 *See also intellectual*
    property
corporate strategy, 93, 95
Costa, Kara, 21
Coudal Partners, 184
creative leadership, 228
critique, 278
CrossGrain Studio, 252
crowdsourced design work, 47
culture, design studio, 212-220, 266-268
    hard building blocks of, 212-218
    process and, 266
    soft building blocks of, 212, 213,
        218-220
Curfman, Corbet, 199
customers, working with. *See briefs,*
    design; business development; client
    service; competition; contracts;
    deliverables; discounts; expectations;
    feedback; meetings; negotiation;
    networking; politics; presentations;

proposals; spec work; strategy

Davidson, Carolyn, 125
deadlines, 140
    contract and, 140
    controlling, 51
    internal, 140
    real, 140
Deck, The, 184
declining work, 24-28
deliverables, 76, 102, 114
    examples, 76
    lopsided, 107
    payment schedule and, 76
deliverables brief, 75
design by committee, 52
Design Client's Bill of Rights, 12-13, 14
Design Commission, 33, 179, 180, 216, 231,
    240
design competitions, 46
design investment curve, 64-65
    versus client expectations, 65
design methodologies, 111-114 *See also agile*
    design methodology; iterative design
    methodology; waterfall design
    methodology
design strategist, 91-93, 97
    necessary skills, 95-96
design strategy, 90-96
    client business aims and, 93-96
Designers Accord, 200
disability insurance, 196
disaster plan, 196
discounts, 61-62, 234
diversification, client, 18
Dubberly, Hugh, 110

Eames, Charles, 91
education, client, 65-66
education events/training, 184
ego, 249
80/20 Rule of New Client Generation, 9
Eisenberg, Tina Roth, 184
employment agreements, 202

More Great Titles from HOW Books

The Designer's Guide to Business and Careers
BY PEG FAIMON

The Designer's Guide to Business and Careers is a comprehensive guide to basic business issues for designers in today's marketplace. You'll find information on how to successfully navigate your design career or start your own studio. From choosing a career path to freelancing to striking out on your own, this must-have guide gives you the tools you need to stay on top of industry trends.

The Corporate Creative
BY ANDY EPSTEIN

The Corporate Creative provides incredibly effective strategies to help you really establish yourself (and your team) as a powerful and efficient force within your company. Finally there is a book that speaks to the all too neglected in-house designer.

The Strategic Designer
BY DAVID HOLSTON

Containing interviews with some of the most respected names in design (Dave Mason, Tim Larson, Stefan Bucher, Ellen Shapiro and more), *The Strategic Designer* looks to help designers become experts in their profession as a whole, not just designing. By adopting a process that considers collaboration, context and accountability, designers move from "makers of things" to "design strategists."

Find these books and many others at MyDesignShop.com or your local bookstore.

Have you ever struggled to complete a design project on time?
Or felt that having a tight deadline stifled your capacity for
maximum creativity? If so, then this book is for you.

You can find it at MyDesignShop.com or your local bookstore.

"Highly recommended for people who want to learn by making, and who have
some design experience but want to grow and stretch their creative abilities."

—*Scott Berkun, author of* The Myths of Innovation

Free chapter: scr.bi/CWBook • *Free teacher's guide:* scr.bi/CWTeachers

6567578R00164

Made in the USA
San Bernardino, CA
10 December 2013